Take Two

Books by Jo Brans

LISTEN TO THE VOICES

MOTHER, I HAVE SOMETHING
TO TELL YOU
Research by Margaret Taylor Smith

JO BRANS

Take Two

DOUBLEDAY

NEW YORK · LONDON · TORONTO · SYDNEY · AUCKLAND

Published by Doubleday, a division of
Bantam Doubleday Dell Publishing Group, Inc.
666 Fifth Avenue, New York, New York 10103

Doubleday and the portrayal of an anchor with a dolphin
are trademarks of Doubleday, a division of
Bantam Doubleday Dell Publishing Group, Inc.

Excerpt from "Our Afterlife I"
from DAY BY DAY, by Robert Lowell.
Copyright © 1975, 1976, 1977, by Robert Lowell.
Reprinted by permission of Farrar, Straus & Giroux, Inc.

Library of Congress Cataloging-in-Publication Data

Brans, Jo.
Take two / by Jo Brans.
— 1st ed.
p.   cm.
1. Self-actualization (Psychology)—Case studies.   2. Change
(Psychology)—Case studies.   I. Title.   II. Title: Take 2.
BF637.S4B69   1989
158′.1—dc19   88-28235

ISBN 0-385-24348-0
Copyright © 1989 by Jo Brans
All Rights Reserved
Printed in the United States of America
May 1989
First Edition

FOR WILLEM

Acknowledgments

Gathering the stories for this book was an adventure I shall never forget. My first and heartiest thanks go to the wonderful people whose lives are represented in the pages to follow.

Next I owe thanks to the many friends who helped in multitudinous ways during my three-year obsession: Edison B. Allen, Tim Allis, Peter Anastos, Ken Bleeth, Lee Cullum, Zoë Cutler, Peyton Lewis, William Edwards, Shelby Hearon, Wilson Henley, Mai-Britt and Jay Hoffman, Cathryn Jakobson, Eloise Kayton, Michael Longo, Jean and Burt Meyers, Kathy Muldoon, Bill Porterfield, Emily and Hugh Salzberg, Muriel and Donald Seldin, Celestine Sibley, Willard Spiegelman, and Harry Weintraub. Alphabetically last but far from least, Sarah Ziegler gave the book its title.

Jill Bagwell, Ellen Cirona, Keith Dawson, Michael Dunne, Jean Roscoe, and Marlene Schiller transcribed the interview tapes. The *New York Times, People, Manhattan,inc.*, and *New York* suggested prospects, as did the nice man at Radio Shack, the woman behind the circulation desk at the library, and much of the rest of the talkative world.

Sally Arteseros at Doubleday was an encouraging presence throughout this, our second project together. A skilled and sympathetic editor, Sally inspired my best efforts as a researcher and a writer. Her creative and insightful editing improved the manuscript considerably. Thanks, too, to her resourceful and helpful assistant, Teresa Scala.

With her sensitivity to a story, her enthusiasm for good writing, her sound judgment, and her unlimited loyal support, Molly Friedrich at the Aaron M. Priest Literary Agency is a writer's dream. Take my right arm if you must, but leave me Molly.

A personal note of thanks to my children, Erin Porterfield and Winton Porterfield, who by negotiating so gracefully the changes I have brought into their lives have taught me a great deal about human resilience.

Finally, from that place at the bottom of my heart, thanks to my husband Willem Brans, who was my companion on all the travels, physical and emotional, that writing this book demanded, and to whom it is most gratefully dedicated.

Jo Brans
New York City

Contents

Introduction: The Gumption to Change
1

PART ONE
THE PROCESS OF CHANGE

DISCONTENT
1   Tending the Human Spirit
17
2   Arrival at Long Last
34

PROVOCATION
3   Designing Woman
53

CRISIS
4   Crisis in a Double Bed
73
5   Outliving a New Suit of Clothes
90

CHOOSING TO CHANGE
6   Going Global
113

PART TWO
THE SKILLS FOR CHANGE

ACCEPTING THE CONSTANCY OF CHANGE
7   Driving Toward the No-Goal
133

ix

CONTENTS

8   To Continue a People
149

LISTENING TO THE INNER VOICE
9   Satisfying the Soul
169
10   The Reasons of the Heart
186

RECOGNIZING AND EXPLORING OPPOSITES
11   What Now? or What Else?
207
12   A Patchwork Life
225

DEVELOPING AN INDEPENDENT EGO
13   Getting Off Your Herculon
241
14   The Next Generation
259
15   Starting Over
278

Conclusion: Take Two
295

take—*noun.*

    6. a. A scene filmed or televised without interrupting the run of the camera.
    b. A recording made in a single session.
    8. *Slang.* Any attempt or try: *He got the answer on the third take.*

—The American Heritage Dictionary

There are no second acts in American lives.

—F. SCOTT FITZGERALD, in his notes for *The Last Tycoon*

Take Two

Introduction

The Gumption to Change

Let me say right away that I have never much liked change. If some are born to change, some achieve change, and some have change thrust upon them, many of the changes in my life have been thrust upon me. Nostalgia is my rightful mode. "Are you trying to make a New York apartment look like your grandfather's house in Mississippi?" a friend teased when I lugged home yet another not-quite antique. The answer is a sheepish but defiant "yes." I know I am revealing a certain Ralph Lauren décor of the mind, but there it is. Given a choice, I am the woman in the group who wants to go back—to the same Chinese restaurant, the same cabin on the same lake, the same husband, the same job, the same, the same, the same.

1

So why am I, a lover of sameness, writing a book about change? This book began at a time several years ago when I revolutionized my life. I achieved a change—achieved it, because it was not in any way thrust upon me—which might not look so dramatic to other people, but which left me, the perpetrator, gasping in disbelief. After sixteen years of teaching in the same school, living in the same city, seeing the same friends, I left Dallas, left a tenured position at the university, left all my family except my husband, and came to New York like any young hopeful to try to make it as a writer. And, frankly, I was terrified.

Oh, come on, you may ask, doesn't everybody change? Isn't change a natural and inevitable part of the human condition? What's the big deal about making a change?

And, of course, what you say is true. We all change, especially in America. Statistics, as well as our own eyes, show us that Americans are, geographically, economically, and socially, much given to change. Each year, half of all Americans move at least once. Half of all Americans change jobs after two or three years, or even sooner. Half of all American marriages end in divorce, which is more often than not followed by remarriage.

Change may be the most constant tradition in this country. America was after all settled by people who left homeland behind; the United States was then founded by those people through revolution. The energy of America, you could argue, has historically been generated by change.

But history is one thing, and personal experience another. However your heart may leap up at the *idea* of beginning again, the powerful pull of the status quo may bring it right back down. When you make a big change in your own life, it's scary.

Call it a lack of gumption, if you like. But "gumption" has two meanings. Once "gumption" meant the practical shrewdness and common sense needed, let's say, to stay put in a job you like. Today "gumption" has come to mean the courage and enterprise necessary to take on something new. I wasn't sure which kind of gumption I lacked, the gumption to stay put or the gumption to change. Could I possibly lack both, I wondered? At that point, I knew I had to do something to get over my fears.

I have always believed in models for behavior, and I began to gravitate, casually at first, toward other people who had changed their lives, who had made changes so dramatic that the change

2

that had traumatized me looked, in comparison, like business as usual. At a party I was introduced to Bubu Arya, who for almost thirty years had led a glamorous life as the wife of Grandhi Arya, an Indian diplomat who eventually became ambassador to the United Nations. When her husband died in 1985, her friends and family expected Bubu to return to the family estate and the entourage of servants in India. But Bubu chose the difficult but free life in America rather than the luxurious but constrained life of an upper-class Indian woman.

To support herself, Bubu cheerfully took a nine-to-five job as a receptionist in Manhattan. This chic, cultured woman, who had dined at the White House, held family celebrations with the prime minister of India, danced with royalty in Monaco, chatted with the dignitaries of Europe at Versailles—how had she met the challenge of her new life? I asked her to tell me about it. When she obligingly came by to talk on her way home from work, she was wearing a designer suit from her old life and the running shoes favored by New York working women from her new life.

Other models for change presented themselves. Shopping for a tape recorder one afternoon, I met Ken Schaffer, an electronics wizard who in the past had helped to wire and amplify performers like Jimi Hendrix and the Rolling Stones, "the gods and demi-gods of the generation," as Ken puts it. At thirty-five, Ken had a change of attitude that reshaped his whole life. "I started realizing something natural and perhaps sacred about the continuity of life as a species."

Kenny gave up the easy money of the rock world. He began to install wires not for "gods" but for mortals, by developing a system through which ordinary Soviet citizens and ordinary United States citizens can communicate with each other by satellite. He gave up a succession of one-night stands—"I was never in love with anyone for more than three nights"—for a serious commitment to a young specialist in Russian studies. His live-and-let-live hedonism of the sixties yielded in the eighties to a messianic devotion to world peace.

Next, I met Sylvia Averbach, who left a successful career as a microbiologist to come, alone, to New York to become an actress. So what, you say? You've heard that story before. So Sylvia was at that time fifty-seven years old, hardly an age to be "discovered" and made into a star.

Sylvia, a small, round, grandmotherly woman, laughed telling me her early adventures—the roach-infested efficiency in which she had lived, the role she got largely because of her perfect Yiddish and her ability to make equally perfect blintzes, the responses of others to her stage-struck ambitions. For example, buying the cheese for the blintzes one night shortly before curtain time, she told the man behind the counter at the deli to please hurry, that she was an actress and had to go on stage soon.

"You're an actress?" he said. "Really? You don't look like one!" *"Really? You Don't Look Like One!"* later became the title of a one-woman show that Sylvia wrote for herself. In the show, she allowed herself the perfect retort: "I'm incognito. Actually, I'm tall, blond, beautiful, and twenty-one."

Sitting in her cozy West Side apartment, I asked Sylvia the questions I had also asked Bubu and Ken: What caused you to make this change in your life? Were you afraid? If you were, how did you get over it? What other obstacles did you have to overcome? What or who helped you? How did your family respond? Has your circle of friends changed? What have you gained or lost by making the change? Are you happy now? Was it worth it? Would you do it again? Would you recommend it to others?

As I listened to the answers, it occurred to me that I was probably not alone in wanting to hear what people like Bubu and Ken and Sylvia had to say. Here were three individuals, not "gods or demi-gods" but ordinary human beings, from three different generations, from widely different backgrounds, acting from very different motives, who had all made radical departures from a former way of life. I called them ordinary—in fact, I don't think they are. Plenty of us dream of changing our lives. We dream, like Bubu, of being independent, of feeling the blood-rush of new challenges. We dream, like Sylvia, of expressing ourselves through words or music or art. We dream, as Ken did, of making the world more harmonious. Instead of acting on those dreams, all too often we succumb to lives of quiet desperation.

Not all dreams should be acted on, of course. I didn't know whether I had taken the right road in changing my life, and I don't know for sure even now. I certainly couldn't, then or now, advocate deliberate change for anybody else. Some people are happy, useful, and content exactly where they are, and I would hope those people have the gumption to stay put.

But sometimes it is our best dreams which loom uncomfortably large and cumbersome in the cold white light of morning. We dream big and settle small. We dream of wiping out infant mortality and colonizing the moon. We settle for a baby Mercedes and two weeks in the Bahamas.

Yet there are exemplary men and women who carry their dreams into everyday reality. When the walls of their waking world are too narrow to accommodate their dreams, they don't trim their dreams. They widen their walls, or knock them down. They have the gumption, that other gumption—the imagination and initiative, the boldness and daring—that it takes to lead innovative lives. I began to look for these extraordinary people, and to ask them for their stories.

Telling ourselves stories, the writer John Cheever once remarked, is the best way we have of comprehending the turn of events in human life. The psychologist Jerome Bruner goes even further, asserting that storytelling is, like logical argument, actually a method of thinking. The way in which a person tells his story, Bruner claims, becomes, both for listener and storyteller, a guide for life, a guide which can be trusted because it incorporates "things like beliefs, desires, expectations, emotions and intentions."

Over the past two years, I have recorded the stories of men and women who have turned the events of their lives to suit themselves. These storytellers span four decades; the youngest is twenty-eight, the oldest sixty-eight. They span the country, too, from New York to California, from Texas to Vermont. They are black, white, and Oriental; single, married, divorced, and widowed; heterosexual and homosexual; poor, rich, and in between. In their diversity, they have one thing in common: all of them have deliberately and daringly made dramatic innovations in the patterns of their lives.

I listened to them tell how and why they did it. In the following pages, as I relate the stories I gathered, I will draw comparisons to indicate a general pattern which I found. But I didn't set out to be scientific, to prove anything about the population as a whole with these narratives. A definitive sociological sample of "subjects" did not interest me, nor did I administer tests, as a psychologist might, of intellectual competency, emotional maturity, or level of achievement.

I did have my own methods, of course. Before the interview, each person received a list of over forty questions, which amplified those questions I had asked Bubu, Ken, and Sylvia. These questions were intended to help stimulate memory and reflection. Heading the questions was the plea to "try to recall particular conversations, scenes, and events." Because I agree with John Cheever that we can comprehend life through stories, I wanted to hear stories in all their particularity. I agree with Bruner also, that those stories become "recipes" for subsequent living. Before I went seeking these storytellers, I needed some sense of the process of change they might have undergone and the qualities or abilities demonstrated. For this purpose, I borrowed the label "innovator" from an economist, William Kingston. I would look for innovators. Though Kingston works the idea out in purely economic terms, his "innovators" link two human worlds and two kinds of human activity—the world of imagination and the world of action.

We usually think of technology as "innovative," Kingston says. In a way, I decided, I wanted to find people who had innovated the machinery of their lives, who had remodeled the mechanistic givens to try something new. Or, as I rephrased it for myself, they would be people with gumption: the imagination to see their own latent potentialities and the active practical energy necessary to develop those potentialities.

What makes such people unusual, I have come to understand over the past several years, is that, desiring a more perfect life, they actively seek change where others would more likely seek stasis. When their lives are happy, they may want to extend the boundaries in order to make them meaningful as well. Sometimes they want to experience how other people live, to walk for a while in the shoes of a ditchdigger, a garbage collector, a homeless person. Or perhaps they glimpse in the distance the gloomy specter of boredom, and make a calculated leap to another level before it catches up. Even when an event or the behavior of someone else serves as a catalyst for the change, the response of the innovator I find remarkable. Few people over fifty, for example, would react to the news that they had cancer as Olive Ann Burns did. Before she left the doctor's office, Olive Ann decided to write her first novel.

As I now use the term, innovators resist being defined and summed up by culture and circumstance. They have an idea, almost a Platonic ideal, of what they are missing in their often well-oiled and smoothly running lives. Resisting their own complacency as well as external disapproval or opposition, they set about to make this idea, this ideal, a functioning part of the way they live.

The changes of the innovators in this book fall roughly into three categories. First, there are professional changes, most often changes from one field to another. In addition to the microbiologist turned actress already mentioned, I have interviewed such innovators as Job Michael Evans, a monk who became a dog psychologist; Jack Coleman, a foundation president who became an innkeeper; Prynn Kaplan, a waitress who started her own construction firm; and Michael Stanford, a sheep farmer who now heads a computer firm.

Other kinds of professional changes are represented also. In one, the innovator stays in the same field but changes the level of responsibility or flexibility in his job. At forty-seven, Ed Mc-Cabe bought himself time by leaving the helm of his advertising firm to become an independent consultant. His first adventure: driving the grueling nine-thousand-mile Paris–Dakar automobile rally. In another, the innovator works out a balance among several careers. In order to satisfy divergent needs in her own life, for example, Martha Ritter maintains three separate careers: actress, writer, and social worker.

In a second category are changes which satisfy aesthetic, spiritual, or emotional longings. The multimillionaire businessman Gilbert Kaplan, who could hardly read music, set himself the herculean labor of learning to conduct Mahler's extraordinarily difficult Second Symphony. Here also belong such stories as that of *Rachel Weissman and Nancy Schwartz. Rachel, who is single and white, adopted two biracial children, the second one seventeen years after the first. Nancy, an adopted child herself, began at sixteen to court disaster by searching for her "real" mother.

* Indicates that the person's name and other identifying characteristics have been changed.

Ten years later, she triumphed over the calamitous situation she found.

Finally, there are changes undertaken to get rid of an emotional or physical burden or constraint, and thus to open up the possibilities of life. In this third category belongs *Waldo Gurewich, who lost sixty-five pounds and revamped his whole life as a result. Betsy Williams, fifty-five years old, moved all the way across the country in order to break off a sixteen-year liaison with a married man. *Brad Warner, a Protestant minister who decided to live as a homosexual after thirty years of marriage and three children, also fits into this category.

Obviously these categories overlap considerably. Rarely is a change purely professional or purely personal. Even a small change in one part of a life will probably make other changes necessary or desirable; a very big life change may begin with one tiny alteration. Regardless of the category of the change, however, the process of change was similar in all of the stories. This process consists of three recognizable stages:

1. DISCONTENT. Because of boredom, frustration, or lack of meaning in life, the individual realizes the need for change.
2. PROVOCATION. Unlike others, who make do with unfulfilled lives, the innovator consciously—or unconsciously—provokes problems that lead to crisis.
3. CRISIS. "What do I really want?" the innovator asks, and then pursues the choice made.

"Choice" is an important word. This book will not deal with the desperate people of the world who have no recourse, who must change to survive. A number of the people I have interviewed describe themselves as having felt desperate to change their lives. Except in a few cases, however, an outsider looking in would see their lives as more fortunate than most. Nor have I taken as my subject people who drift into change, who put up so little resistance that life takes them where it will.

The people of this book, the innovators, went out and sought change. Nothing was wrong, at least on the surface, with their lives. On the contrary, much was right. For most of them, the old life contained a plenitude of comfort, security, acceptance—all the things that usually make for happiness. The new life spelled discomfort of various kinds, insecurity, loss of status, and skepticism or rejection from others. Yet the innovators chose to move into uncertainty and risk, chose to gamble with their lives.

One of the questions that I consistently asked of the innovators is "Do you consider yourself 'different' from other people?" Most of them do. They usually don't know exactly how or why they are different, but they can see that they operate differently; they live differently from others.

Emily Korzenik calls herself an "activist." "I react strongly to things," she says. "I can't throw things off." Though sometimes this intensity causes her to "impose" her convictions on others, it gave her the strength to begin rabbinical school when she was forty-seven, and to become an ordained rabbi at fifty-two.

"Of course I'm different," says Sylvia Averbach. "I'm a little crazy." But, she adds, "everyone is entitled to a year of craziness."

And *Dominique Leclerc, a former nun who left the convent after more than twenty years because she felt spiritually and emotionally stultified, described herself as "a seeker and a survivor." She identified in herself "a very decided determination to learn, to grow, to experience, to understand, and to stretch a little bit further than my perceived limits, constantly, always."

The willingness to act, to take risks. High aspirations. Determination. Optimism. These are the qualities the innovators most frequently cited in answer to the question "Are you different?" As human beings, to use Dominique's words, innovators describe themselves as seekers and survivors. They insist on living their lives on different terms from those of their friends and acquaintances. Even within their families, they think, they are mavericks. Most of them describe their parents and siblings, and sometimes their children, as having far more stable, routine lives than their own.

Their essential difference from others lies not so much in what they are or in what they have, as in what they do. Some of the innovators, like Gil Kaplan, have money. A few have prominence, like A. Bartlett Giamatti, head of the National League of baseball when I interviewed him and later baseball commissioner, or Katherine Fanning, then editor of *The Christian Science Monitor*. One has even achieved and then discarded royalty— Hope Cooke, once the Queen of Sikkim, now a social historian living in Brooklyn.

But for what makes them special, I tend to agree with *Alma Whitman, poor, black, barely literate, who says proudly, "I'm not different, but I *did* something different." Alma, unmarried and childless, decided at forty that she wanted a child but not from any of the "sorry" husband material she saw around her. So she had her little son by artificial insemination. "Blacks just don't do what I did," Alma says.

By their fruits shall ye know them, and to my mind, it is the doing that distinguishes innovators. They have learned four important skills in living. I prefer to speak of skills rather than of qualities because to me "qualities" suggests something innate and fixed, givens of genetics and conditioning. "Skills," on the other hand, like speaking French or riding a bicycle, are not givens. Skills can be acquired. Though a natural proficiency never hurts, any normal, healthy person who tries hard enough can learn them.

The four skills in living which the innovators possess are:

1. ACCEPTING THE CONSTANCY OF CHANGE. Through such acceptance, innovators become active rather than passive in their attitude toward change. They make changes themselves rather than wait to be the victims of change.

2. LISTENING TO THE INNER VOICE. Innovators use not only the intellect, but also hunches, feelings, dreams, "signs," and intuitions, in deciding what they want for their lives. They pay attention to the hidden self.

3. RECOGNIZING AND EXPLORING OPPOSITES. For innovators, everything has a recognizable and intriguing opposite: order/disorder; male/female; what is/what might be. Thus they are open to the complex possibilities of the world.

4. DEVELOPING A STRONG, INDEPENDENT EGO. This skill gives innovators the desire and the courage to break with convention and overcome obstacles in order to follow their dreams.

Is there any advantage for the rest of us to seeing these skills in action in the lives of those who have mastered them? Will we gain any advantage in trying to learn the skills ourselves, whether or not we ever plan to make a dramatic change in our own lives? I think there is, and we will. As Jerome Kagan of Harvard recently pointed out, change is a far more common experience in human development and in all human affairs than continuity. We prepare for continuity, but it is change we must learn to expect.

In our hearts, we already know that truth. Any realistic, mature person has already begun work on the first of the four skills, accepting the constancy of change. The more thoroughly we master these four simple but profound skills in living, the more fully we are able to live. Accepting the fact that change is the law of nature; listening to the inner voice that tells us what we ourselves desire; paying attention to the rich array of opposites that the world offers; building an ego strong enough to go after the things in the world that we want—thus we gain power over our own lives.

Natural as it is for me personally to crave security, and to revere, cling to, and seek to resurrect my past, I have learned that power over my life depends on how well I negotiate change. I often long to cry out like Virginia Woolf's Mrs. Ramsay, "Life, stand still here!" But there's less power in trying to hold back than in making ready to go forth. "Power," Emerson wrote in 1841, "ceases in the instant of repose; it resides in the moment of transition from a past to a new state, in the shooting of the gulf, in the darting to an aim. This one fact the world hates: that the soul *becomes.*"

We hate the fact of constant change because we fear it. We fear *becoming* as I feared leaving my old life and becoming the person who is writing these words. Maybe innovators feel less fear— they live as if they do. Innovators can, quite simply, tolerate higher levels of uncertainty, of tension and paradox, than other people can. They can live with equanimity and even enjoyment in the midst of degrees of flux and ambiguity that others would find at best distracting and at worst seriously damaging. In fact, innovators like to shake things up, to keep things moving. They want to give their feelings and minds room to play. They are as curious and frequently as spontaneous as children.

In any situation, they want to know "What would happen if . . . ?" They don't want to miss anything. Stubbornly, they will maintain their right to know "what would happen if"—and to experience it also—in the face of all kinds of caution, orthodoxy, convention, and outright restraint.

More than almost anything, innovators hate to feel bored. They tend to be more afraid of boredom than of change. They

11

may sit in an office in a three-piece suit—for the moment—but their hearts are with Huck Finn in his overalls, lighting out for the Territory and a future of his own making. "I think you have to keep moving," Bill Emerson told me, "from security into insecurity. Intuitively, you know you have to undertake things that you're not certain you can do. You keep changing life at whatever risk, because the risk of being bored is a much deadlier risk."

Another remark which Bill made in our interview has been a touchstone for me as I have sought to comprehend the peculiar breed of person I call the innovator, of which Bill is a prime example. When we talked, Bill had already made many changes during his sixty-three years, and he was contemplating yet another. I interviewed him in Columbia, South Carolina, where he was a tenured university professor. Five months later, he was once again a freelance writer, living in Atlanta.

On the scorching July day of the interview, Bill was talking, with zest and enthusiasm, about the upcoming change he and his wife Lucy were planning. "Every nine years," he said, "I make a big change."

I looked around me at the accoutrements of their pleasant life, the comforts of a university home in which money is neither an object nor a problem. I knew the affection and esteem with which his students regarded Bill. I was mindful of the battles he had already fought, the respect he had won from his peers as a professional journalist who had placed himself pugnaciously among academicians.

How difficult, after a lifetime of change, another change could be for Bill at the age of sixty-three, I thought. How hard he might find this change, which took him away from students and colleagues, company he clearly enjoyed with every atom of his courtly, combative, contradictory self, and threw him back on his own solitary resources.

Yet here he was saying, with every appearance of genuine relish, "Every nine years, I make a big change."

"Even when you're happy?" I asked.

Bill looked at me quizzically for a moment. Then came the emphatic retort, "Especially when I'm happy."

Part One

The Process of Change

Live all you can; it's a mistake not to. It doesn't so much matter what you do in particular, so long as you have your life. . . . Live!

—HENRY JAMES, *The Ambassadors*

Discontent

Because of boredom,
frustration, or lack of meaning
in life, the innovator realizes
the need for change.

1

Tending the
Human Spirit

By and large, statisticians tell us, Americans are a contented people. Three out of four of the men and women who responded to a Gallup Poll taken during the Reagan administration, John L. Goodman, Jr., reports, claimed to be satisfied with their personal lives and their jobs. We don't know, of course, what these three out of four Americans mean by "satisfied." Polls deal in quantity, not quality. Nevertheless, if the people who confided their satisfaction to Gallup are at all representative of the population as a whole, most Americans are satisfied, or say that they are.

The innovator, on the other hand, is very often dissatisfied. Ask an innovator, "Are you satisfied?" Chances are, the answer will be, "Yes, but . . ." or "I will be when . . ." However enviable his or her situation may look to others, the innovator feels that life holds unexplored possibilities, unrealized potentialities; something has been left undone.

Sylvia Averbach had wanted to be an actress for over forty years. When she finished high school and planned to go on the stage, her Russian immigrant father discouraged her. "It isn't nice for a Jewish girl to be an actress," he said.

Sylvia's father—"my vocational guidance counselor," she calls him in her one-woman show—was a window-washer for a large dairy in Philadelphia. He told Sylvia, "I see through the windows men working with white laboratory coats, like doctors, and they have clean hands. I know the president of the company, so when you graduate from college, I'll be able to get you a job. You'll be a microbiologist."

Sylvia became a microbiologist. During the Second World War, she joined the WAVES and married a young Navy doctor. Three children and "a beautiful life" later, her husband died. Out came the old discontent she had nearly forgotten.

"I was fifty-seven," she says, "and I was desperate. I made a list of all the things I had never done in my life because I was married and a mother, and I was surprised at the long list that I had. I wrote anything I thought of—walk across the Brooklyn Bridge, fly an airplane, go scuba diving in Israel, walk down the middle of the street nude—anything that came to my mind that I hadn't done and in my fantasies wanted to do. One thing that cropped up time and time again was that I wanted to go to New York and be an actress." So she did it.

Sylvia wanted to become an actress. Cecilia deWolf, already an actress, became frustrated and miserable in the very world of New York theater that Sylvia craved. What the innovator does in particular doesn't so much matter, as Henry James puts it, "as long as you have had your life." Feeling that something is missing, that life is meaningless, generates a discontent which, with the right provocation, becomes a challenge.

"At twenty-nine and a half, I realized I was discontented. My dream had been to play Desdemona, and here I was selling dog food. I had thought that by the time I was thirty I would be

making an impact on the world. Instead, my whole life felt just—
I don't know, weightless," says Cecilia deWolf.

"So all of sudden I went, 'Hey, wait a minute. I'm an adult.
I've got to *do* something.' "

A cold rain falls steadily outside the Manhattan apartment
building where Cecilia lives with her musician husband, but
Cecilia's kitchen is as warm and cheerful as Cecilia herself. On
the blue-checked cloth of the small round table at which we are
sitting, my tape recorder is flanked by a bowl of oranges and
green apples and a small ceramic candleholder with a fat orange
candle. I realize that the pretty blonde who is talking so animat-
edly across the table cares about the quality of daily life. Cecilia,
thirty-five, is wearing slacks and a green shirt tied at the waist.
Her blue eyes sparkle in her animated face. Concern for the
quality of life, she is saying, caused her to change her career.

When she decided to innovate her life, Cecilia had already
"done something" by most standards. Next to the youngest in
an upper-middle-class Long Island family, she had seen her
father die when she was nine and her widowed mother struggle
to cope with the "crazy household" of eight children, the four
older ones "steps." Cecilia, who began acting at six, was good
enough to make her own way. At college in Denver, she worked
in local dinner and cabaret theaters. Graduate school at Penn
State was financed by an assistantship which paid full tuition
plus a weekly salary.

Even in New York, where another name for "actor" is often
"waiter," Cecilia had acting work. Soon after her arrival in the
city, she joined a top improvisation company, Chicago City Limits. With her improv work and the money she made doing television commercials, she supported herself.

But Cecilia wasn't happy. She had wanted to be a serious
actress, a "Meryl Streep or Maggie Smith, to make a contribution." Instead, "I was earning a living, being very silly on stage
with Chicago City Limits, and selling dog food and cleansers to
pay the rent." And no one was about to give her a shot at playing
Desdemona.

She couldn't even get a theatrical agent. "I had done weird
things," she says. Her father's death and the family's subsequent
trauma had marked the sensitive girl. She learned "to be good
and do things right" to protect herself, but under her docile

19

surface Cecilia was seething with questions: "what it means to be human, and why get up in the morning—those basic questions that some of us get plagued with. I was always searching for the solution to the human dilemma."

This existential search had led her, before she came to New York, to join a radical feminist theater company in Minneapolis, a particularly "weird" move to theatrical agents who think of Broadway as the center of the known world. "At the Foot of the Mountain Theater," a well-funded Equity company, later became the biggest and most successful feminist theater group in the country. But the Minneapolis company began with only eight women, "heavy duty" playwrights, directors, and actresses, according to Cecilia. Still in graduate school when she was first approached by the group, Cecilia was the youngest pioneer member.

United by a common political vision, the eight women lived together as well. They created and produced feminist plays on such subjects as rape, madness, marriage, and the relationship between mothers and daughters. The mutual support, the serious involvement in work, and the group's idealism—"We were working to change the world"—appealed to Cecilia. "I bought the platform," she says. "I was so angry at the way the world was, and I decided that men must be the problem."

At length Cecilia began to find the closeness of the tight little community oppressive. Her life turned "dark and heavy"—literally "heavy," as slender Cecilia ate her weight up to 185 pounds. "Desperately angry" and desperately unhappy as well, she did what many of the seekers of the seventies were doing—she signed up for est training. "I had heard about it, and I just did it."

Like "primal scream" therapy, Gestalt therapy, and Esalen, est is an outgrowth of the Human Potential Movement of the sixties. According to its most articulate spokesman, the psychologist Abraham Maslow, this movement replaced the concept of maturity, as the goal of human development, with the doctrine of growth. Freud and his followers studied unhealthy and neurotic personalities. Maslow studied those whom he considered to be supremely healthy.

In *Toward a Psychology of Being,* Maslow described his ideal for human development. The "self-actualizing" individual, to use his term, is a person whose basic needs are satisfied, who is free of neurosis, and, most important, who continues to grow. By moving from one "peak experience" to another, even into old age, all human beings can exercise their potential for development.

This new psychology attracted numerous enthusiasts, some of them famous. Carl Rogers, Aldous Huxley, Arnold Toynbee, Buckminster Fuller, and Joseph Campbell have all been associated with the Esalen Institute at Big Sur. Est training was originated by Werner Erhardt, a handsome, charismatic man who had been Jack Rosenberg before the road-to-Damascus experience that, as he told his thousands of followers, had "transformed" him. In "training sessions" across the country conducted by his disciples, Erhardt shared his methods of transformation with others. Those methods have been softened and individualized in recent years, but the old tactics inspired belief also. In his biography of Erhardt, W. W. Bartley III quotes the singer John Denver: "Est epitomizes what it is to be human."

But there have been detractors of the Human Potential Movement, and of est. At its worst, these critics point out, self-actualization is just another word for plain old selfishness—the syndrome of "I'm sorry to leave you and the nine children, dear, but I must go out and fulfill my potential." And est has been described as what passes for spirituality in a secular society—a hyped-up amalgamation of *The Power of Positive Thinking, How to Win Friends and Influence People,* and that old-time religion.

Est doesn't work for everyone who tries it. After a training session which cost three hundred dollars and involved several hundred people, one disenchanted seeker complained, "You have to get IT. They keep you in the same room for hours and won't let you leave even to go to the bathroom until you get IT. But nobody will tell you what IT is."

Est did, however, work for Cecilia. An est session served as a catalyst for her growth out of a narrowly feminist perspective and into one more broadly human. The leader of the session, she says, was a man who "acted like an animal." All day long Cecilia sat silently seething, watching him pick his nose, take off his shoes, scratch his genitals, "let it all hang out," in the parlance of the times. Disgusted with his boorishness, she didn't hear a word he was saying.

Finally she stood up and shouted at him. "I have been watching you," she screamed, "and I think you are a pig, a boor! You look like Stanley Kowalski in *Streetcar Named Desire*. You are everything I hate in men. I hate you, I hate you!"

"It was the first time in my life I'd ever told a man *the truth,*" she remembers. "And as I was spewing it all out, I realized that he didn't look like Stanley Kowalski to me at all. He looked like the young Marlon Brando."

With that realization, she stopped her tirade in mid-sentence. In front of three hundred people, she said, "Oh, my God—I am incredibly attracted to you. I really find you the most attractive thing."

"Then that fell away," Cecilia remembers, "and what was left was this fear. He was a man and I didn't know *how* to be with him. And it struck me that that was the truth about me and men—in all my life I had never known what to do with men. They were these strange beings, this other species, and I hated them because I was terrified."

Cecilia, I suppose, found IT. She had been searching for "the panacea, the belief system," the single solution to all her pain. In a series of est moments, she realized that, like all human beings, she was too complex for such simple answers. The fatherless child, the daughter of her struggling middle-class mother, the capitalist who had worked all her life for money, the socialist in the sisterhood, the actress trying to express humanity, the feminist who knew nothing about men—they were all Cecilia. "I had never experienced myself as anything bigger than the content of my life," she says. "Est helped me see that I was the context that holds the content." She was the person she was, in fact, exactly because of all the paradoxes she contained.

Groping for words with which to communicate the insight she gained through est and which has dominated her life since, Cecilia catches sight of the bowl of apples and oranges on the table between us. "I had an experience of myself," she says, "as the bowl that holds the fruit. But all those pieces of fruit were in fact parts of me. You can live at the level of one piece of fruit in the bowl. But you are a self, and a self is free to *do.*"

Back in Minneapolis, the "At the Foot of the Mountain" company sat down together to debate the merits of a script Cecilia thought was "wonderful." But one of the members suggested that the play was "counterrevolutionary" because the female characters in it had relationships with men. A heated battle ensued.

"There we were," Cecilia remembers, "sitting at this table, under the tapestry of a vagina, right?, with our shaved heads and our work shirts. And I just started laughing. I mean, I loved these women deeply. But I knew I just didn't want to fight this battle anymore." At twenty-seven, Cecilia, the "baby" of the group, had grown beyond it. With her enlarged view of life and of herself, Cecilia saw that they had been preaching only to the converted. So she left Minneapolis and moved to New York. "As an actor," she says, "I wanted to speak to the world."

After two years in Manhattan, she realized that, aside from the improvised comedy at Chicago City Limits, she was speaking largely to television audiences about dog food. So much for all her noble ambitions. Aspiring, optimistic, determined Cecilia was in despair.

Fortunately she was also in therapy. "I'd go in week after week, and I'd sit down and say, 'I just hate what I'm doing, it's not what I planned on. I'm not doing anything of any worth.'"

For a while the therapist, who really was "a great friend," just listened sympathetically. Then—"I'm sure she just got sick of hearing how I hated my life"—one week she asked, "Look, Cecilia, is there anything else that you've ever wanted to do in your whole life?"

Cecilia thought. "When I was real little," she answered, "I wanted to be a nurse. I used to get all dressed up in my nurse's uniform and take care of my dolls."

"You have an assignment for next week," the therapist said. "Make a list of the nursing programs in this area." Desperate enough to do anything, Cecilia complied. As she was checking sources in the public library, it dawned on her: "I could do this. It's not beyond me to do this."

The thought freed her. "It was like saying I could expand, I could just take a rocket ship, go to another place, create some more territory to live in."

So, on the last day of fall registration, Cecilia signed up for chemistry and physics courses to fulfill the science requirement. Optimistically, she applied at the same time for admission to a special two-year intensive program in nursing at Columbia-Pres-byterian, which started in January. "I'll become a nurse," she thought. "Acting is expressing the human spirit, and nursing is tending it."

Medicine is the career of several of Cecilia's family members. Her oldest half-brother, nearly sixty, is a brilliant and respected cancer specialist, "a big heavyweight doctor." As smart and ambitious as she is, I asked Cecilia, had she thought of becoming a doctor instead of a nurse?

No, she told me in very decided tones. It was not the pathol-ogy that interested her, but the person enduring the pathology. "Nurses keep the patient alive. We're there."

Cecilia did, however, consult her physician brother about the advisability of a nursing career. He was appalled at the idea. "Why do you want to leave a good profession like acting to go into nursing? Nursing is a terrible profession," he said. "You'll be a slop cleaner. It's a repulsive, menial job—you don't want to do that."

"But I want to make a contribution to life," Cecilia told him.

"Oh, you young people," he said. "You have this airy fairy outlook. Do what you're trained to do. Life is about getting bread on the table."

Cecilia thanked him for his advice and left. "I thought, that's just a doctor's point of view. It was my decision to make."

Or so she thought. It never occurred to her that Columbia-Presbyterian might not want her in their nursing program. Run-ning back and forth to auditions for commercials to raise the high tuition, Cecilia studied physics and especially chemistry. Chemistry, she decided, was a bad joke designed to drive her crazy—she couldn't believe in molecules. "What do you mean—molecules? All I see is air."

With the help of a tutor, she toughed out good grades in both. When her stamina flagged, she cheered herself on by thinking, "In two years I'll be a nurse." Meanwhile, she waited to hear from the nursing school admissions office.

Cecilia opened the letter from Columbia-Presbyterian in the chilly casting office of an agent known in the acting business, for obvious reasons, as the Prince of Darkness. Waiting for the Prince to deign to admit her to his royal presence, she stared in disbelief at the kind but firm words of rejection. "Take some biology courses and try again in the fall," the letter ended.

"I can't accept this," Cecilia said aloud. The Prince's frosty receptionist looked at her oddly. "I can't accept this," Cecilia repeated. "May I use your phone?"

She called the admissions office. "I can't accept this refusal," she told the voice on the other end. "I have decided to become a nurse, and I can't accept this rejection."

"Um, yes," said the voice. "I see. Well."

"You have got to understand. I've already decided my whole life here. I have to do this." Cecilia felt a big est scream coming on.

"Let me get Dr. Carter," the voice said faintly.

Another, firmer voice came on the line. "Now then, Miss deWolf," it said, "the problem is that you don't have enough biology. You will never pass Anatomy and Physiology—that's our weeding-out course—with high school biology. You'll be swamped. Do yourself a favor and come back when you've had some biology courses."

At this point, Cecilia began begging. "You don't understand, Dr. Carter. I have changed my whole life. I took physics, I even took chemistry. I have to do it now. I can't wait. I would go crazy. I would kill myself."

She laughs as she remembers her histrionics. "I may not have said I would kill myself," she hedges. Whatever she said must have been good. The admissions board decided to gamble on Cecilia; she was admitted for one term on probation.

She *was* swamped. "Having dissected a rabbit twelve years earlier just didn't do it," she says. "I didn't know anything, not even the difference between a vein and an artery. I opened my books that first day, and I went, holy Jesus, I'm gonna die."

She didn't, of course. She made it, with the help of a sympathetic agent named David Elliot. For Cecilia was lacking not only in science but in money as well. In a city where actors take menial jobs in order to act, she had to act in commercials in order to prepare herself for a "menial job." Just making a living had previously taken all her energy. Now, in addition, she had huge school expenses and less time to work. "But I was too busy to worry about money," Cecilia says. "I threw my hands up and said, 'I trust that the universe will take care of me somehow.'"

The universe took the form of Dave Elliot, who put himself out to book her for television commercials in spite of her trying schedule. "He'd call my machine and say, 'I know you have that physiology exam at twelve-thirty, Ceci, but can you get downtown by two?' And I would finish the exam and race downtown from 168th Street on the A train. I'd be all flushed; the curls would be out, and I'd look like a rag. But I'd do the shoot, and then I'd race back up for class."

Halfway into December, toward the end of her first year in school, Cecilia had not paid December's rent and was down to "the very bottom" of her checking account. Dave told her, "I have a booking for you, a three-day shoot in New Orleans, but it's in the middle of exam week."

She went. She had to. "I came to school with my bags packed to fly to New Orleans, took two exams early, and then went down with all these nursing books on the shoot, and returned to take three more exams. It was really not fun. It was very hard."

One of the hardest parts was the loneliness. "You're on this lonely road, and nobody knows really what you're doing. I couldn't tell people in nursing school about the acting—they would have thought I was flaky—and other actors would never have understood the nursing thing."

On Tuesdays, Cecilia got into the late-night habit of dropping by a jazz club, the Red Blazer Too, to listen to a set or two before bedtime. On her graduation night in 1984, she and her friends celebrated there, and Cecilia, in an exuberant mood, at last mustered up the nerve to speak to Andy Stein, one of the musicians whose music she'd been listening to so regularly. On their third date Andy asked Cecilia to marry him.

The two were married in 1986. Cecilia credits nursing school for giving her her husband. "Before I went into nursing, I was a girl reeking of adolescence. Making that lonely individual choice to expand my life, to become a nurse, to give myself a foothold on this planet—I became a woman. I became a person ready to be a wife and a mother. I became a grownup."

Cecilia describes becoming a nurse as a spiritual training. "Here I was, this crazy theater person, and I had to get down, to humble myself, to go back to zero." She still remembers a humbling experience when she started making the rounds as a student nurse. Her teacher said, "Here's a pan and water, Cecilia. Now you go into that room, please, and give that man a bedbath."

"What?" Cecilia said. "You mean his body?"

"Yes, wash him. He's old, he can't walk, he can't breathe, he can't move. Wash him."

"His whole body?" Cecilia asked. "You mean his penis? How do you wash a penis?"

"You pick it up, you wash it, you rinse it, and you lay it down."

"I stood out in the hall shaking, going, 'I can't! I just can't!' This was new territory, some level of human intimacy that I knew nothing about," Cecilia recalls.

"But I went in, and when I finished the sheets were soaked, the floor was soaked, and I was soaked. But that man was *clean.*"

All her life Cecilia had been struggling with her own questions: What does it mean to be human, and how can I endure the suffering that is my life? Now she was seeing other people in desperate straits, with a head nurse yelling, "Get a bucket! This man is hemorrhaging!" And in a split second Cecilia would be watching someone bleed to death.

As she watched, helpless, she thought, "God, how little my life has been. All those years I've been on stage trying to express 'truth.' Who the hell did I think I was? All our lives, we live trying to cope by not looking and not seeing and keeping our wounds bandaged and our foot on the trap door and getting through with as little pain as possible. But in the face of death, people finally wake up."

Cecilia became a good nurse. As she began to see that the will to live, or to take pleasure in what life was left, made a difference in her patients, she sometimes used her skills in acting. While she was still at Columbia, for example, she was doing a rotation on the cancer ward. "There was this one black man, missing a leg. He was a street person, no visitors, nobody. He weighed sixty pounds, and he'd had so much radiation that— Well, he had no vocal cords left, and he couldn't talk, he never smiled, never had any expression, just a living dead man.

"The nurses just wheeled him around, and nobody talked to him because you couldn't get any response. He was an enigma, because he should have been dead, but he had hung on.

"And one day, I was changing his sheets right underneath

him. Here I was, a human being in his presence, and he was staring straight ahead; he didn't acknowledge that I was there.

"I was in a crazy mood, I guess, so I started singing 'Embrace me' and dancing around the bed. I was acting; I started really seducing him. I flipped the sheets.

"And he looked at me. *He looked at me.*

"I just kept on singing and dancing with the sheets and the pillows. And all of a sudden he started laughing and he had no vocal cords but he was laughing. I sang louder and I was dancing and he was laughing and a permanent nurse on the floor came in and she just started crying because she had never seen him respond to anything."

In the face of death, people wake up. One woman who couldn't eat anything asked for, and got, a pizza. "She took one bite, but she had her pizza."

Today, in the clinic which she runs in Long Island City, Nurse-Therapist Cecilia deWolf tries to teach her patients to raise the quality of their lives, as she has raised the quality of hers, by pursuing whatever gives them real joy. She wants them to wake up while there is still time to enjoy the pleasures available to them.

"Just yesterday," she tells me, "a man came in, an executive, who's having a hard time just living. He gets up at five to get to work early. He gets so angry and frustrated at work that he has four or five glasses of wine at lunch. Then he comes home in the evening to his wife and five kids, and he drinks heavily every night. Basically he's an alcoholic." However, he came to Cecilia because of hypertension.

Wearing his mirror sunglasses, he sat down in her office. "How are you feeling?" she asked him.

"Fine," he told her.

Cecilia rolls her eyes and laughs. "But here he is, sitting in front of me, wearing these mirror sunglasses!"

She told the patient, "I really need to see your eyes to talk to you."

He pulled his glasses off slowly, reluctantly. "They're blue," he said.

"And they're bloodshot," said Cecilia.

"Because I drink," he told her. "But I have to. I can't stand it

otherwise. I'm going crazy. It's the only way I can get through."
His blue, bloodshot eyes pleaded with her for help.

"He's gotten a lot of conversations about his drinking, his
drinking, his drinking," Cecilia says. She tried a different tactic.
"When is your time for you?" she asked.

"There is no time for me," he told her. "I don't have time for
me."

Cecilia studied him for a minute. She remembered the therapist who had helped her change her life by asking, "Did you ever
want to be anything besides an actress?" Maybe there was some
pleasure to be resurrected from this man's past. She knew that
the patient lived in an affluent suburb by the beach. "Do you like
to swim?" she asked.

For the first time, the man smiled. "I used to be a lifeguard,"
he said. "I loved it."

"Make a pact with me," Cecilia told him. "Three times this
week, when you come home, before you start drinking—you can
have a drink afterward—take half an hour and go for a swim. Just
go to that beach and be with *you.*"

"Who knows what he'll do?" Cecilia says, shrugging realistically. "But he needed somebody just to give him permission to
change his life, to put some pleasure just for himself back into
his day."

Oddly enough, since Cecilia became a nurse, her acting career
has taken a definite upswing. Although she hasn't played Desdemona, serious roles are coming her way. Cecilia attributes this
new lease on acting both to her increased empathy for human
feelings and to the fact that she is not desperate for acting jobs.
Released from the necessity to make a living by acting, she can
bring more of herself, the real, the grownup Cecilia, to a role.

Her life has a balance that it didn't have before, the balance of
an artistically arranged bowl of fruit. One piece of fruit is the
acting, another the nursing, another her marriage, still another
the child she would like to have in the next few years. But Cecilia
is the bowl that holds all of these separate pieces of organic life.
She has a strong sense of herself and of what she can do. "I can
do anything on this planet and I'll still be me and I'll be fine."

Her joy in acting has been restored. She tries to explain what
makes acting such a joy for her. "When my father died, life was
difficult. Theater taught me that we can create an alternative

reality to the difficult reality of life. I just did a play up in Woodstock about a family that loves each other and that makes a huge change. Such a hopeful play. I love that. I love it that, in spite of all the bullshit that's going on all the time in life, we are able to create another reality, at *this* moment in *this* world."

At Woodstock, another cast member, a man who had already had a cancerous lung removed, made the mistake of smoking in rehearsals. Cecilia watched for a while. "I was so angry, so angry, but I stayed out of it, not being in my nurse mode, you know."

Then one night she just couldn't stand seeing him smoke. She walked over to the man, snatched the cigarette out of his hand, grabbed him by the neck, and shook him. "That's the dumbest thing I ever saw," she told him. "I care about you. Please, please, stop it! Don't fuck with life!"

No nurse wins them all, of course. Of all her patients, Cecilia remembers with the most regret one man whom she nursed for six months before he died of cancer of the throat. "He was a mensch. Oh, he looked ridiculous—emaciated, three hairs on top of his head. But I just loved this guy from the minute we met. I went in to do a very unpleasant procedure on him, and I said, 'I'm so sorry I have to do this.' He said, 'That's okay, fire away, I'm used to it.'

"The months went by and he was having many, many procedures done on him. He kept getting thinner, and they took more and more of his throat out. He had one of those slate boards, a Mighty Mouse board, and he would write me notes because he couldn't talk. We just had this great friendship.

"Then there was a long bout when he really couldn't swallow anymore. The doctors decided to put a tube right into his stomach so we could feed him directly."

The night he was to go into surgery, he wrote on his Mighty Mouse board, "Remember that line from *Macbeth,* 'My mind is full of demons'?"

"I've got it," Cecilia told him. "Your mind is full of demons. Let's get you a clean pillow case." Then she sat down beside him to talk until he went down into surgery to have the gastrotube inserted.

At midnight, when Cecilia was supposed to go off duty, her

friend had still not returned from surgery. She waited. She wanted to take him back to the recovery room and sit with him until he came to.

Cecilia was glad she had waited because, when his eyes opened, they were full of terror. "I mean, it was just the end of the rope for him."

About two o'clock in the morning, back in his room, the patient motioned for his Mighty Mouse pad. Pointing to his stomach, he wrote, "I haven't seen it yet."

She nodded.

Slowly he wrote, "I don't think I can look." Then he underlined the words.

Cecilia nodded again.

"So we gave him the Valium that had been prescribed for him," Cecilia says. After the Valium, she gave her patient the unwritten prescription of good nursing. "I loved him so much that I basically just got up in the bed with him and put my arms around him and just held him."

She told him, "I love you as a person. This tube is just one more physical piece of all this shit, this torturous physical hell you've gone through. But I want you to know that I think you are a great man, and I love you." Cecilia held him until he went to sleep. When she came in the next morning, she learned that he had slipped off peacefully in the night.

Easter came a week later. "I went out to see my mom and to go to the little Episcopal church on Long Island that I grew up in, this beautiful church. It was a sunny day, and I was with my mother and my family. The handbells started going, and the first hymn was 'Christ our Lord is risen today.'

"Well, I started crying. I hadn't ever cried for this patient, and I cried so hard. Every single hymn—'The strife is o'er,' everything—made me cry harder. He was dead, but I had loved his spirit, not his body, and his spirit wasn't dead.

"Nursing has put me face to face with what it means to be human, with my own mortality. It has said, 'You know what, you are dying.' I don't have a disease yet, but I'm dying. We're all dying.

"Before I went into nursing, I was always in despair. But you're with these people, and you see they can't walk, they're vomiting from radiation, they can't say a word. But you know what, right now, right here, they're alive.

"And if I can get up and swing my feet over the side of the bed, God damn it, what else fucking matters? I'm alive. I'm doing well."

For Cecilia, the process of innovating her life began with a metaphysical discontent in Cecilia herself. Trusting in the validity of that discontent, Cecilia deliberately introduced provocations for growth into her experience. The feminist theater company, est, the therapist, were catalysts. Through them Cecilia changed from docile daughter to "good" student to radical feminist to aspiring actress to caring nurse and finally to a self, as she puts it, capable of containing all those roles and many others.

But these catalysts worked because Cecilia allowed them to. They were not acts of God, imposed from above. Cecilia herself invited these catalytic experiences to do their work in her life. To grow, she faced up, first, to the fears that lay under her radical feminism; next, to her unwillingness to trivialize her talent as an actress; then to her deep desire to be of use in the world. When her inner voice spoke, Cecilia listened. Then she acted on what she heard. She chose to change in order to grow.

She has grown up through understanding something about the opposites of existence. She learned that she had to harden her ego in order to hone the skills of her compassion. Determined and optimistic, Cecilia pushed shamelessly to get into nursing school, scrabbled to make up her deficiencies and to earn her own way, disregarded talk about the horrors of nursing, and quelled her personal squeamishness. She had to get tough in order to give love.

Cecilia refused to lead a disappointed life, to borrow a phrase from Saul Bellow. When the hero of Bellow's classic American novel, *The Adventures of Augie March,* can't get satisfaction in one pursuit, he tries another. "I . . . go at things as I have taught myself, free-style, and will make the record in my own way," says Augie, who is an archetypal American character. Augie has gumption. So has Cecilia deWolf.

Augie winds up at the top, married to Stella, a movie star. We could call Cecilia's success horizontal rather than vertical. As an actress, she imagined herself a star, high on a stage, "expressing the human spirit." As a nurse, she came humbly to realize what a stranger that spirit had been to her, how little she had known to express. Whether or not "Cecilia deWolf" is ever spelled out in lights on Broadway, Cecilia has learned to see, through the travail and courage of the failing flesh, how immense the possibilities of the human spirit really are. Tend the body and you tend the soul. The girl who demanded a sweeping solution to all the world's ills has yielded to a woman who knows the value of a clean pillowcase and a loving touch.

2

Arrival
at Long Last

Sometimes the discontent of the innovator arises from the gap between ideal and reality, from a mental image, which the real world cannot match, of what life can be at its best. "We all possess inner worlds," writes the psychologist Anthony Storr, "which are, to varying degrees, at odds with the external world."

The most creative people, Storr goes on, "find, in their work, a new path of reconciliation." Jack Coleman became obsessed with the desire to know, firsthand, what it is like to live lives other than his own. Out of his experiences came a gnawing discontent with the injustice and inhumanity of the world. From that discontent emerged a dream of perfection. That dream Jack has tried to bring to fruition in a little town in Vermont.

"We are all deprived; we are all disappointed; and therefore we are all, in some sense, idealists," Storr writes. "The need to link the real and the ideal is a perpetual tension, never resolved so long as life persists, but always productive of new, attempted solutions." For that divided creature, man, these attempts at synthesis provide the "deepest consolations" and the "greatest glories."

Thus it is that an extraordinary man like Jack captures the imagination of many ordinary citizens.

The best of the leaves are gone this late in the season, the natives at gas stations and restaurants tell us. No connoisseurs, we are pleased with the leavings. Enticed by their glint, several times we have exited I-91 or Route 103 to meander down winding lanes of rusty red and tarnished gold. So by the time we arrive in the tiny town of Chester, in southeastern Vermont, it is almost five o'clock. There's even a smell of snow in the dark October afternoon when we finally pull up in front of the welcoming lights and the wide porch of the Inn at Long Last.

Inside the inn, all is glowing and warm. Glancing around the spacious, high-ceilinged living room while my husband checks us in, I take grateful note of a fire burning cheerfully in the large fieldstone fireplace. Big armchairs and deep leather couches invite us to sit. Books and good reading lamps on antique tables suggest we stay awhile. Polished floors, bright quilts on the wall, a hand-carved sign in the front window, a whiff of garlic (and can that be duck?) from the kitchen, a curving staircase to other comforts I can imagine on the two floors above—we'll stay, we'll stay, I think, as I stretch my car-weary bones.

The young woman behind the counter hands us our key. A tall, slender man with an aquiline face and a neatly trimmed gray beard comes forward to take our luggage. I recognize him as the man pictured in the recent *New York Times* story which has brought us to Vermont, the man we have come to see. "Dr. Coleman?" I ask.

"Yes," he answers, smiling, "but let's get you settled before we talk." And brushing aside our protests, he shoves one bag under his arm, takes the other two in his hands, and sets off briskly up the stairs. Bemused, we follow. Our bellboy is a nationally prominent labor economist, a past president of

Haverford College, a former chairman of the board of the Federal Reserve Bank in Philadelphia, the author of seven books (including one co-authored by Secretary of State George Schultz), and for the last ten years was president of the Edna McConnell Clark Foundation, a $400 million charitable fund in New York City. He is John R. Coleman, Ph.D., or, as he prefers to be called, plain Jack Coleman.

In May 1986, at the age of sixty-four, Jack left his prestigious post at the Clark Foundation to open this inn, with his son Paul and his daughter-in-law Ami as partners. Jack was acting on his own advice, he told the *Times* writer, to "obey that feeling you have at two o'clock in the morning when you wake up and you know what you really want to do." Reading this comment, I was curious. How had this man "known" he wanted to open an inn? What discontent had given him the gumption, at an age when others retire into a satisfied maturity, to start all over again in a business at which he was the greenest adolescent? Five months later, I have come to Vermont to hear the latest chapter in the story of Jack's innovative life.

Earlier chapters I already know. In preparation for this meeting, I have read Jack's 1974 book, *Blue-Collar Journal: A College President's Sabbatical,* which was made into a television movie, *The Secret Life of John Chapman.* In a variation of the traditional "How I Spent My Summer Vacation" genre, Jack describes a sabbatical he took while he was president of Haverford College. Instead of reading and writing, or visiting Europe, the usual practices of academics on leave, Jack worked incognito as a ditchdigger on a sewer project in Georgia, as a garbage man in Maryland, and as a salad-and-sandwich chef at the Union Oyster House in Boston.

While making sandwiches, he says in *Blue-Collar Journal,* Jack first conceived the idea of having a place of his own. Watching Joey, the owner of the Oyster House, happily commanding his kitchen, Jack muses, "I often ask myself nowadays why I'm doing what I do. Why am I in academics rather than, say, doing what Joey does? The answer is far from clear." And he wonders— whimsically or seriously?—"if Joey would like to switch jobs."

The highly praised book, a detailed and matter-of-fact account of what it is like to be a greenhorn at hard labor, offers little explanation of Jack's motives beyond "I needed some other experiences. I wanted another me to come out from time to time." What sort of "me" is the Jack Coleman who, carrying three heavy bags, has just beaten us up two flights of stairs and is not even winded?

But first comes a whirlwind tour of the inn. Though daughter-in-law Ami selected wallpaper, paint, and linens throughout the rambling white country house, Jack himself chose a theme and located appropriate books, paintings, and other art objects for each of the more than thirty guest rooms, he tells us. Thus, the whole inn is like a giant Rorschach given significance by Jack's imagination and diverse intellectual interests. The Audubon Room has reproductions of the famous prints. The Isaac Sharpless Room recognizes Jack's distinguished predecessor as president of Haverford College. There are the Charles Dickens Room, very elegant and Victorian; the Robert Frost Room; the E. B. White Room; other rooms honoring architects, opera singers, and artists, representing a dizzying array of the enthusiasms of a restless and questing spirit.

I stop in front of the George Orwell Room. "Orwell is one of my heroes," Jack says. I remember Orwell's autobiographical *Down and Out in Paris and London,* describing a time of severe poverty in which he worked at a series of ill-paid jobs. He came to hate every form of man's dominion over man.

"Maybe that's Jack's impetus," I tell my husband later. Jack has left us to wend our way down to the bar/library, in which Jack's own books nestle inconspicuously in a corner, and then in to dinner, where, yes, there is duck. I study my husband across the candles, the flowers, the starched linen. "Maybe he's a sort of democratic socialist, like Orwell."

"No socialist created this duck," says my husband. "This duck is aristocratic." And indeed it is, duck, or rather duckling, roasted with garlic and fresh rosemary, glazed with brandy and honey. And the wines are fine, and there's hazelnut cheesecake with Frangelica, and Remy Martin after our coffee. Jack himself is everywhere at once, checking on the kitchen, greeting the guests, encouraging the waiters, a genial and attentive host. An enigmatic man, Jack Coleman.

The next afternoon I take my tape recorder to Jack's apartment next door to the inn. My mission: to dispel the enigma. Jack laughs heartily when I ask him if he is a socialist. "Only in

37

the way my mother was," he says. "Politically, she was middle of the road, but she had a very, very deep belief in the dignity of every human being." Jack grew up, the middle child of three, in Copper Cliff, a mining company town in northern Ontario, Canada. His father, a metallurgist with a college degree, came from a "very smug, very proud" Church of England family, which lived "the civilized life" in Toronto. Loving but reserved, the elder Coleman was "a hard man to know."

Jack describes himself as much more like his mother in temperament. Unlike Jack's father, she grew up in Copper Cliff, the daughter of a poor, semi-literate family; she herself never finished high school. Her central quality, according to her son, was her democratic attitude. "Let people put on airs and she was unforgiving. They didn't get a second chance with her. But so long as they were good, open, honest people, my mother loved them all.

"She was very close friends with the mayor, the company manager, the garbage man, the guy who delivered the ice, and the only two people in town who were on welfare. Mother was the same with every one of them. I never saw any difference in the way she spoke about anybody at all."

The son shares his mother's innate regard for the dignity of every human being, a regard which shapes his religious life also. Some twenty years ago Jack, acting on his belief that God is in every person, became a Quaker. Perhaps to test that belief, more obviously to test himself, Jack has constantly sought to discover through firsthand experience exactly what it means to live another's life. Concerned with the balance of power between employers and workers, for example, he specialized in labor economics in graduate school. But the abstract study wasn't enough for him, which explains his desire to become a worker himself for a time. In his blue-collar jobs, Jack "learned things about other people that you can't learn from a book."

Later, he extended his study of human nature to include criminals, their keepers, and the homeless. On several occasions, with his identity kept secret from the other inmates, Jack voluntarily served time in jail, once even on a chain gang in South Carolina. "I was curious to know what it is like to be in prison, to have your freedom taken away from you." He learned that "you look for any way, even the smallest way, to establish that you're an independent person."

Jack, for example, would unscrew the light bulb in the top of his cell so that the guard doing the head count had to look in *twice* to check his prisoner's whereabouts. Seeing the guard do a double-take, Jack says, "Jeez, I felt good. I was saying, 'There's a real person in here, not just any old thing.'"

It was not the guard who was the real enemy, Jack came to realize, but the situation itself, the fact that some were prisoners and some their keepers. Guards had problems too. To understand the other side, Jack did guard duty, including a three-week stint on Death Row in Texas. He learned, to his dismay, that he was not immune from the corruption that comes from power, the "guard mentality." Even the simple act of putting on a uniform can corrupt, Jack says. When his older daughter saw him once in a police uniform, she told him, "Jack, as soon as you put that uniform on, you strut."

By far "the most searing and important experience" of walking in another's shoes came to Jack in 1983 when he lived for ten days as a homeless person on the streets of New York. "I cannot claim that I know much at all about what it's like to be homeless," he says. "For me it was phony. I was never more than a hundred and twenty blocks, at most, from my apartment, and I could walk back any time I wanted to." Nevertheless, those ten days have marked Jack Coleman's soul permanently.

"When you're a homeless person, you're nothing," he says. At the time, Jack was the head of the prestigious Clark Foundation. People bowed and scraped when he came into a room. With a change of clothes and of manner, "homeless" Jack became invisible. "People I knew walked by me and didn't see me—a guy who lived in my apartment building; a man who had been in an intensive training program with me just weeks before; the guy from Arthur Anderson who handled the Clark account. They looked right at me, I thought I had eye contact with them, and *they didn't see me.* That's nothingness."

It was January when Jack took to the streets. His first night out, the temperature dropped to fourteen degrees. Two years later, in late 1985, the city would begin picking up the homeless and forcing them into shelters on very cold nights, but in 1983 "you could freeze to death very, very easily."

The first act of kindness he experienced came not from the authorities but from another of the homeless. As the night grew late, Jack couldn't find a place to sleep. Everywhere he went to find some kind of protection from the cold, the police kicked him out. At length he remembered a grate on Forty-seventh Street between Fifth and Madison on which, when he walked by on his way to work every morning, he often saw a man sleeping. He made his way there. The grate was occupied. Cold and discouraged, Jack went up to the permanent resident. "I asked him if he would share his grate with me. The man immediately moved over to make room, without any questions at all."

During those ten days on the streets, Jack discovered that you could go hungry even when you had a little money. He never begged, as many of the homeless do, so every night he allowed himself a dollar for a bowl of soup at a greasy spoon restaurant. For people like him, he discovered, a special routine existed: first he had to surrender his money, then he was served. By the third or fourth night on the streets, "because of the way I looked and maybe the way I smelled," Jack says, he was turned away at first even when he showed his money. At last the restaurant owner agreed to take his dollar and Jack was permitted to eat, but in a corner by himself so that his presence wouldn't offend other customers.

Back at the Clark Foundation, his self-imposed exile with the homeless over, Jack found himself once again discontented. It wasn't that he was unhappy, exactly. "I loved that job. It was a wonderful job. But I had been there ten years, and that's long enough."

Why long enough, if he was happy? "Arrogance," Jack says. "One of the diseases to which all foundation officers are susceptible is arrogance. Once you become head of a foundation, no one speaks the truth to you from then on." People want the money the foundation is set up specifically to give away, so "they say what they think you want to hear." After a while, certainly by the tenth year or so, "you begin to take them seriously—'Maybe I *am* that wonderful person they say.'"

Simultaneously, according to Jack, because of the power you have to control charitable gifts, you begin to think of the foundation money as yours. You begin to feel, as he puts it, " 'Aren't I nice to be giving all this money away?' When those things start happening to you, you should be out of there." Those who stay too long grow little by little so accustomed to the office, the salary, the praise, that they're unwilling to think of anything else to which they can give their lives.

"Where do you go?" Jack asks. "If you've been president of a college, you can move to a foundation. But if you've been president of a foundation, what do you do next? Most people don't want to become innkeepers."

But then Jack Coleman is not most people. Where he got the notion of opening an inn, Jack is not quite sure. He had learned to cook of necessity in 1966 when he and his wife Mary, the mother of his three sons and two daughters, were divorced after twenty-three years of marriage. Over the next fifteen years, he developed a passion for feeding his friends. A happy day for him might mean having thirty-five or forty people for dinner—all by himself preparing the meal, welcoming his guests, planning entertainments for them, cleaning up afterward, doing what Jack calls "playing house."

Sometime in the late seventies, Jack described his pleasure in "playing house" to a female friend. She told him, "You know, Jack, you ought to be an innkeeper, because that's where you could really shine at these things you say you want to do." Jack laughed, then put the thought out of his mind—his conscious mind.

But Jack is a man who trusts the workings of his subconscious. Somewhere below the surface of his administrator's rationality, the idea of "playing house" full time took root and began to send up tentative, exploratory shoots.

As the years advanced, Jack began to have "a quiet sense" that the time for change from foundation president to innkeeper was upon him. "I had a realization that there are probably only so many years left in my life," he says, "that there are dreams left yet to be fulfilled, and there's nothing in the world to stop me from fulfilling them."

Earlier in our conversation, Jack and I had discovered a shared enthusiasm for the work of the Canadian writer Robertson Davies. As I listened to Jack describe the change that had come over him as he recognized his own mortality and the importance of acting on his dreams, I was reminded of Davies's comments on Carl Jung in his essay "The Conscience of the Writer." "Jung is insistent," Davies writes, "on a particular type of development in the mind of anyone who meets the problems of life successfully; it is the change, the alteration of viewpoint, the transformation of aims and ambitions, that overtakes everybody somewhere in the middle of life." Jack had met the problems of life superlatively well; the time had come for transformation.

At this stage, Robertson Davies goes on, such a person

> realizes that some day he is really going to die and that the way he approaches death is of importance to him; he finds that without God (using that name to comprehend all the great and inexplicable things and the redemptive or destructive powers that lie outside human command and understanding) his life lacks a factor that it greatly needs; he finds that, in Jung's phrase, he is not the master of his fate except in a very modest degree and that he is in fact the object of a supraordinate subject. And he seeks wisdom rather than power—though the circumstances of his early life may continue to thrust power into his hands.

Paradoxically, Davies concludes, this change does not make a person "old." "What will make him an old man is a frightened clinging to the values of the first half of life." He will age physically, of course, as he moves into "the new realm of values and emotions," but "his intellectual and spiritual growth will continue, and will give satisfaction to himself and to all those associated with him." Such people, according to Davies, "are on better terms with youth than the shrivelled Peter Pans who dare not be their age." Odd as it may seem, since we rarely think of opening an inn as being the path to higher wisdom, for Jack it was exactly that.

His experiences as president of Haverford College from 1967 to 1977 had no doubt fed Jack's dreams of what such an inn would mean for him. Haverford, a Quaker men's college in Pennsylvania, has had since its founding in 1833 a tradition of gentlemanly civility. During the student unrest which damaged

42

the manners and morale of other universities during the seventies, Jack says he never let Haverford students lose sight of their own good fortune.

"No matter how sordid and ugly the world in which you find yourself after you leave here may be," he remembers telling the men of Haverford, "you know it doesn't have to be that way. You will recall that once in your life you were in a place where people treated one another civilly, decently, openly, and honestly. You can never use the excuse for bad behavior that men cannot live together, because you have seen here at Haverford that they can."

After living with the criminals and the homeless, the disenfranchised of the world, Jack had a renewed awareness of the value of a place which could, by its example, remind people that civilized living in the best sense of the term is possible. In 1981, Jack at last mentioned that he'd like to open an inn to someone —to his son Paul, who was then twenty-six. To Jack's surprise, Paul responded enthusiastically, "That's what I want to do, too!" Paul's young wife Ami was equally enthusiastic.

Jack was elated. "Things broke for me that made it possible for me to do what I wanted—good health, children who love me and believe in me, a large amount of curiosity about the outcome. Even the fact that I'm divorced may have helped, because you can't take a jump like this unless you have a partner who really wants to do it with you."

Jack took the jump. After a good deal of talk and planning— and after a seminar in inn management which spelled out the long hours and financial difficulties of their project—during the summer of 1985 he, Paul, and Ami began a serious search for the right inn. At first the monstrous, dilapidated structure, painted flesh-pink, on the town square in Chester, seemed more nightmare than dream. But the location, four hours from Manhattan, two and a half hours from Boston, and a half hour from six ski slopes, was hard to beat. And the house had an eccentric charm that began to appeal to them more and more. Finally, they bought it for $500,000 from the bank that had taken it over when, after eight months as an innkeeper, the previous owner had gone bankrupt.

Some of his acquaintances thought Jack was crazy—"acquaintances, not friends. My friends *know* I'm crazy, or at least the idea that I would do something that was crazy to other people was not unusual to them." But people who knew him less well expressed vehement doubts. "Why take on a thing like that at this stage in your life?" they asked. "That," says Jack, "came from people who think I'm old now because I'm sixty-five."

But Paul and Ami were full of youthful confidence, and Jack felt as young as they. So, with the bank's backing, the three proceeded to spend almost as much on the renovation as they had on buying the inn. They painted the exterior white, replaced the leaky boiler in the basement with two new ones, rewired the basement, renovated the lobby, installed new showers and new toilet seats throughout the entire building. New beds and mattresses went into the guest rooms.

Local craftsmen came in to do this work, as well as to build the fireplace and bar in the library. Relations between employers and workers were so amicable that the men and women who worked on the carpentry and painting had their names inscribed on a brass plaque for the library. The Colemans had worried that Chester might not accept outlanders, but they made friends quickly. For one thing, the abandoned inn and the two empty stores connected to it cast a real pall, physical and financial, over the small village. "For us to come in, put money into the place, brighten it up, have cars out in front—people wanted us to be here and to succeed."

But Jack, people-smart as always, had other ideas that made friends for them in Chester, too. The Colemans held a giant sale of all of the discarded furniture, china, and silverware from the inn, and gave the proceeds to Chester. One third was donated to the town library, one third to the volunteer fire department (which Paul joined), and one third to a fund for a band shell on the village green. "The people liked that," Jack says, "and they've done extremely well by us. Our prices are high for the meals, but people do come, not only from Chester, but from other towns around."

If harmony reigned between the Colemans and the village, the collaboration among the three Colemans had its stormy moments. To purchase the property, they formed a partnership, then created a family corporation to lease the inn from the partnership. Of the corporation, Jack became president, with controlling interest, Paul vice president, and Ami secretary. Great, on paper—all the lawyers approved. But in a real life human family, things were not always so neat.

First came their joint disappointment in realizing that Jack could not realistically handle the kitchen. "There's a big difference," he says, "in doing all the work yourself for an occasional dinner party, and in cooking for seventy people, several meals a day, day in, day out. I exaggerated how competent I was in the kitchen." They hired chef Michael Brown, a graduate of the Culinary Institute of America, with a real talent in the kitchen and an artistic temperament to match.

But Jack found it hard to get out of the way. "You can't hover over that guy—he's too damned good—but I hovered beside him or something." When the inevitable conflicts came, Jack walked away in a huff.

"The biggest problem Paul and Ami had with me," Jack says, "and it is an ongoing problem, is that I am very critical, and I have a real inability to give up *control*. The control thing is big with me. I try to too great an extent to make everything a one-man show."

Jack didn't tangle with Paul, but he tangled with Ami. The first big blow-up came over the curtains in the new library. Ami had chosen them and Jack thought they were "godawful." "I had been loud in my praise of the fabrics, the wallpaper, the colors, that she had selected throughout the whole building, but I didn't like those—God, I didn't like them!—and it hurt her very, very deeply that I didn't like them."

He wanted them changed, Jack said. Ami said Jack didn't respect her taste. Jack said he had liked everything else she'd done, but not this. Ami said Paul liked the curtains. Paul looked pained. "It's funny now," Jack says, "but you know blow-ups usually occur between people over terribly small things. We had a royal blow-up."

Who won, I ask?

"There are different curtains down there," Jack says, grinning, "but Ami hasn't forgiven me, and Paul doesn't like the new ones."

Of course, they were all exhausted, they were all tense, they were all under tremendous pressure to succeed, especially Jack. "When you're a college president," he says, "and something goes wrong, you can blame it on the goddamfaculty—that's all one word among college presidents—or you can blame the trustees or you can blame the economy.

"When you're president of a foundation, about the only excuse you can use is that you're trying to solve intractable problems, problems that hardly anyone could make a dent in. Prison reform or unemployment among severely disadvantaged teenagers, for example.

"But here, short of a disastrous freak of nature, there's nobody to blame if we fail in this. It would be a failure of me personally, not of Paul and Ami, but of *me*."

Jack had another problem that Paul and Ami became aware of first. They watched him carefully during the first three months the inn was open, consulted other members of the family for their opinion, and only after being sure they were right did they approach Jack himself. Jack, the younger Colemans realized, was an alcoholic.

"I had been drinking for thirty years or more, I guess," Jack says, "and as far as I know the effects didn't show, particularly. But in the three months here, it began to take over. I was drinking less and less, but I had no tolerance whatsoever. My moods were up and down, in and out. When I woke up in the morning, people had no idea what I was going to be like, whether I was in a good mood or a bad mood. I couldn't make decisions, I didn't open my mail, it was incredible!"

Jack knew something was wrong, but he didn't know, or didn't want to know, what it was. "What I really thought was happening was that my mind was going. I just seemed to have lost control of myself—which is the definition of an alcoholic: you lose control, your life becomes unmanageable.

"I wasn't falling on my face, or blacking out, or committing stupid acts behind the wheel of a car. I was just no longer the person that I had been before, or the person I wanted to be. I was desperate. I make no secret of the fact that I was very seriously planning suicide. I just felt my life was falling apart, and that was the way out."

One Saturday morning, John, Jack's oldest son, showed up suddenly in the living room of the inn. "Jack," John said, "there's a crisis. You've got to come with me."

"My God," Jack thought, "one of my kids!" He didn't ask a question, but just followed John silently down the street to Paul's house. They walked into the living room. There sat Jack's two daughters, his youngest son, and Paul. Two members of the Clark Foundation staff who are close friends were there, as well as another man whom Jack didn't recognize.

"What's going on?" Jack asked. "What's this all about?"

"Then they just started," he says. "It was a Family Intervention, where your family and others who care really deeply about you confront you with your alcoholism. It's all very carefully orchestrated and rehearsed." The unknown man turned out to be a professional counselor for alcoholics.

Jack's reaction was typical. "I just clammed up and tried to walk away. I used to think that was noble, and that's what I wanted to do." It didn't work. The children insisted he stay to hear them, and then they insisted that he go into treatment. "I resisted for two days. I fought and fought. I went back to my apartment and poured out all my vintage wine. I tried making promises. I tried appealing to their affections, their loyalty, their filial respect. I tried being tender and loving. I found that I couldn't get any one of them to weaken. So I went. It was the best thing that ever happened to me!"

After spending a month in the hospital, for the next three months Jack was to go back for therapy on an outpatient basis (we talked in his second month). He also joined Alcoholics Anonymous, for which he has nothing but praise. Not only did the group help him with his drinking problem, but it pleased him by bringing him into contact with all kinds of people. "I defy you to name another institution in this society that brings together such a wide range of people in one room as AA does— from those who are clearly illiterate, young and old, to those who are highly educated and very successful, with a full spectrum in between. And there's an openness and honesty that's just absolutely beautiful."

Through his therapy, Jack got a new look at himself. He learned that he had been deceiving himself in several ways. After scoring one test to measure aptitude and preference, for example, the psychologist who tested Jack in the clinic told him he had never seen a score quite like his. "You absolutely went off

the page on caring for other people!" he said. "You're dominated by that." Jack smiled and nodded.

But the psychologist went on. "You have to watch that. Caring
too much about others can be an excuse for avoiding your own
problems."

Jack also had always prided himself on using his mind. "I
don't think of myself as an intellectual," he says, "but I know I'm
intelligent. One of the messages I celebrated most powerfully in
my teaching was, 'Use your mind.' "

Imagine his chagrin when he learned that in recovering from
alcoholism, intelligence is a disadvantage. "You try to figure this
thing out, and you're lost, because it's a chemical dependency.
It's not a moral weakness, or an intellectual weakness. It really is
a disease, and it's clearly terminal. Statistically, thirty-four out of
thirty-six alcoholics will die of it. There's no real cure, and only
one or two in thirty-six have any chance at all of keeping it in
remission."

Jack is right, I learned later. Research has shown that, because
of an excessive amount of Cytochrome P-450, an enzyme in the
liver, the alcoholic metabolizes alcohol differently from the social drinker. You have little chance of permanent remission, as
Jack emphasizes, if you try to outwit the disease. "KISS is one of
the mottoes of AA: Keep it simple, stupid. And that was very,
very hard for me, to be told over and over, 'Jack, stop trying to
intellectualize this thing.' "

Jack prided himself on his control of others and of himself.
Even as a child, he remembers, "I played with younger children,
and I organized them. I have enough imagination so that they
were willing because I could think of interesting things to do.
But it was control."

His alcoholism was the first thing ever that Jack Coleman
could not control without help. The introspection, the soul-
searching, that Jack went through he describes as "the most
profound of the changes that I have made in my life. And alcoholism brought me to it. That's why I say, thank God I'm an
alcoholic." In spite of his intelligence and education, in spite of
the position and power he gained in the world, in spite of his
earnest Quakerism and his great capacity for friendship, it took
his bout with alcoholism to confer on Jack's life a blessing he
would not have wanted to miss.

It changed his view of God—the name, you will remember, that Davies uses to refer to "the redemptive or destructive powers that lie outside human command and understanding." "Before," Jack says, "my God had been a standard to which men and women can aspire, what men and women can be at their very best. It never occurred to me to ask for God's help—God would have been much too busy to help, busy setting this standard to bring out the best in me.

"But when I clearly needed help, I had to alter that picture. Now I believe that God does have control over my life, that if I pray 'Let Thy will be done,' as in the Lord's Prayer, I've got a very good chance of making it."

Like Cecilia deWolf, Jack Coleman felt a "divine discontent," to use Charles Kingsley's phrase, which led him to change his life. Jack has done good in the world as a teacher, as a college president, as the head of a great philanthropic institution. But he may be at his best, both for himself and for others, "playing house" as the host at the Inn at Long Last.

Ultimately, what Jack means by "playing house" is sharing an ideal pattern of living with others. Discontented with the world he has experienced through his vicarious excursions into other lives, particularly the lives of the homeless, what really impels Jack is the desire to create a perfect, though temporary, "home" for others. Jack wants to bring his inner, imagined world, which is a place of harmony, equality, and joy, into actual existence. "It's my dream," he says, "that the inn will provide an image of perfection which people can take away with them when they leave. It isn't perfect yet."

It may never be perfect, as it will never be a permanent home for anyone, never even a temporary refuge that everyone can afford. As an image of perfection, the inn is for Jack what the ideal republic was for Plato. Plato's republic has never been seen on earth. To exist, these ideal structures must be built and managed by fallible human beings—that's the catch. Like Plato, like idealists everywhere, Jack is probably doomed to fail. But there's glory in the attempt.

49

Provocation

The innovator
consciously or unconsciously
provokes problems that lead
to crisis.

3

Designing Woman

Often people accept feelings of frustration, boredom, meaning-lessness, or "something missing" as part of the human condition. Innovators do not. Instead of an acceptance of life's givens, innovators have a curiosity about life's possibilities. To find out "what would happen if," they provoke a crisis which leads to change.

Sometimes the will to change is unconsciously or half-consciously provoked. When *Mark Murdoch, an actor, began volunteer work in a soup kitchen in his Times Square neighborhood, he had no idea that it would lead him, at the age of forty, to become a priest. Nor did Anselm Atkins, a Trappist monk, realize that his pursuit of knowledge would, after fifteen years,

53

lead him away from his vocation in the Church into another profession, and into marriage. Each man's pilgrimage—Anselm calls his an "unpilgrimage"—began as a faint, barely conscious stirring in the center of his being. A longing for honesty, for a coherence between thoughts, feelings, and work, caused each eventually to reshape his life.

The story of Lois Grant is even stranger. The provocation to change began for her as an overwhelming sense of unhappiness with the way she spent her days. When Lois was frustrated in her attempt to act on this feeling, she developed painful and crippling symptoms of rheumatoid arthritis. Lois, an intelligent and highly rational woman, firmly believes that the arthritis was an outward sign of her inward misery. And she is just as firmly convinced that the arthritis was driven into remission only because she completely redesigned her life.

Disparate as their stories are, the change for each of these people began at thirty-five, the age when Dante's pilgrim "came to myself in a dark wood where the straight way was lost." How, following the half-conscious provocations of the psyche, each found a new road indicates that the destiny that shapes our ends is certainly as resourceful as any television scriptwriter. For these three people, that destiny worked its will from the inside of the human being out. As a man thinketh in his heart, so is he. Or, if he is an innovator, so doth he become.

"There are three good tests for deciding whether you're doing the right work," a wise old priest told Mark Murdoch. "Ask yourself: Do you do it well? Does anyone else want you to do it? Do you get a kick out of doing it?"

If your work is somehow deficient in the kick department, the thought of changing your life by doing something entirely different can be tempting. For example, Joel Conarroe, president of the Guggenheim Foundation, attributes a number of changes in his life to "the seduction of the job interview." "You begin to get interested," Joel says, "begin to envision what your hour-by-hour life would be like in such a setting. And then at a certain point you've started living the life in your mind, and you can't say no." In just such a natural, instinctive fashion did Mark Murdoch change not only his job, but his profession as well.

A tall, dark, handsome fellow with brooding brown eyes and a romantic profile, Mark had been an actor for seventeen years at the time he began asking himself the test questions his priest suggested. After graduate school, he had studied at the prestigious Lee Strasberg Institute. Like his friend Cecilia deWolf, Mark had done work on commercials, but he had been more blessed than Cecilia with work in legitimate theater. As a proven performing artist, he had lived for ten years in a subsidized Times Square apartment complex for actors, surrounded by theater celebrities. Tennessee Williams had once lived down the hall. Angela Lansbury was Mark's next-door neighbor. Mark could only conclude, from steady signs of recognition and support of his acting, that he did it well, and that others wanted him to do it.

But did he get a kick out of doing it? By introducing a provocation for change into his life, Mark unconsciously tested the kick and found it wanting. He realized that he got a far greater kick out of something else. A cradle Catholic, Mark first began working in a soup kitchen for the homeless and indigent to help out in a project which was run by his parish church.

The soup kitchen led to his involvement, with other concerned members of his church, in starting a shelter near Times Square which, night after night, housed some twenty homeless women. Mark raised funds for the shelter, wrote grant applications, asked for donations. In addition, he worked in the shelter himself. Several nights a week he assigned beds, handled problems, counseled the troubled. Doing these jobs, he felt useful and happy.

Above all, he *empathized* with those who were down on their luck. He credits his theater training, which had taught him to tap into himself for universal human feelings, for his ability to empathize. "You know," Mark says, "there's a bag person in me. By recognizing that, I think I was able to give these women, who had been ignored or looked down on, a sense of dignity as human beings." And he got a kick out of doing it.

Mark gave more and more time to his volunteer work. After watching Mark for several years, his priest friend confronted him. "Look, Mark," the priest said, "you know what's going on here, don't you?"

"Of course I did," Mark says. "I knew right away what he was talking about. He meant my life." Mark was showing through his

55

behavior that his heart lay, not with his avowed vocation in theater, but with the avocation he so plainly loved.

"Yeah," Mark told the priest. "I have to do something about my life." In his late thirties, Mark went into the seminary, and he became a priest at forty. He hopes through the Church to work fulltime with "his" people in the Times Square theater district. With the volunteer work, Mark introduced into his life a provocation for drastic change.

"You don't just *decide* to change," Mark says. "I think change has to come as a matter of honesty with yourself, asking 'Is what I'm doing what I really want to do?' What I'm doing—becoming a priest at forty—is unusual. But I can't let myself off the hook. I'm really pursuing truth and authenticity in my life."

If the pursuit of authenticity led Mark Murdoch *into* the church, the same pursuit led Anselm Atkins *out* of the church. From a non-Catholic family, Anselm converted to Catholicism at sixteen, and spent fifteen years of his young manhood as a Trappist monk and priest. "During this period," he says, "I considered myself living totally for God, doing exactly what God wanted as best I could. No earthly thing truly mattered, only eternity."

Nevertheless, he brought into his life several provocations for change. His questing mind led him to acquire, first, some reputation as a young American theologian particularly interested in amending Catholic doctrine. Then he became a cartoonist. And Anselm was the first Trappist monk ever, he thinks, to commute to a neighboring college for a Ph.D. degree in literature. He went on to gain new respect by publishing a dozen articles of literary criticism. He wanted to live honestly by the light of his restless mind. Leaving the monastery at thirty-five, he went through a series of spiritual revolutions which he describes as "monk-priest to priest ex-monk, then ex-priest, then ex-Catholic, then ex-Christian, then ex-theist," though "I'm certainly no nihilist."

Though gradual, Anselm's spiritual innovation was not always smooth. "Deciding that you don't believe in God at all can be scary," he says. "If you're wrong, you're in big trouble. If you're right, the problem of death becomes much more troubling. In the face of this, you just have to continue to hold to what you think is right, and face the consequences."

In an essay, "From City of God to City of Man," in which he described his "unpilgrimage," Anselm recalls a frightening experience. He was alone in the dim stacks of the monastic library, surrounded by volumes attesting to the ongoing human search through the ages for truth—"literature, anthropology, comparative religion, philosophy, and science." Suddenly, "an insidious thought stabbed me: What if all this Jesus stuff *really isn't* true? That thought had to be juggled like hot ice. It would require a total readjustment of life and mind."

To live an authentic life, Anselm made such a total readjustment. Deciding, as he puts it, that he wanted "to window-shop in the world of ideas, trying on whatever clothes-philosophy seems to fit," he left the monastery and then the priesthood, receiving a papal dispensation. He married Margaret Kavanaugh, a practical nurse who had been a Carmelite nun for eight years. Though still vaguely considering themselves Christian, he and Margaret became social activists in the seventies, heavily embroiled in improving the City of Man. Ecologically minded, they built their own energy-efficient pine and cedar house in the middle of two wooded Georgia acres that have been declared a wildlife sanctuary by the Audubon Society. And they talked. Over their more than fifteen years of marriage, Anselm and Margaret, "talking a lot, reading together, neither overtly pressuring the other," have changed, Anselm says, "from whole-hog Christianity to atheism."

He respects the Catholic heritage, and refers to the Church as "the most magnificent work of art ever constructed by man." No other faith could ever take the place of Catholicism for him, so he prefers to live without religious faith, a self-avowed "lover of the earth." Anselm questions whether any Christian can ever truly claim the latter distinction, tied as the Christian vision is to the hereafter rather than to the here and now. He has decided that, for him, living an authentic life means living in the here and now.

"There is a definite loss of status in being an 'atheist,'" Anselm says. "It implies that you hate pink sunsets and kick small dogs. As a Christian, I would definitely have disapproved of the change we have made, because it went against everything

I stood for. I would not have considered it possible—until it happened."

When it happened, Anselm could not honestly refuse to acknowledge it, to take up his rightful residence in the City of Man. Today he and Margaret live in the house they built, seeking the good life together. That means "loving another person, trying to be creative, being aware of as much as possible, trying to cut through to the most important things and the best, and trying to pass something on." An acclaimed artist working in stained glass, a skill he learned in the monastery, Anselm recalls a design he made for a window for an interfaith chapel. The design is called "Life on Earth."

Working in a soup kitchen and in a shelter for homeless women, Mark Murdoch came to realize that he wanted to become a priest; he took his place in the City of God. Leading the examined life, Anselm Atkins acquired a new appreciation of the City of Man, particularly of the intimacy of marriage. Change came naturally and gradually to each as he responded with sensitivity and without hypocrisy to his own inner demands. For Lois Grant, the change began when she acknowledged to herself that she was not getting much of a kick out of anything in her life.

Lois says that she was brought up to believe in the "maturity myth." "You know, if you're a good girl, if you do all the right things—marry the right person, buy the right house, live in the right town, get the right job—you live happily ever after.

"Well, I had done all of these things. I had two beautiful children, a nice house in a nice suburb, a nice husband. Material things were not a problem. So why wasn't I living happily ever after?

"That was the big question. I had been a good girl. Why wasn't I happy?"

In answering that question, Lois Grant completely redesigned her life.

At almost fifty, Lois, a small, attractive woman with ginger hair and candid blue eyes, is happy. We sit side by side on the sofa in the modern Georgia condo which she shares with her second husband, Keith. While Keith, an architect, is working upstairs through a hot Saturday afternoon, Lois tells me how she reached her present state of happiness. It took her fifteen years.

When Lois allowed herself to realize, at the age of thirty-five or so, exactly how unhappy she really was, her first thought was that *she* had failed. "Maybe there was something wrong with me, that I hadn't been a good girl." What more, she asked herself, should she have done?

"The maturity myth," as Lois understood it, imposed certain limits on life, particularly on a girl's life. As a bright child growing up in Illinois, Lois loved science and chemistry; she knew if she were a man, she would become a doctor. But when she went to the state university in 1955, "girls didn't go to medical school." Instead, Lois decided on home economics, an acceptable "female" major which required some science. Her freshman year, she was pinned to John, an engineering student at Illinois (he would later become a lawyer). John was familiar; he came from her neighborhood back home and went to her church. When Lois was a senior, she and John married. Before long they settled down to raise a son and a daughter in the upper-middle-class suburb of Birmingham, Michigan.

In Birmingham, Lois energetically took up the kind of life her mother had had. She aspired toward perfection in domestic and community work. "I did needlepoint; I made découpage purses. I made all of my daughter's clothes and some of my son's clothes. I made the curtains for the house, pillows, artsy-craftsy things—I was always designing something, creating, sewing.

"I taught piano lessons, and I took voice lessons. I was very active in the church, and sang in the church choir. Then there was the PTA, the Birmingham Musicale, and this and this and this. I was very busy. And one morning I sat in my car in the driveway, and I said, 'Wait a moment. Is this the third Tuesday or the fourth Wednesday, and which meeting am I supposed to go to?' " She was miserable to realize that "nothing I was doing was adding up to anything."

So, when the children were in junior high school, Lois took on a couple of part-time jobs. She worked for a while as a behavioral analyst for a real estate consulting firm, evaluating applicants for sales positions. During another period, she wrote material for radio documentaries, eventually turning out forty-eight scripts which netted her a grand 4 percent in royalties. For these jobs, Lois got little recognition and less reward. "If a man were writing those scripts, Lois," her sister told her, "he would be making big money."

Lois knew her sister was right. But for Lois, money wasn't the point, at least not then. "I was just a housewife looking for some mental stimulation. I would go to the library and get all of these books. Then I could read to my heart's content and say that I was working."

Her responsibilities as mother diminished as the children grew older, but the job of perfect wife increased. Lois served as hostess to her husband's business associates, at events ranging from casual midweek dinners to what she calls "fabulous parties." "I would take three days to make a dinner party—a day cleaning, a day shopping, another day cooking. There wasn't any food that I couldn't produce—the world's greatest cheesecake, Napoleons from scratch. And after the dinner was over, I would entertain them—play ragtime, or we would all sing around the piano."

Lois liked the challenge of dinner parties, as she liked the challenge of writing or of music. Routine housework bored her to distraction, however, and over the next two years she grew more conscious daily that most housework *is* routine. By 1975, when she and John had been married for sixteen years, Lois felt hopeless and frustrated. She believed that her frustration was insidiously ruinous to her children. The kids were growing up, but she kept right on doing too much for them, not letting them go as she knew she should. She needed some use for her leftover energy; she needed a new challenge. "I wasn't making any money. I didn't have any sense of mission or growth. Everything was just scattered."

Everywhere in the seventies, women like Lois were moving en masse into the job market. But conservative John was "very uncomfortable" with the idea of his perfect wife working out in the world. They didn't need the money, he argued. Why did Lois want to work if he could provide everything they needed? The truth was that while the children were less and less dependent on a stay-at-home mother, John himself was accustomed to living in a style that was possible only if Lois remained a housewife.

Though John grudgingly agreed that Lois could perhaps think of a job in her old field of home economics, he wasn't too enthusiastic. Nor was Lois, for a different reason: though she wanted work, she had had all the home economics she could stomach. She was ready for something completely different.

One night at the dinner table, Lois remarked that volunteer activities were being recognized by some firms as valid job experience. She had certainly done a lot of volunteer work, she said. Maybe, she told her family, she could after all find work that was unrelated to home economics, something really demanding.

The children were enthusiastic. They eagerly interrupted each other with grand plans for what Mom could become when she grew up. Cheered by their encouragement, Lois turned to her husband. "What do you think, John?" she asked, wanting his opinion, wanting even more his support.

John blew it. "If you get a full-time job, Lois," he said, "who's going to do the menial work?"

Menial—exactly the term used by Cecilia deWolf's doctor brother to describe the work of nurses—is all too often a word applied to the traditional tasks of women. Lois seethed at its use, and at John's tone. Menial! Was that how he saw what she had done—raising the children, creating a home for him, entertaining his colleagues? Was that the way he regarded the enormous efforts women like her had made for families and communities across the country? Lois vowed that she would find work which she could do well, which somebody else wanted her to do, and, above all, which she got a kick out of doing. And it would be work John could not disdain as menial.

Not long afterward, Lois visited her sister in New York. Once out of her pumpkin shell, with the encouragement of her sister, Lois decided to go to an expert in aptitude testing. Was she suited only for traditional women's work, or was it possible that she had a latent ability that John would have to respect?

For the aptitude evaluation, on April 5, 1975, Lois took a battery of tests at a place called Human Engineering on East Sixty-second Street in Manhattan. Then she sat down with a counselor, George Wyatt. "It's amazing," Wyatt told her. "The average person has three or four aptitudes. You have nineteen! What are you doing with all this ability?"

Lois flushed with pleasure. Then she began to explain—her volunteer work, her part-time jobs, her home, her family. "Stop," Wyatt said. "Don't you see? You need more than that.

You are wasting your energy and your ability. *You need a life's work."*

" 'You need a life's work,' " Lois remembers, smiling. "Those words just rang. I knew instantly that he was right." Raising two fine children could not be a life's work—that wasn't fair to the kids, for heaven's sake. Nor could singing in a church choir and giving elaborate dinner parties. Being a perfect wife wasn't enough. "I needed something to do for me. I needed a life's work."

Wyatt further won her confidence by telling her—how could his tests have fixed so clearly on the dream of her young heart?— that medicine was one of her three strongest aptitudes. She would make a fine doctor, he said. But Lois felt that her time for medical school had passed.

A second aptitude was musical composition, which didn't surprise Lois. "I had thought about composing, because music is an important part of my life. But composing is lonely. I'm very sociable, and love to work with people."

A third aptitude, which did surprise her, was architecture. "To be an architect—I would never have thought of it for myself. I didn't even know any architects. Here we were, in this beautiful old mansion on the Upper East Side with the curved stairway going up, and the wrought-iron balustrade, with carved decoration and wood paneling and all this ornate stuff. And I started looking at it all, and I started thinking about becoming an architect."

Back home in Birmingham, Lois went to the library "to find out what architects do." When she learned that there were three schools of architecture in southeastern Michigan, one of them only fifteen minutes from her house, Lois felt an incredible ebullience, the same thrill of recognition that Cecilia deWolf felt about nursing school. She could do this!

John punctured that ebullience very quickly, with his skepticism about architecture as a career path for women and especially for his wife. Today, Lois makes allowances for John's attitude. "It was just the way he was raised," she says, "in a very conservative German family—you know, Kinder, Küche, Kirche. He didn't believe I should think very far beyond that, and he just couldn't understand why I couldn't be happy in the house."

In 1975, John was not the only person skeptical about female

62

architects. According to a study issued in 1988 by the research arm of the Congressional Caucus for Women's Issues, that year there were proportionately more female welders (4.4 percent) in this country than female architects (4.3 percent). If, earlier, Lois had felt medicine was an outrageous choice for a woman, in 1975 architecture was equally or more outrageous.

Nevertheless, Lois determined to muster up the gumption to try it. John protested, but she enrolled anyway. Classes were to begin in June, just before her thirty-eighth birthday. During May, the atmosphere in the household became heavily charged. Lois stubbornly persisted in her plan; just as stubbornly, John opposed it. In the middle of the tension created by this deadlock, Lois felt the first pangs of arthritis.

In recent years, an ancient controversy over the connection between personality and disease has grown stronger. An increasingly widespread theory today is that one can sometimes actually forestall disease by maintaining "a positive attitude." This simplistic notion thus holds the sick person responsible for her sickness: She "brought it on herself" by having a bad attitude or the wrong emotion. Such an exaggeration has been rightly denounced, by Susan Sontag among others, because it adds an unfair emotional burden to the physical trials of the sick person.

Nevertheless, a recent "meta-analysis" by Howard Friedman and Stephanie Booth-Kewley, psychologists at the University of California at Riverside, brings together data from over one hundred previous studies to demonstrate that chronic, ongoing depression of the kind from which Lois suffered is implicated in a number of diseases, chief among them arthritis. Whatever research can prove or not prove, Lois herself links her arthritis to psychological factors. When George Wyatt said to her, "You need a life's work," and she saw that she would have to jeopardize her marriage to go after that life's work, she believes her immune system faltered. Her defenses dropped, so that psychologically she became more susceptible to arthritis. Arthritis was the outward manifestation, which had to be dealt with, of an inner state which she would have preferred to ignore.

She experienced the first symptoms of the disease in May before school started, but she began her studies in June anyway.

Over the next three or four months, as Lois sat in classes and grappled with homework after a fifteen-year hiatus, the pain began traveling. "I started having pains in my knees, then I would have a pain in my ankle, then my shoulder would hurt, then my wrist would hurt, then I'd hurt my hand, and then I'd have a stiff neck." She went to an internist, who suggested arthritis. Lois went to the library and started reading about arthritis.

"You can't read very much about it," she says, "without getting into the psychosomatic factors. The average rheumatoid arthritic represses emotion, especially anger, has a domineering mother, and first experiences symptoms in the middle thirties after a dramatic change in her life. I thought, my God, take me away, I'm a textbook case."

It was all there. First, there was the repressed anger. "My sister and I were raised never to be angry," Lois says. "We were never allowed to fight. I remember one time when I was in high school I was shaking my foot, and my mother said, 'Why are you shaking your foot? Are you nervous? Don't do that!' We weren't even allowed to be nervous.

"So all my life, I repressed what I was feeling. I put all my tensions in my jaw. When I started voice lessons, my teacher said to me immediately, 'You're singing with tension in your jaw. Relax it. You can't really sing very well with such a tight jaw.' "

Part of the "maturity myth" with which Lois had been brought up consisted of the storybook marriage, an image of family togetherness as the standard. "If you ever got angry with your husband, your marriage was a total failure," she says. Now she was very angry indeed with John, and he with her. The arthritis would not allow her to ignore this anger.

In addition to the anger, the outbreak of arthritis signaled the dramatic and difficult change Lois was making in her life. "There are a few women my age who have been in the field of architecture all their lives," she says, "and there are a lot of younger women who are going into the field now. But I don't know anyone else exactly like me. When I started back to school, nearly forty years old, out of some twelve hundred people in the program, there were exactly four women." She was almost always the only woman in every class she took.

Lois likes men, and was able to make friends and to find study mates. "I still have as friends guys that I went to school with. They're twenty-eight or thirty years old, living in different parts of the country now, but we still keep in touch."

She ran into friendly professors too. Early on, one of her professors made copies of her first quiz, titled the copies "How to Write a Quiz," and then handed out the copies to the class. Eventually this professor made her his teaching assistant, telling Lois that she was the best student he had. Through his influence, she became the slide curator of the school, "working with all the slides of this beautiful stuff, and I loved it."

Meanwhile, in spite of her success at school, the arthritis continued. At certain periods, the pain would be so bad that she would not be able to sleep. She tried cortisone injections and a spectrum of drugs. As she learned more and more about the disease, however, Lois decided to attack the arthritis on every front, psychosomatic as well as medical. She started going to a psychologist.

"The arthritis really drove me into therapy. I just decided it was time. I had thought about it many times before, but now I had a really good reason." In therapy, she learned "how to become angry, to realize that I had a right to be angry, that everybody gets angry. The problem is not to do away with your anger but deciding what to do about it. Are you going to hit somebody in the nose, or are you going to talk about it?"

Unfortunately, Lois was not able to go home and talk problems over with her spouse. After his initial obstinacy about her going back to school, John expressed his continuing disapproval in a subtle process of undermining that rarely let up. For her birthday the first year she was in school, her next-door neighbor Cathy brought over a big package. With John and Cathy looking on, Lois opened it to find a book called *Architects on Architecture*.

"Oh, how wonderful!" Lois said, holding it up for John to see.

John glanced at the book, and then looked over at Cathy with a little frown on his face. "Cathy, why are you encouraging her?" he demanded.

On another occasion, an instructor in a design class asked Lois to make a sculpture out of cardboard, using only rectangles. After hours of painstaking experimentation, Lois came up with a charming little design which she painted. When the sculpture was returned with the professor's praise, Lois brought the little piece home and put it proudly on a shelf in the den.

One of John's office associates came over for dinner and noticed it. "That's really interesting," he said, taking the sculpture up and examining it with respect. "What in the world is it?"

John looked at it contemptuously. "We call that 'Lois's Folly,' " he said dryly.

"That hurt," Lois remembers. "I was going through all this growth and change. I tried to bring John with me, but he wouldn't come. He just didn't want to give up any of his cherished ideas about women and how things ought to be."

It took Lois five years to get a degree in architecture. "I started out kind of slow, taking twelve hours at a time, because I still had my husband and teenaged kids to care for," she says. From the beginning, she knew she had to give up some things.

First to go were her piano students. That was painful. "I mean, I just loved those kids. My last piano recital for them was difficult. I sat there thinking, 'This is the last time I'm going to do this—set this up, get the chairs, have everybody play the piano.' It was a very poignant moment."

She lost some friends too. Not all of her friends were as supportive as Cathy. When Lois told one woman, who had been a friend for years, that she was getting a degree in architecture, "she started to laugh. And she laughed, and laughed, and laughed. It was bizarre, a very strange situation. She's a migraine person—I don't think she knew what was going on inside of her."

But Lois's sister was wonderfully supportive, a fact which strengthened their already strong relationship, and so were Lois's two children. She needed all the support she could get; getting through the tough program took a lot of gumption. "I just dreamed I could do something," she says. "I said, 'I can do this,' and then I had to get down there and do it."

Early on, she had to drop one of her first math classes because she didn't have the right background for it. She took the class again later and got a good grade. "So I just chipped away at these little pieces. There wasn't any magic." She stops and smiles. "Well, it may have been magic that I passed calculus. I had a hell of a time with calculus, but at least I didn't flunk out like some people did.

"And the kids helped. My son heard me say that calculus was the weeding-out course, and he would ask me ever so often, 'Hey, Mom, are you being weeded yet?' "

In spite of the difficulties, in spite of John's opposition, in spite of the arthritis that continued to plague her, Lois knew from the beginning that she had made the right decision in seeking the change. "Suddenly, all of this diffuse scattered stuff that I mentioned earlier disappeared. I had school and my family, two foci for my life. It just made so much more sense. I felt that I had a sense of purpose and a goal, a real goal that I could put my energies into."

After four successful years in architecture school, Lois decided to go for the fifth year, which meant a professional degree with an area of specialization. Because of her interest in medicine, Lois did her thesis on hospital emergency rooms. "That was wonderful, visiting emergency rooms, and talking to people about how the rooms worked and how they had to be designed. The medical director of the first emergency room that I visited said, 'Well, I can't wait to talk to you—I always wanted to be an architect!' And I said, 'Well, guess what? I always wanted to be a doctor.' And it was just great, bringing those interests together."

In 1980, Lois was awarded a degree in architecture, and immediately went to work for a Michigan firm. She had promised John—and herself—that she would repay her school expenses, approximately six thousand dollars, in her first year of work. To her delight, she was able to make good on the promise.

Things were no better between the two of them, however. In November 1981, when Lois was laid off because of the Michigan economy, the bottom fell out of her life. "I was very, very sick. The weather that winter was the worst I can ever remember. I could hardly walk. I was hobbling. And I was terribly depressed." Before the winter was out, she had lost twenty-five pounds. "I was gaunt," she recalls.

This desperate state forced her to recognize that she could not go on with John. For her own health, she thought, she had to make the change that she had postponed for at least seven years. In April, she left her husband, telling him, "I have to find out if the stress of living without you is as great as the stress of living with you."

Lois dreaded announcing the split to the children, who were both away at college. That turned out to be the least of her worries. Diane, the younger, who was a college freshman, said, "I've known this was going to happen since I was ten years old. In fact, we had a bet that it would happen when I went away to school."

"Children are very sensitive," Lois says. "They knew that we just couldn't continue the way we were."

"Here—I've listed all the changes that I made," Lois tells me, thrusting it toward me. "I quit going to church, I left my husband, I divorced my husband, I went to court to change my name back to my maiden name, and then I changed my handwriting."

"You changed your handwriting?" I say, baffled.

"Just my signature," she says. "When I changed my name, I designed my signature the way I wanted it. I didn't want it to be the old curlicue way."

I laugh. "I know adolescents do that," I tell Lois. "I can remember experimenting with two lines under my name, or a special little loop. But, Lois, you were much older than—"

"I was forty-six," she says, "but I felt like I had just been born. I was a new person, with a new life. I didn't like the way the other signature looked. It looked old-fashioned. You know, when you're in architecture, you design things. The first thing a designer designs is herself."

The new Lois Grant has at last driven her arthritis into remission. Soon after she left John, she and her doctor hit on a pattern of medication that for some reason—who knows what?—was more effective than anything she had tried before. At the same time, Lois began meditating faithfully twice a day. "I think that defuses stress more than anything else you can do or any drug you can take," she says. "And I really believe that helped me, because then I got my job back."

A friend told Lois right after her divorce that it was only a matter of time before she would meet a man who was right for the new Lois. The prediction turned out to be accurate. In 1985, at an architectural seminar, she met Keith. His wife had died of multiple sclerosis the year before, he told her, as they sat getting acquainted over dinner.

She told Keith of the arthritis and of her divorce, then, jokingly, mentioned her friend's prediction. "Are you the one?" she asked, teasing.

"Lois," Keith answered, not laughing at all, "I hope I am the one. I want to be."

Keith was, and is, the one. He and Lois were married not long after they met. Their marriage, Lois says, has little to do with traditional wife and husband roles. It is a union of two compatible adults, not least a marriage between two architects. "I think architecture is very special, and I think people who are in architecture are special. You have to understand sociology, you have to understand urban planning and technical things, and then there's the aesthetic dimension—it's a great big piece of life that you can share with somebody."

Today, Lois and Keith live in a southern city where the weather is warm, the days are long, and the light fades slowly. John, too, has married again. His second wife, says Lois, is very much like the Lois she used to be. Both kids are doing fine. Lois is especially pleased that her daughter has a solid four point average—not bad for a girl in her second year of medical school.

Crisis

"What do I really want?"
the innovator asks, and then pursues
the choice made.

4

Crisis in a
Double Bed

At the point of greatest tension in the process of change, the innovator realizes that he is putting his whole life on the line. He must make a choice: "What do I really want?" Answering that question honestly creates a crisis, external, or internal, or both. The crisis, while agonizing at the time, leads an innovative person to make a dramatic change in the pattern of his life.

An innovator usually has provoked the crisis he faces, but he does not always choose the time or the setting for the crisis. For *Bradford Warner, a high school English teacher and the father of three children, the crisis came unexpectedly one cold Saturday morning in March of 1980. The setting was the live-in mas-

73

ter bedroom of the Warners' comfortable, middle-class house in a large city in Tennessee.

*Margaret Warner, Brad's wife of thirty years—he was twenty, she nineteen when they married—sat in a rocker sewing and listening to Vivaldi on the radio. Half-asleep in their double bed, Brad lay comfortably watching Margaret's restful motions with the needle. Margaret had gained a little weight over the years, he reflected, but in her rose flannel robe, her long blond hair loose down her back, she was every bit as pretty as she had been when they got married in 1950. Maybe even prettier—he liked her rounder look.

Lulled into security by the cozy domesticity of the scene, Brad decided to risk it. He raised himself on his elbow. "Honey," he told Margaret, "I think I'll go to New Orleans next weekend with Lewis and Al. They need me to help drive."

Margaret threw down the dress she was hemming and burst out, "I don't understand why you spend so much time with all your faggot friends. What's wrong with me that you never want to go anywhere with me? You and I never do anything together. Don't you even like me anymore?"

Brad recognized that the moment had come, the showdown that he had done everything to provoke but nevertheless dreaded. "I felt trapped," he says. "I felt guilty. I felt frustrated. I felt helpless and confused. I was tired of keeping up the charade, exhausted." He knew that things had to change.

"But I was also afraid," he says, "afraid of hurting Margaret, the children, my parents, my friends. Maybe afraid most of all of hurting myself."

Tears were running down Margaret's cheeks. Brad looked at her face, the face he had known so long and so well, the pretty face which was now filled with misery. He forced himself to speak. "It's not your fault," he told her. "It's my fault. There's nothing wrong with you. There's something wrong with me."

"What do you mean?" she said, fear in her voice. "What's wrong with you?"

"I don't know how I did it," Brad says. "I still don't know what I said exactly. The next half hour was the most traumatic of my life. But somehow I managed to tell her that I had known for years that I was, and am, homosexual."

Even six years after that crisis, Brad Warner finds it hard to talk about. "I still get short of breath just thinking about it. The anxiety that comes with this kind of disclosure is unspeakable. You can't ever say afterward, 'Oh, I made a mistake, I didn't really mean I'm gay.' You can never recall those words."

A tall, thin man with a gentle intensity, Brad peers earnestly at me over his wirerimmed glasses. "It's the only thing like that I have ever experienced in my life," he tells me. "Once you've crossed that line, there's no going back. I felt that something very significant was taking place, like a death."

For Brad, the change loomed, profound and terrifying. "Like death, it was irrevocable, final, and I didn't know what the results of that finality would be. But I knew that things would never be the same again."

We are sitting in the breakfast room of the small house Brad bought several years after he and Margaret divorced and which he shares with a male friend, not a lover. Since the divorce, Brad has never again lived in the kind of domesticity that he and Margaret had for three decades. He sometimes misses it, and he would like to find a permanent partner. "I suppose what I miss most," he says, "is having someone present for the little things that go on in life, just sharing in the daily act of living." But the partner for whom Brad longs would be a man, not a woman.

Brad insists that his change from a respectable married man to an acknowledged member of what he calls "a despised minority" does not mean that he "changed into" a homosexual. "You don't change into a gay, though some people think you do. Sexual orientation is a given. I didn't go to a gay bar, see all these attractive men, and *decide* to be gay. The change I made was in accepting who I really am."

Accepting "who I really am" on Brad's part meant a considerable act of acceptance on Margaret's part as well. How does a man ask for such acceptance of a woman who has slept at his side for thirty years, who has borne his children, and who expects to grow old with him and to lie by his side for eternity? What in the world does a woman feel when her husband tells her he's gay, I wonder aloud?

"Would you like to talk with Margaret also?" Brad asks. "I think she would be willing."

"Yes," I say, "but not with you there."

He calls Margaret, who is indeed willing. The next afternoon,

Margaret and I talk for a couple of hours, sitting together on the sofa in the pleasant family home Brad left when he admitted to himself, to Margaret, to their children, and to the world that he is homosexual. From these two conversations, as well as from letters and journals which both have given me, I have pieced together the crazy quilt story, the story of a family's change that began with a crisis in a double bed.

The story of Brad and Margaret began in 1951, a notoriously uptight year, in a small church college in rural Tennessee. The two were sophomores who had been dating since their freshman year. "I thought, and still think, I was in love with Margaret," Brad says. Brad was an intelligent, serious boy from an uneducated farm family. The only child of strict fundamentalist parents, Margaret was quiet and a little shy, Brad remembers. "She looked up to me, depended on me for things, and I enjoyed being depended on. Her roommate was dating my roommate, and we were just naturally thrown together."

Into this ordinary boy-girl affair came an extraordinary offer. Brad, who planned to go into the ministry, was offered the opportunity to pastor a rural church and to transfer, with all expenses paid, to a larger state school. There was a catch, however. The church authority making the offer told Brad that the pastorate "really wouldn't be appropriate unless you were married."

"Aren't you dating some girl?" the church leader asked. Brad acknowledged that he was.

"Well," said the official, "why don't you marry her this summer? Then I'll appoint you to that church, and you can start your ministry while you finish school."

Nineteen-year-old Brad was intrigued. Here was a chance to skip some steps in becoming an adult, or to "play grownup," as he puts it now. Margaret was willing, glad enough to exchange her dictatorial parents for a husband her own age. Though each had private reservations, they decided to marry, and Brad's parents gave them their blessing.

Margaret's parents consented more reluctantly, with some conditions. "We will let you get married," her mother told Margaret, "but do not have any children until you get out of college." Her father even paid for the honeymoon, after he set a

wedding date convenient for him, but which happened to coin-
cide with Margaret's menstrual period. Mute with embarrassment and unable to protest, the new Mr. and Mrs. Brad Warner
"went off on a honeymoon and spent the first night just sort of
lying in bed thinking about things," Brad says. "I was very angry
at Margaret's father for doing this and disappointed in Margaret
for letting him."

They returned to orchestrate a revival in Brad's new church.
An out-of-town preacher stayed with them in the little parsonage for the first two weeks of their marriage. "We had no privacy," Brad says. "It was a bad start."

It goes without saying they were both virgins. "I was a very
good girl," says Margaret. "I think if I had been thirty when I
married, I would still have been a virgin. That's just the way I
was."

Brad, too, calls himself "a good little boy." Because of his
youth and inexperience, he disregarded the fact that in high
school, and even earlier, his sexual feelings were aroused mostly
by other boys. Those high school crushes had never been con-
summated, and, he says, "it just never even occurred to me that
they were anything to be concerned about." Homosexuality
"was never even an option."

Both Brad and Margaret unconsciously believed that marriage would fix everything. Today, Margaret thinks that she and
their children were victimized by Brad's naïveté. "That idea that
'if I just get married, it'll fix itself, and I'll be socially accepted'
makes me damn mad," she says. However, in 1951 she too had
her secret agenda, a mutiny against her strict parents. Her first
act of rebellion was to get pregnant, against her mother's express instructions, and to drop out of school a semester before
graduation. Young as they were, neither Brad nor Margaret
recalls being distressed by the pregnancy. As Brad puts it, "I
thought when you got married you were supposed to go on, be
married, just get on with it."

So he and Margaret "got on with it." With the birth of their
daughter, Norma, two years later a son, Mack, and then a second
son, Tommy, Margaret found an outlet for the feelings that, to
her surprise, had not been satisfied by marriage. "I never really
had any great sex drive," she says, "though I see now that may
not have been totally my fault. Then I thought it was." Instead,

she took refuge in motherhood. "I always wanted a large family because I was not in a large family," she says. Soon she added a fourth child to her roster: Brad himself. Mothering Brad became her way of establishing intimacy in her marriage.

Margaret's nurturing turned Brad off. He didn't want a mother; he wanted a sex partner. For whatever reason, "sex was always a problem with us," he says. "I don't think I 'turned' homosexual because Margaret did or didn't do something. It's very likely that had she been Gypsy Rose Lee she couldn't have satisfied me sexually.

"But I sometimes wonder: If the general sexual needs of a person are fulfilled in some way, even if it's not the primary, desired way, can things be managed? I won't ever know that."

Five years into the marriage, Brad had been graduated from college and from the seminary, and had moved his family to his first regular church position in a large Tennessee town. There, he remembers being frustrated both sexually and psychologically. He was troubled by a recurrent dream of a huge tarantula that was trying to kill him and that he couldn't overcome. Finally, he developed terrible stomach problems for which he consulted a Nashville specialist. The specialist couldn't find anything physically wrong, but he speculated that the spider in Brad's dream indicated some kind of sexual problem. Brad might not be getting enough sexual fulfillment in marriage, he suggested. "And I bought that one quite readily," Brad says, "because that's what it felt like to me. What it felt like was that Margaret wasn't giving me what I wanted."

"And, sure enough," he adds, smiling grimly, "she wasn't."

Margaret liked the status and security of being a pastor's wife. Although she thinks she did well enough in the role, Brad doesn't agree. "I actually had church members come to me and say—this is the shorthand version—'Unless you get your wife to shape up, you're in big trouble.' And Margaret just couldn't and wouldn't do it."

In Margaret's behalf, Brad admits that the job of the wife of a small-town preacher is tough. First of all, there were always money problems. After Margaret left college, she had steady work as a secretary, but their income was still extremely limited. "I think we must have been married twenty years before we could ever balance the budget," she says.

Then there were the moves, seven or eight of them in their first fourteen years of marriage. Brad recalls, "You move from house to house to house, but the houses are always furnished, down to the pictures on the wall and the ashtrays. And there's always a parsonage committee to see that you don't change a thing."

This sense of being constantly on display was a serious problem for them. Once a parsonage committee came in and found that some of Margaret's cooking pots had made black marks in the sink. They came to Brad later and said, "You know, you're not keeping this house up right."

"They'd never confront her," he says. "It was always me— 'you take care of this situation.' I was responsible for her."

Worse, Margaret felt protective of Brad. She tried to run interference between him and his parishioners. "If anybody tried to take me to task about something (which was a constant thing), she would jump to my defense. She would not do it subtly. She was very direct and harsh, and she lacked tact." He characterizes her attitude toward him as "possessive and domineering." In both her public and private roles as a minister's wife, Brad saw Margaret as far removed from the shy, quiet girl he had married. The happy times that they had with the children—family vacations and so on—could not really compensate for the unhappiness he felt with her much of the time.

In the middle sixties, Brad rolled all of his unhappiness up in one ball and left, not Margaret, but the ministry. It wasn't so much a calculated decision as a spontaneous one. He never suffered a lapse of religious faith and, in fact, still maintains his ministerial credentials. But he felt that a life out of the pastoral ministry would be better for him and his family. By commuting, he got a graduate degree in English from a state university. Soon after, the family moved to one of the largest cities in the state and Brad took the high school teaching position he still holds.

Graduate school, the first big change Brad made in his life, was for him, in the relaxed university climate of the period, "like floating up from the bottom of a very deep ocean." As a minister, he had gotten up at six in the morning, showered, and donned a suit and tie. "I had to be presentable because I never knew when somebody was going to come by just to see if I were up and about." Now, in the anonymity of the big city, he felt as if he were "coming up to air, and the freedom I experienced there was incredible."

In this atmosphere, his long-repressed homosexuality slowly began to awaken. Up until that time, Brad had never in the least understood his own sexual nature. "The subtle kinds of things that I think almost always go on among gay people at some level —even as a pastor, what I felt around church camps or in men's fellowship or whatever—had always seemed more like camaraderie than anything else. It was not a sexual thing at all—consciously." By 1970, when Brad was thirty-nine, for the first time in his life he began to meet "people who would own up to the fact of being gay. I began to get some idea of what goes on in the world." What he describes as "the delicate dance" of his own coming out took another ten years.

An important step in this dance was a visit to a gay bar as, of all things, a "field trip" in a graduate school sociology class—this was the age of Aquarius, remember, and such outings were the very stuff of a seventies education. Until that time, Brad held the stereotypical view that a homosexual was "an effeminate, flaky, unemployed person who thought only about sex. I didn't want to be one." Superficially, he had liberal attitudes toward homosexuality. Below the surface, a strange, ambivalent brew of emotions simmered. Brad unconsciously felt attracted to other men and was at the same time repelled by that attraction.

In the bar, he says, "I was absolutely petrified." Nevertheless, the visit, which "seemed to last for days and days but probably only lasted an hour," was a revelation. "There were all these good-looking, masculine men who I couldn't believe were gay. Seeing them gave me permission to explore the issues further. The experience didn't change my nature, but it was the beginning of a change in my behavior. I began to pay attention to myself."

He had his first real homosexual experience in 1971 with a maintenance man in his high school, "a very attractive young man, who told me one morning that he was a frustrated writer of poetry. So I said, 'I'd like to hear it sometime.' He came to my classroom one night late, and for about two hours he read his poetry, sort of off-the-wall Ferlinghetti. Interesting.

"But I would have listened to it if it had been drivel. Because there was something in the air, just an absolute—how do you put it into words? Attention, electricity. I wanted to move and he wanted to move. But he wasn't about to do anything without feeling the situation out, and I didn't know what to do, so that's the reason I guess he read poetry for about two hours.

"Then he put his hand on my knee, and I didn't jump and run, and things moved on from there. It was all of the—the ocean crashing on the shore, the waterfalls, all the things that you—It was also guilt-provoking, the self-loathing, the last twinges of homophobia, all of that. It was wonderful." Brad was forty years old, and this was the first fully satisfying sexual experience he says he had ever had. He wanted more.

Over the next several years, Brad did what many married homosexuals do: he began to lead a double life. In 1978 (according to Brenda Maddox, author of *Married and Gay*) a Kinsey Institute study of acknowledged homosexuals in San Francisco found that one-fifth of the men and one-third of the women interviewed had been married at some time in their lives. Such gays who have not "come out" lead lives of secret homosexuality. They rarely go to gay bars, never march in Gay Pride parades, don't fight for gay rights. Some are open about their sexual preference to a private gay circle; many engage in occasional or frequent homosexual encounters while scarcely admitting the truth to themselves. Often calling themselves "bisexual," they try to straddle two worlds. For about five years, this was Brad's life.

Living in this fashion, Brad felt an often "paralyzing ambivalence." Going into a gay bar, for example, he says, "You've got this feeling that the minute you walk up to the door, the television cameras will be there, the news media will be there, lights will go on, your wife will be waiting in the car outside. It's totally irrational, but the feeling is there: you're going public." Though Brad hated the secrecy, he was certainly not ready to go public. Instead, he began to make friends with selected gay men.

"The interesting thing," he says, "is that Margaret liked these people too. She knew that they were gay, though it took a while for her to figure this out. Then she even permitted me to go out with them, to parties occasionally and so on.

"It was a great subterfuge for me. She says she didn't suspect that I was gay. We had always been a liberal family, and it was a sort of 'I think I will befriend these poor gay people and be their token heterosexual.' It served my purpose well.''

Even without Brad's "subterfuge," in the swinging seventies, liberals like the Warners would naturally have numbered a few gay couples among their acquaintances. But one day in the late seventies Margaret suddenly realized that *"all* our friends were gay couples. I had depended on Brad so much for our friends, and I observed that it was nothing for me to be the only woman at a dinner party with seven or eight men. We hardly had any heterosexual couples as friends." She began to suspect that her husband was gay.

Margaret did not express her fears openly for a long time. Instead, her response to this hidden concern took, from Brad's point of view, a particularly unpleasant form: Margaret began to cry. Whenever any friction occurred, she says, "I would probably cry." Throughout their marriage, she had been prone to mild depressions, and "Brad would bring flowers or something," she remembers. Now, as Margaret turned into a veritable fountain, the flowers stopped. "I think he was just fed up."

If tears which she could not control were often Margaret's response to the tension between them, Brad responded, as he had done before, with stomach problems. "Everything affected his stomach," Margaret remembers, "and he would go to bed. I'd say, 'What can I do? Can I bring you this or that?' and he'd get angry. I liked to be nurtured, but he didn't."

Both Brad and Margaret had plenty to worry about. In addition to Brad's awakening homosexuality, both of their sons became involved with drugs, especially Tommy, the youngest of the three children. When Tommy was fifteen, he began running away from home. Usually he would stay away one or two days, but once he was gone for a month. "I had no idea where he was," Margaret says. "His brother knew, but he wouldn't tell me. Mack would say, 'Don't worry; he's okay. He is just not ready to come home.'"

In the concern for the boys, another long-term friction in the marriage escalated. Brad and Margaret had never agreed on how to discipline their children. "My parental theory," Brad says, "was 'Love them and leave them alone.' Margaret's was 'Find out what they are doing every minute and make sure that it's right.'" This disagreement between the parents exacerbated the situation for the troubled children, and, as Brad says, "produced great anxiety for everybody."

Understandably, Margaret was giving Tommy a lot of grief over his drug abuse. Brad was trying another tactic, a strong system of support. One day an argument arose between mother and son. When Brad spoke out in Tommy's defense, Margaret turned on them both "viciously," Brad says. The boy appealed to his father, "Can't we leave? I can't take it here anymore."

Brad saw this appeal as a provocation for his own change. It was "a way to get out. I used the excuse of Tommy and the great strife, but I really knew I was leaving because of my sexual identity." In spite of the money problems, Brad had somehow managed to save eight hundred dollars to buy a sailboat. Instead, he rented a room for himself and Tommy, and set himself the task for the next six months of dealing with the problems created by Tommy's drug involvement.

Those problems were traumatic and took their toll on Brad. At the same time, however, he says he breathed more easily away from the wife who was a constant, nagging reminder of the sexual confusions of his life. "I felt like a cheat and a liar, but I also felt so good, so wonderful, so free."

Margaret took the separation to heart. They both had individual therapy for a while, and she went on with group therapy for well over a year. "I decided that something was really wrong with me and I had to fix it." In therapy, she began to forgive her domineering parents, who were both dead. The group taught her the limits of responsibility for others. "You ain't the mama of everybody," she puts it. And it taught her the limits of responsibility for herself. "I guess I grew up and decided that I didn't have to be perfect.

"I think," Margaret says, "that probably I had one of the most successful group experiences that anybody ever had." She moved from abject emotional dependence to relative independence. "I felt like I came out of it a completely different person. Otherwise, I don't know whether I could have even lived through what was coming with Brad." What was coming was the crisis that culminated in a major change in both their lives.

After a six-month separation, Brad came home. "Margaret had worked very, very hard," Brad says, "and had become a much more lovable person." He had never been honest with her or the therapist about "the sexual thing," and he thought, "She's making the changes that I asked her to make, so I've got to go back." He didn't want to, but he wanted to be fair and kind. Now he realizes that "in the long run it was probably not a kind thing to do because it provided us with four more years of negotiations and problems."

For Margaret, Brad's return was at first "beautiful, like a honeymoon." She felt strong and independent, and Brad was attentive and sweet. They made a pact for "free nights out, no questions asked. That was his idea." Brad mentioned going to movies or to see friends; she would go out for drinks or dinner with the people in her therapy group. She even had a couple of male friends whom she saw, with Brad's encouragement.

Margaret allowed her therapy group to convince her that her fear that Brad was homosexual was illogical and unfounded. In the meantime, as she found out later, Brad was continuing his double life. And as two, then three, years went by, her suspicion emerged again in the realm, beyond logic, of her dreams. "I had terrible dreams," she said, "about him and other women, then in the same dream about him and other men." After one of these dreams, she went so far as to ask Brad, "Would you ever have sex with another man?"

"I said that I probably would," Brad remembers. "Then she said, 'I've got to go and fix dinner,' and turned around and went into the kitchen."

"I suspected, but I really didn't want to face knowing," Margaret said.

Brad, too, was beset with bad dreams at this period. In a recurrent one, he was driving a car. When he stepped on the brakes, they didn't work. He knew that he was out of control of his life, plummeting toward a showdown of some kind.

In another dream, he was again a minister, getting ready to perform a marriage ceremony. First, he couldn't find his prayer book which contained the vows. Then, he realized he had no coat on. He tried to borrow a coat, then a robe. But the only robe was much too wrinkled and dirty for him to wear. At length he was suitably dressed, but he could no longer find the wedding party, and he couldn't remember the way to the church. "The predominant feelings in the dream were loneliness and irresponsibility. I was letting everyone down."

Margaret remembers a "particularly awful dream. I was on a sinking ship and I could feel the water coming across the boards of the deck I was standing on. Then in the dream someone came to me and said, 'You're okay. You're not going to drown. You'll be all right.' I never put a face to this person, but I managed to get out of the dream alive. I woke up screaming, but it was all right."

Not long after that dream came the crisis. "Brad told me that he was gay. That kind of stopped the dreams, just knowing the truth."

That day after he told Margaret the truth, Brad went downstairs and brought up to the bedroom a bottle of champagne that they had been saving for a special occasion. He wanted not to celebrate exactly but to mark the day that would change their lives. Besides, he thought they both needed a drink. Margaret felt an enormous confusion of anger and pity at his foolishness. "It's as if you had told me you have cancer," she said to him. "I'm not going to throw you out. I married you forever, and that's that." But she certainly didn't want champagne.

She wanted to get her feet on the ground, to know where she stood. "Could you live as a celibate?" she asked Brad. He said no. Margaret knew that counseling hardly ever helps a gay man to live a heterosexual life. Such therapy is very intensive and expensive. "He'd have to want to do it awfully bad, and there was no guarantee. If he was not willing to give up any of his gay friends or to remain celibate, therapy just would not have helped."

"I could fight another woman," Margaret says. "I could not fight this. He told me the first of March, and we stayed together till the first of August. It was pure hell. It was just awful. We tried everything, you know. We tried different bedrooms, and I tried winning him back and all that. It just didn't work.

"The different bedrooms idea was horrendous. You meet this stranger coming down the hall. He goes into the bedroom across the hall from you and you go into yours. You close the doors, and you both go to sleep. Maybe."

Margaret tried to understand. "She really tried," Brad says. "She just could not." Ironically, in his opinion, it was not Brad's gumption but Margaret's attempt to understand that drove them toward an honest evaluation of their marriage. "Her constant attempt to understand was our final undoing. We had to rehearse the whole bloody mess every day—and being basically a coward who cannot take constant conflict, I felt I had to get away to save my life. I truly began to feel I would die if I didn't get some relief from the constant tension."

Together they decided that halfway measures were not enough. A complete innovation in their lives was necessary. Brad must leave. Together they told the children what was going on. Norma, the oldest, was married, with a home of her own, but the boys were still living with them. All of the kids cried, but all said they had suspected that something was seriously wrong. They even had a pretty good idea of what that something was.

The children were more understanding and accepting than almost anyone else Brad told about the decision to leave and the reason. His parents were old, and he just told them that he and Margaret were unhappy together. Even that was devastating to them, and he certainly couldn't unload anything else on them. His straight friends had a hard time with the revelation. To Brad's surprise, even some members of the gay community tried to discourage him. "You're crazy, when you're nearly fifty years old, to come out into this vicious gay world where looks are everything," they told him. "Being gay and gray is no fun. You'll spend the rest of your life a lonely old man."

"I probably will," Brad said, "but that's not the issue. I hope desperately that there might be a real relationship of some kind out there for me, but I don't expect anything. I just need to be me, whoever 'me' is."

In August 1980, Brad moved into a small apartment near the school where he teaches. He took hardly anything with him—no family photographs, no memorabilia, none of the keepsakes of the past thirty years of his life—just his clothes and a few dishes. The week he left, Brad revealed some of his feelings in a letter to a gay and married friend who had not come out. "I feel very sad," he wrote, "and guilty as hell, but I know that I have done the right thing. And I also believe that, while Margaret is hurt, confused, and afraid now, she will be happier in the future. I hope we can remain close, for I still love Margaret. Perhaps you are the only one I know who will understand that."

Over the years, Brad's domestic situation has improved. He

has bought and furnished his lovely little house, and found a sympathetic gay housemate. His emotional situation is even better. He has a loving relationship with his kids, though he and they are all a little slack about keeping in touch—Margaret is the one more apt to call and write. He has a lover, a man of his age with whom he is compatible, though neither is quite ready to set up housekeeping together. Best of all, Brad has no guilty secrets. "I'm no longer afraid," he says. "I have settled my religious worries, I've settled my social concerns. I have nothing left to be afraid of."

So this story has a happy ending. Though neither could have predicted it, Brad and Margaret are both happier since the dramatic change in their lives. Six months after Brad left home, Margaret filed for divorce. "I had to get on with my life," she says. "I was in limbo. I didn't feel married and I didn't feel single —I still wore my wedding ring. I needed to get some closure to the situation." The divorce became final in May, one day after Brad's fiftieth birthday—"I didn't want to do it on his birthday. I was cool at the court, then I came home and fell apart. We were married officially thirty years and nine months to the day. The waste, the waste—thirty years."

Margaret stayed on in the house the family had lived in for fifteen years. She needed that continuity for herself and for the children. And, she thought, for Brad too. The advice her therapist gave her was, "Cut Brad out of your life. Forget you ever knew him. Don't ever let him in your home again."

"I said, 'Well, maybe,' " Margaret says. But once the dust of the divorce had settled, she realized that she and her former husband "had too much invested in our friendship to see it all go down the drain." That Thanksgiving, she invited Brad to dinner with all three children and their friends or mates. Brad brought a gay friend, and all the kids had partners. "I was the only one without a guest, the only one 'out' that year," Margaret says. "Around the table, it was two, two, two, two, and Margaret."

No longer is Margaret the one out. In 1984, she changed jobs. One of her new colleagues was *Jim Short, an older man whose wife had just died of cancer after a lingering illness. Jim, a quiet and gentle man, had tended his wife for years and been devastated by her death. Margaret's nurturing heart went out to him, but in his grief Jim was a loner; he never joined the others for their occasional happy hour relaxation. He just didn't seem interested.

When Margaret had known Jim for about a year, she had car trouble one evening and Jim offered to take her home. On the way, he asked her to go out for his favorite Mexican food. "I said sure," Margaret says, "and we went out once. He was terrified. He shook all evening." But when he took her to her door, he chuckled and told Margaret that "it was a lot easier than he expected."

A couple of weeks later, Jim saw Margaret at work one day and said, "Whenever you want Mexican food again, hold up your hand."

"I held up my hand right quick," Margaret says. That was the beginning. "I liked him very much and he got very easygoing with me after that." On a trip the two took to Michigan to visit his brother, Jim asked Margaret to marry him.

Before she said yes, Margaret had to be sure that Jim could accept her ongoing friendship with Brad. "That was difficult for Jim," she says. "I had to convince him that Brad was not going to ask to come back to me."

The children helped to convince Jim that he should accept their father. "Jim," Mack told him, "if you want to be in this family, you might as well accept Dad, because Dad's going to be around. We've gone through so much together. Tommy and I took drugs. Not many kids have to live down having a queer father. Mom and Dad divorced, Norma has been divorced. This family has come through all that. This family means a lot."

At length, conservative Jim was convinced. He and Margaret married just before Christmas 1985, and Jim moved into the Warner house with Margaret. "He was willing to come into my world, that's essentially what he's done," Margaret, the nurturer, says happily. She has plenty to nurture these days. She describes her world as a "circus," especially at Christmas.

"Christmases we have a mixed group, to say the least." Tommy has married Susy, a girl he met in a drug abuse program. Susy and Tommy are there, with their little boy. Susy's mother is a lesbian; she and the woman she lives with come at Christmas.

Then there's Mack, who hasn't married, and Norma, with her second husband and the daughter by her first husband.

And, of course, there's Brad. "Last Christmas I went to Margaret's house," Brad says. "My roommate Donald went, and then Malcolm, my current lover, joined us. It was sort of like a nice, happy family.

"Margaret's husband was there, of course—Jim, a nice guy. He had a very difficult time accepting me in the beginning, but he's worked it out. Margaret just said, 'You either accept Brad, or we're never going to get married.' " Brad sounds proud.

So straight and gay, old family and new, they gather once a year at Margaret's table. They toast each other and their personal successes. And they toast the achievement of a family innovative enough to have survived a crisis in a double bed.

5

Outliving a New Suit of Clothes

"Are you afraid to die?" I ask Joel Conarroe.

We are sitting in his office at the Guggenheim Foundation on Park Avenue. Joel's spacious, sunny quarters are on the thirty-third floor. New York City is at our feet. Looking out of the wall of windows facing south, I can see across the tops of buildings toward the Statue of Liberty; through the windows on the east, I glimpse the Empire State Building and the glistening waters of the East River. In more ways than one, Joel, president of a foundation which influences the lives of hundreds of artists and intellectuals, is at the top of American culture. A warm, vital person with a host of friends, Joel might be said to have put into place every bastion that human achievement can erect against the fear of death.

"Are you afraid of death, Joel?" I ask again.

"I'm terrified of death," he answers. "Aren't you?"

I am. Death is the great change which induces the ultimate human crisis. The common denominator which will reduce us all, death is both the riddle unsolved by restless minds and the quietus to such enterprise and ambition. We fear death because we fear the unknown. We also fear time is running out. We dread leaving this glorious green globe, this arena for love and hate, for pleasure and challenge. We dread dying without having fully lived.

"I don't believe in tombstones," Jack Coleman told me. "I don't believe in burial. But if I were to have a tombstone, I would hope somebody would put the words on it, 'I'm glad I did' —'I'm glad I did' rather than 'I wish I had.' And that's the way I want to lead my life, so that I can really say, 'I'm glad I did.' "

Innovators often feel like Jack; they often have what Joel Conarroe calls a "strong sense of mortality—the awareness of the pitifully short time that we have for all sorts of terrible and wonderful experiences." This sense of mortality, Joel says, has a powerful effect on the choices anyone makes. The awareness of death can be a catalyst for changing your life.

Joel's own sense of mortality was heightened by several experiences with early death. His parents died young; a brother died at thirty; his closest college friend died at twenty-nine of leukemia, "just on the brink of an astonishing career." "For me," Joel says, "it's a great gift, being able to live past the age that my father died." Gratitude for this "bonus" has left Joel determined to avoid "a stagnation that is a kind of death."

The closer death comes, the more powerful the crisis it imposes. It's one thing to realize abstractly, as Cecilia deWolf says, that "we are all dying." It's another to nurse the dying as they cross the last threshold, as she does. It is more impressive still to see your family and your good friends die before their time, as Joel has. Then there is the terror—Joel's word is right—of your own death. How can you conquer the instinctive, terrified recoiling in the face of death? Can the experiences of others help?

Maybe not. I'm not sure. Though birth and death are the great universals, each person's death is his own. I would never presume to offer a prescription for "a good death." But I can tell you how two of the people I interviewed faced death, and how they changed their lives because of that confrontation.

Perhaps the most bizarre story I heard was that of Paul Shields. The crisis of Paul's encounter with death occurred when he was thirty-five and a newscaster for Channel Five in Atlanta. In December 1969, he woke up in a hospital, having no idea how he got there. He opened his eyes and felt himself all over for bandages, for splints or casts, for pains. He had none. Mary Ellen, his wife of four years, and their young daughters, Brooke and Stacey, were nowhere to be seen. At the foot of the bed, his parents sat, their faces haggard. His mother was crying softly. His father's eyes were closed, as if in pain or exhaustion. Behind them, ignored, a television set announced the evening news. Channel Five, Paul's show.

Paul watched the newscast for a moment through half-closed eyes and could not believe what he saw. Delivering the news was Ray Moore, Paul's competitor—his toughest competitor—who was supposed to be on Channel Two. Why was Ray doing his job, Paul wondered indignantly, and why was he himself in this hospital bed when he felt perfectly fine? Was he dreaming? Was this a Kafkaesque nightmare from which he would awaken?

Paul panicked. He tried to get out of bed. When his parents saw that he was awake and alert, they told him at first only that he had been ill. Bit by bit he learned the full truth: that he had at that time been in various hospitals for almost a year, in critical condition with a rare brain disease. More than once, he had been on the verge of death. Paul remembered nothing of any of this.

Oddly enough, Paul was told, he had fallen ill on the way to a funeral, driving with a group of men who worked with him at the station to Tuscaloosa, Alabama, for the last rites of a friend. All the way over and all the way back, Paul sat slumped and silent in the back seat of the car. Paul is usually a jovial, outgoing man, a talker and joke-teller, and his friends were alarmed by this unusual silence. When they finally got back to Atlanta after the whirlwind trip, one of the men said, "Come on back to my house and call Mary Ellen, Paul, and have her come out and pick you up. You shouldn't try to drive, the state you're in."

All this Paul was told later. He remembers nothing about the four or five months before that episode, nothing about the episode itself, nothing at all of the eighteen months or so that preceded his dramatic hospital awakening. He doesn't recall leaving newscasting for sales because of his political ambitions that prompted him to avoid possible conflicts of interest. He doesn't remember holding a sales job at all, and certainly not being the station's top salesman the month he was taken ill. He doesn't remember being appointed by the mayor to the Community Relations Commission, which was actively involved in race relations in Atlanta. He remembers his busy social life with Mary Ellen and his tender feelings toward the little girls, but recalls nothing at all about the troubled teenager he and Mary Ellen had taken into their home as a foster son. All that is gone, probably forever, from Paul's memory.

Death came close to Paul a number of times. Channel Five chartered a plane to fly their desperately ill employee to Johns Hopkins in Baltimore. There, Paul was diagnosed as having Jakob-Creutzfeldt syndrome, a rare neurological disorder, usually fatal, which is manifested in violent epileptic seizures. Mary Ellen and Paul's parents were told that Paul probably had about six months to live. His parents, who live in Baltimore, put Paul into a nursing home near them. The family steeled themselves for Paul's death.

"My mother later told me," Paul says, "that on three separate occasions they got a call from the nursing home that I wouldn't make it through the night. After the second call, they took a pair of pajamas to the local funeral home and left them. Then they arranged to have me laid out for one night in Baltimore, then shipped back to Atlanta for the funeral."

But Paul hung on past the allotted six months, so in September 1969 Mary Ellen had him taken to Georgia Regional Hospital in De Kalb County, near Atlanta. In December, he nearly died again, and was hustled off to Grady Hospital. His parents were summoned from Baltimore for the end. Then, as I have described, Paul awoke, a modern Rip Van Winkle, to "a strange, strange world. I didn't know what year it was, or where I was, or what had happened to my life. It was like coming out of the tomb."

As he had escaped death again, back Paul went to Georgia Regional, which at the time was a brand-new mental health center. In addition to the violent *grand mal* seizures, which Paul and his family found terrifying, the hospital discovered that Paul was also having as many as a hundred and fifty *petit mal* seizures a day, most of which he didn't recognize as such. John Pirino, a young psychologist at Georgia Regional, took a special interest in Paul's case. He taught Paul to identify those small seizures and to log the situations in which they occurred. Through this systematic tracking, Pirino concluded that tension triggered the seizures. Paul's physical problems, Pirino thought, were related to psychological problems. With medication and relaxation techniques, the number of seizures was gradually reduced.

By May 1970, Paul felt ready to go home, but Mary Ellen told him that the hospital would not release him and held out little hope for his full recovery. Paul was shocked; he had thought he was doing a lot better. He was even more shocked when one day his wife took him into a corner of the day room and asked him for a divorce. Paul began to cry. After a while, with difficulty, he got himself under control. "Come back tomorrow and we'll talk about it," he said.

When Mary Ellen came back the next day, Paul agreed to the divorce. "I thought then I was a hopeless case," he says, "and I couldn't see holding someone who didn't want to stay." He turned the house they owned over to her, and voluntarily relinquished all rights to the girls. "I don't know when, if ever, I will get out of here," he said when his mother protested. "I have seen too many children being fought over in the midst of broken homes, and they end up being the victims."

A week after the divorce was final, Mary Ellen married a family friend whom Paul had trusted and respected. Shortly afterward, the newly married couple departed Atlanta with Brooke and Stacey, leaving no hint of their destination. Years later, Paul learned that they had told the little girls that their father was dead. In a way, he was.

"How in the world did you do it?" I say. We are sitting at the game table in the den of the tree-shaded modern home in the outskirts of Atlanta where Paul lives with his second wife, Dale. Paul is Saturday-comfortable in his striped shirt and khakis, and pretty, trim Dale sticks her head in the door to say hello before heading for the mall with their two young teenagers. Clearly

Paul has made it back with a vengeance. "Where did you get the heart, the just plain gumption," I ask, "to come back from the dead and construct a life as good as the one you lost?"

"Better," Paul says. "My life is far better now; it's a far more meaningful life than it was before. Being in the hospital was probably the best education I ever had." Though a news story shortly after his hospitalization described Paul as "a man who seemed always to give more than he took," Paul disagrees. Before he went into the mental hospital, Paul says he was a young man who came from a beer family but who had champagne tastes. Aspiring to what he had never had, he claims that he was a "huge snob" who judged people by their family background, where they lived, what kind of car they drove—the externals.

"I've always been a rather pompous jackass when it comes to the way I dress, for example. I've always liked to wear a coat and tie. Had I met John Pirino, my psychologist, on the street before my illness, I would have thought of him, with his jeans and his long hair, as a hippie kid and would have had nothing to do with him."

Even his marriage suffered from his snobbishness, Paul believes. "I was wrapped up in my own career, and we were too concerned with going and doing rather than sitting and talking. I say *we,* but I had the biggest hand in it. We had to have dinner parties every Saturday night, invite just the right people, do things just the right way." So the marriage was built on externals also. When Paul became ill, the marriage turned out to lack the substance required to hold him and Mary Ellen together.

"I began to grow up inside the walls of the hospital," Paul says. "I learned to accept people as they are. They had an old school bus, and once a week they'd load us on the bus and take us shopping. We would just wander through the stores, have a day on the town, like going to Broadway for an evening. And I was with a group of crazies, but they were my friends."

He also learned something about friendship, he says, when Saturday-night-dinner-party friends turned out to be more. One couple, Sally and Lee Robbins, called the hospital after the divorce. "Can Paul come home?" they asked. "We've been trying to get him out of here for weeks," the hospital administration told them. So the Robbins family "adopted" Paul. "I spent virtually every weekend with them and their four children from June until I was released four months later.''

In September 1970, Paul came out of the hospital. The station, which had kept him on full pay during his entire hospitalization, gave him a part-time job. He began going out with Dale, who worked there. The two were married in December, and within two years Paul was back on the air as a newscaster.

One of the first stories he did was an interview with Rosalyn Carter, whom he had met when her interest in mental health had led her to work as a volunteer at Georgia Regional while Paul was a patient there. The governor's wife knew Paul's story, and she and Paul had had many conversations about the problems of caring for the mentally ill. When her husband became President, Mrs. Carter put Paul on a White House task force on mental health and the media. Later, as chairman of the Georgia Mental Health Association, Paul began to talk widely about his own illness and its positive outcome. He called the talk, which he made over and over for various groups around the country, "I Left My Pajamas at the Undertaker's."

"Mental illness can strike anyone," Paul says. "No one's above it. I don't know whether I belonged in a mental institution, but I'm very happy I was there and can go on record about it. I'll never forget an old man in Baltimore, in and out of the hospital for years. His name was Henry Ludwig, but everybody in the neighborhood called him Crazy Henry. I could have been a Crazy Paul, stuck down at the state asylum for the rest of my life. But there is hope for all of us crazies."

Paul Shields woke up to find himself on the brink of physical and mental death. Why this happened is for all practical purposes inexplicable. Even if we accept, as Paul does, John Pirino's theory of psychological causes, we can hardly claim that Paul engineered this extraordinary crisis in order to innovate his life. Today, Paul himself is not much interested in what caused his illness. It was a *coup de foudre,* a thunderbolt.

That his life is better after the thunderbolt than before attests to the gumption with which Paul triumphed over the crisis in which he found himself. What counts now for him, and thus for us to whom he told his story, are the benefits he gained in overcoming his bizarre disorder: stronger and more genuine human bonds, and a conviction that positive change can come even out of madness. Paul left the asylum—the word is his—and came back into the world with an enlarged and humanized vision of the meaning of life.

Paul was a bonus for me, a story I heard about while I was in Atlanta and couldn't bear to pass up. I really went to Atlanta to interview Olive Ann Burns. Very few of us will "wake up" one day to discover, as Paul did, that we have inexplicably lost a year and a half of our lives. It's a little difficult to think what we would do under such extraordinary circumstances, but I suspect that most of us would do what Paul did: pick up the pieces of our lives and start over.

The crisis in which Olive Ann found herself is far more usual. In some corner of our minds I daresay we are always trying to prepare ourselves for the kind of news which Olive Ann got and which led her to change her life. I, for one, play the scenario out every time I go in for a routine physical examination. What would I do, I ask myself, if the doctor found something? Something frightening and life-threatening, something which awakened in me the latent but ever-present fear of death? What is unusual in her case is the response Olive Ann made to the news. She adopted a plan of action so innovative I have come to her Atlanta living room to talk about it.

Everywhere in that cool room which is traditional enough to be called a parlor I observe reminders of illness and mortality. The basket of get well cards on a delicate antique table. The lived-in look of a four-poster bed I glimpse through an open door into the bedroom. The pain lines on the face of this tall, slender, elegant woman across from me, and the somewhat too abundant hair of what must surely be a wig. The lacy black shawl, a sick person's shawl, draped around the shoulders of her smart maroon dress.

Yet there are humor and acceptance as well as pain in the dark eyes with which Olive Ann surveys me and my tape recorder, and she and her husband Andy are welcoming and hospitable. Andy has baked oatmeal cookies and made a fresh pot of coffee, and Olive Ann urges, "Stay and spend the night with us." When I quickly decline, "Southerners always want to have company even when they know they shouldn't," she says. And she laughs, a hearty, cheerful laugh, a well person's laugh. This same gusto and good cheer sound in the rich Southern voice with which Olive Ann tells the story of the way she changed her life in the face of that frightening, life-threatening *something*.

In 1975, when the crisis occurred, Olive Ann Burns was fifty-one years old. For most of those years, she had been a working journalist and, that oddity in her time and place, a "career woman." "Really," Olive Ann says, "I was just particular in who I wanted to marry." In a friend's novel, *Desperate Women,* she insists, she was "the chief desperate woman, because here I was in a career and what I really wanted to do was to get married and have children."

For over eight years, working on the Sunday magazine staff of an Atlanta paper, she sat next to a "real nice person and a good talker" named Andy Sparks. She still laughs at their names, Burns and Sparks. Andy struck fire in her heart. "I used to say he was one of the few people I'd ever met that I would like to marry, but just my luck—he obviously thought of me as a sister." Fraternity turned into more, and at length the two married, when Olive Ann was thirty-two and Andy thirty-seven.

"I married a man who respected me," she says, so she never had to fight for turf, for the opportunity to do her work. They agreed early in their marriage to live on Andy's salary, and use whatever Olive Ann made for extras. Thus, by choice, Olive Ann could retire from journalism briefly when a daughter, Becky, and then a son, John, came along. But when John was four months old, she began writing a weekly advice column for the paper under the name of Amy Larkin. "I lived like a queen the seven years I did that advice column," she says. "I looked after the children and did the column and had a maid."

When she wearied of the limitations of the column, Olive Ann went back to features for the paper and freelance journalism. From time to time she thought about writing a book, always nonfiction because that was her training. One plan was for a book about "the other woman," based on some of the letters she got when she was writing the advice column. Another was for a book called *How to Be Sick,* based on attitudes she had learned through the respiratory ailments that had plagued her from childhood. "But nothing ever gripped me enough to make me get at it." She really never expected to publish a book herself.

Her parents died within a year of each other in the early

1970s. "Trying to keep them alive," she began writing down some of their favorite family stories. Soon she had collected two thick volumes of family lore, which she put away for Becky and John. "I thought it would be nice for the children to know something about their roots." What got her started was a lively tale of a forebear who buried his wife of thirty years and immediately announced his plans to remarry within three weeks—"actually, it was seven weeks, we found out later. A little more respectable." She loved the story, loved the gutsy triumph over death, and she thought as she typed it out, "This would make a great first chapter for a novel."

She thought then that she had gotten over her own fear of death. When Olive Ann was about thirty-four, Andy's aunt had died. In the way of Southern families at the time, the Sparkses "sat up with the body." Olive Ann was asked to take her turn one night. "I didn't want to *not* do it, and I didn't want to do it—I just thought I couldn't do it. I had been in a panic about dying all my life; I'd just wake up in the night and shake, you know." She had never told her fears to anyone. Now she sat down and told Andy everything that had ever frightened her about death. The telling worked like therapy to allay her fears.

Until death came closer. "Death," says Olive Ann, "is like having a book published. It always happens to somebody else, never to you."

But at the end of 1974, death blew its hot breath on her neck. During her annual physical examination, her doctor said, "Your blood picture is like what you'd have with mono or some other virus. But you don't have a virus. You aren't even sick now. But I think this is going to develop into leukemia or lymphoma."

Both her parents and an older sister had had cancer, so Olive Ann understood fully what he was telling her. She listened and asked the right questions. How long before they would know?

"It could happen in two months, it could be two years," he told her.

"I think I did listen to him," Olive Ann says, "but I was desperately looking for a way out—not a way out of having cancer, but a way out of having to be obsessed with *if* and *when* I would have cancer. I wanted a way out of having this as the main thing I thought about." Her mind raced as she listened to the doctor sum up her chances.

"It could even go away," he concluded. "But I don't think it will." As she looked absently into his concerned face, Olive Ann came up with the plan which was to be her "way out."

"I know!" she thought. "I'll write a novel! I already have the first chapter."

She had never written any fiction and had never thought of writing a novel before in her life, and the outrageousness of the scheme thrilled her immediately. "I kept on listening and asking questions about the possibility of cancer," she says. "But it was as if I didn't listen. All I could think about was the excitement of writing a novel."

Before she left the doctor's office, she called Andy and told him the news—both pieces of news. She might possibly have cancer, and she was definitely going to write a novel. "Because when I said I was going to write a novel, that was definite. I had all this material. And, being a person who never started anything I didn't finish, there was no question that I would write a novel."

Publication was another matter entirely. "I thought for sure it wouldn't be published, because who's going to publish a book by somebody who doesn't know how to write one?" She didn't know a thing about fiction; she hadn't even read much contemporary fiction. Olive Ann knew she had a lot to learn, and that was part of the fun. She remembers a story her parents told. Traveling through Europe, they struck up a conversation with an American couple they had met at an outdoor cafe in Vienna. Where had the other couple been, Mr. and Mrs. Burns asked, and where did they plan to go next?

The husband began to recite their itinerary when the wife interrupted. "Actually, I didn't want to come on this trip," the woman complained. "I really don't like to go anywhere I haven't been before."

"Nobody in our family was ever like that." Olive Ann describes the Burns clan as "talkers and achievers. My father liked change; he was challenged by anything that was new and difficult." Her mother dealt with change by finding the comfortably familiar in the apparently strange. Olive Ann has something of both parents in her makeup. She welcomed the challenge of fiction, but she began to plan her novel by assessing and capitalizing on what she had learned writing for newspapers.

100

First, she knew, she had the ability to communicate. "Newspapers will only publish something that a lot of people will read. You've got to grab the reader in the first paragraph, and anywhere it bogs down, he may quit reading." She had a great natural "lead"—a wedding three weeks after a funeral.

Second, because of her journalistic training, she had an interest in the way people really speak—"the rhythm of the speech and everything about it, because that reveals so much about the person. So I was used to all that, and liked that a lot."

Her new venture didn't dispel the fear of cancer, of course; in the back of her mind that dark specter loomed. In spite of her excitement about writing a novel, Olive Ann didn't come home and write "Chapter One" at the top of a page immediately. "I was too 'excited' about the possibility of cancer at that point," she explains matter-of-factly.

Soon after, however, on a month-long visit to her sister in Pennsylvania, she wrote the first chapter. Then she mailed it to Andy, back in Atlanta. His response was "I think you better try it again."

"Uh-oh," she thought. "I thought this chapter was a natural. This may take a while."

It took her nine years. "It was like a hobby, you know, like a Sunday painter. Sometimes I might go a month without writing, sometimes I might write steadily for a month. I might even get up in the night and work on it if I got an idea. But there was none of this writing every morning, like keeping office hours. I did it because it interested me."

Part of her fun was "figuring out how to spell the Southern accent." Her son, who was fifteen, read one page of the first chapter and threw it down. " 'Sump'n' is a dumb-looking word," he announced. "I wouldn't read any book that started with that. I don't even know what it means."

"If you're real smart, you could figure out what it means," Olive Ann answered, crushed.

"Well, people don't want to figure out what something means," John said. Olive Ann realized he was right. "I satisfied my yearning for the dialect by having a paragraph in which I explain that although I'm not doing it all the way through, my people say 'sump'n' for 'something' and 'ast' for 'asked' and so on."

The big bugaboo for her in writing fiction was "How do you put it together?" Sometimes Olive Ann got discouraged with the narrative because "I really didn't know how to do it." Various friends and relatives, none of them experts, helped her to learn. Her next-door neighbor pointed out that Olive Ann derailed the main story whenever she wanted to tell a funny anecdote. "You've just put in all the funny stories your daddy ever told you," she told Olive Ann. "Here you are for thirty-five pages talking about letting rats loose in the school play, while I'm wondering what happened to Grandpa and Miss Love."

Another friend said, "Look here, Olive Ann—you just can't have flashbacks within flashbacks within flashbacks, because the reader gets lost."

"I was just writing a lot of episodes with the same characters," says Olive Ann. "I couldn't figure out how to interweave what was going on."

Then Andy's mother got sick and came to visit. Mrs. Sparks was an avid soap-opera fan, and Olive Ann watched her favorites with her every day while they had lunch. "Soap opera writers are masters at interweaving," Olive Ann says. "One story will be ending, and one will be in the middle, and one will be starting with just a gleam in the man's eye as he looks at his wife's brother—I mean, his wife's sister—well, anyway, the brother's happened too."

After "about a year" of watching the soaps, "all of a sudden I understood how they did it. Then I had the problem of how to wean myself from the soap operas."

Meanwhile, over a two-year period the doctor's prediction had come true. Olive Ann's mysterious blood picture bloomed into fullblown lymphoma. To begin with, the symptoms didn't show externally. The disease attacked her bone marrow and her blood.

Then she developed "a big fever." After she spent ten days in the hospital having a series of tests, the doctor decided it was time to start chemotherapy. "I'd been going to the doctor for blood checks every month, but, except for that to remind me, I hadn't dwelt on it. I had begun to feel invincible. Then all of a sudden this happened, and it was really brought home to me what I had."

She was scared. "I thought of it as being scared of the chemotherapy, but I think I was really scared of cancer and of dying."

Olive Ann, whose religion she describes as unorthodox but very important to her, wanted to pray, but she didn't know how. A woman of iron-clad integrity, she wanted to play fair with God. "I had gotten this feeling that it wasn't fair to pray, 'God, make me well,' because you've got to die sometime. When my mother was having cancer surgery, I prayed all the way to the hospital, 'God, please don't let it be inoperable.' Well, that was a stupid prayer because it was already inoperable, and my praying that didn't make it any different. And after that I couldn't ask for anything because I didn't think it was fair."

But Christ said, "Ask and it shall be given," and Olive Ann believed an explicit statement like that must mean something. She concluded that you shouldn't pray for material things— "and your body is a very material thing"—but for "things of the spirit like courage and patience and understanding."

Her crisis came. "I was supposed to have chemotherapy the next day. I was scared to death." While Andy finished his day's work and the children were at school, she contemplated the ordeal before her and began to pray. "There was nobody here, and all I prayed was, 'God, help me not to be afraid.'

"I said it over and over. I must have said it for thirty minutes. I was saying it out loud, and I was saying it LOUD, too. And I was crying. And that was all in the world I said, was, 'God, help me not to be afraid.' I was truly in a panic.

"But when I got up, I was not afraid.

"I didn't see any flashing lights. I didn't hear any God speak to me. I have a friend who said she heard God. She said it was a male voice, and he told her a lot. I didn't hear anything. But I was absolutely unafraid, and I never had to re-pray that prayer.

"I've been religious all my life, but this prayer thing—it was like a miracle."

Olive Ann needed a miracle for what lay in store. Her illness attacked her energy, her control, even her vanity—the chemotherapy caused her to lose her hair. She found baldness terribly embarrassing. "I looked pinheaded. I just had a fringe of hair at the hairline, and it *floated*—we called it 'the Octopus Look.' "

One night she came into the living room with a towel on her

arm. "I'm going to wash my hairs," she announced, "both of them."

Her teenaged son protested; he couldn't bear the thought of his mother losing her hair. "Don't make jokes about it," he begged. "It's not funny."

"You'd rather I cry?" she asked.

"I could have cried," she says. "I wanted to cry, and I just about did. But that night we all laughed, and after that I didn't feel as embarrassed."

Throughout the illness and the chemotherapy, Olive Ann continued to do her usual work. "I would be weak, so I'd go to bed." Her family would have done anything and everything, she says, "but I took great pride in not letting Andy come home and have to cook dinner. So I would fix a salad and go back to bed. Then I would do a vegetable and go back to bed, and then fix a chicken and go back to bed. But that's just cooking meals, which is not the same as having your mind busy."

She also wrote articles from time to time, but what really kept her mind busy was writing the novel. By 1979, Olive Ann had written four hundred pages of her first attempt at fiction. She had talked to Andy about the work, but she hadn't let him read it "because it was so scribbled over it was unreadable."

Now Olive Ann typed out a clean copy and handed it to her husband. "Read it quick," she said, "before I mess it up again."

"He read it, and I saw him wipe tears from his eyes. Then I saw him sitting there, laughing out loud. When he got through, he said, 'Drop everything else and finish this.' "

"Andy's not a person of lots of words," Olive Ann says, "so I knew he meant it. He really understood what I was trying to do." She took Andy's advice, and began to work on the novel as hard as she could.

Miraculously free from fear, she now experienced another miracle, though in this case she rejects the word "miracle": remission of the cancer for the next eight years. Olive Ann also rejects the word "remission." She told her doctor, "I'm not in remission, I'm well. If you have a cold and it goes away, you don't say, 'I'm in remission from the cold.' You say, 'I'm over that cold,' even though you know you may get another cold later on."

A surgeon friend agrees with Olive Ann's theory that the

freedom from fear was instrumental in her "getting well." "If you're not afraid," he told her, "it leaves the body free to get well. Our bodies have a lot of ability to get well, but fear causes so many problems that get in the way." Olive Ann approves of this reasoning, in part because it does away with the idea of the "miracle" of healing.

Why can't she call her mysterious remission a miracle, as she did her loss of fear? Because fear is a spiritual illness, and cancer only physical. The cancer might come back, because we are all going to die. The body is destined to fail, if not through cancer then through some other mortal illness. Mortality is the essence of humanity. "If you say God sent a miracle to cure you," Olive Ann says, "if the cancer comes back, do you say God took the miracle back? To me, the true miracle is accepting death and not being afraid of it."

Olive Ann was warned that the cancer could return at any time, and she went through a number of false alarms over the next seven years. She refused to panic again. "There's no point in being nervous," she told herself. "Anybody, anywhere could die any time, without warning. But they don't think, 'Oh, next week I may die on the expressway, so I had better stop driving.' So why should I think, 'Next year I may be dead of cancer,' and just stop living?"

Instead, she was grateful for the warning she had had. Awareness of her mortality led her to change the way she lived. "I had been a great worrier. If something happened to my sister, or my children, or anyone, I would lie awake all night thinking what they should do—you know, the advice columnist coming out. That was my most obnoxious trait."

In the face of death, she quit worrying. "I realized that the only way you can live is one day at a time. I found myself observing the world, seeing how the sunlight on a leaf was white. Just suddenly I realized that it didn't matter how long you lived, it was *how* you lived and whether you really enjoyed every day."

"Let us go and risk our lives unnecessarily," writes that other heroic woman Isak Dinesen in *Out of Africa*. "For if they have got any value at all it is this that they have got none." And Dinesen adds, *"Frei lebt wer sterben kann."* He who can accept death lives freely.

Olive Ann accepted death. She could have been cautious with the time remaining to her. Instead, she risked the precious hours of her life unnecessarily, choosing to spend all the time she could find in seclusion, writing a book which she had little hope of getting published. Why? Because by taking that risk, she put death into perspective. With her courageous action, she defied death. What is more important than the fact of death, she was saying, is the wisdom about life which I can put into this novel. "And by that point," Olive Ann says, "I was so into the book that I could write any time and anywhere."

The book, *Cold Sassy Tree*, tells the story of Grandpa Blakeslee's precipitous remarriage from the point of view of Grandpa's fourteen-year-old grandson, Will Tweedie. Will admires the new bride, Miss Love, a milliner working in Grandpa's store, and bestows a somewhat uncomprehending approval on the courtship and wedding. The book is set in 1906 in the small town of Cold Sassy Tree, a time and place of tight social forms—though three weeks of mourning hardly seem sufficient even in our own fallen world! The rest of Grandpa's family and the inhabitants of Cold Sassy heartily disapprove of Grandpa's behavior. They consider Grandpa disrespectful of Grandma, barely in the ground, and exploitative of Miss Love, whom they think the old skinflint is marrying so he won't have to hire a housekeeper.

Olive Ann says her intention was to write of the love story between Grandpa and Miss Love, and of Will Tweedie's attempts to comprehend adult love. She put no explicit sex scenes in her book, but she did try to express what she calls the "tension," the "lyric wonder and electric yearning" of a real romance. To her mind, Grandpa is "human but fundamentally decent." He is "true to himself," but "free of the burden of perfectionism." Above all, she says, "I wanted him to live with courage and gusto, and know how to look death in the face."

To her surprise, the book was not only published but went on to become a bestseller. The real change in her life, Olive Ann says, came more from the publication than the writing. She had been "a real hermit" from 1980 on, trying to finish the book, and "to get out with people again was just wonderful." When the book came out in 1984, the publisher, Ticknor and Fields, threw a party for several hundred people at the Atlanta Historical Society.

106

A good number of the people in attendance were relatives of Olive Ann and Andy. "At some point, I got up and said over the loud speaker, 'Can I introduce my family?' And then I'd call this one up and that one up—there were about twenty-five cousins and sisters and brothers and nephews and nieces and all Andy's crowd. And my publisher said, 'This room is like a ship, and it's listing to starboard as this family comes forth.' His theory was that the theme of the book was family, but I don't know—I never have known what things like 'theme' are."

After the party, Olive Ann expected things to settle down with *Cold Sassy Tree.* "I liked the book so much myself that it never surprised me that other people liked it, but I thought it would maybe sell a couple of thousand copies. All my friends said, 'A first novel, you just don't break your heart, Olive Ann—it will sell at the most seven thousand.'"

Certainly, she didn't expect to make any money with *Cold Sassy Tree,* even the modest amount of money it would take to achieve her definition of riches. "I was brought up in the Depression when you didn't waste food, so the only rich I wanted to be was rich enough to throw out the soup if it wasn't good. When I think of all the time I've spent trying to make the soup better, when all I did was just to make it bigger."

Olive Ann has thrown out the soup twice since the publication of the book she worked on for nearly a decade. When I last heard from her in January 1988, nearly four hundred thousand copies of *Cold Sassy Tree* were in print. Four years after publication, the book was still on several national bestseller lists, and Faye Dunaway had taken an option for the movie rights. The American Library Association and the New York Public Library had both put *Cold Sassy Tree* on their lists of recommended books for teenagers, where, Olive Ann was thrilled to note, she occupies a place of honor between Emily Brontë and Willa Cather. "Of course, that's just alphabetical," she says, "but I never thought I'd be in such company."

This unexpected notoriety has brought her a new kind of problem. As a well-known author, she is often invited to address groups, and "I like to speak. I'm a real ham. I just love to see people laugh, and here's my chance, and you get paid for it." But she declines. Why? A simple matter of time and priority.

"The big difference between being a writer and being an author is that writers write and authors speak. And I'm a writer."

Her new life is not without some familiar old perils. In October 1986, the lymphoma returned. For the first time, it caused a tumor, which grew to frightening proportions in her stomach. "My stomach kept getting bigger. It looked as if I was about five months pregnant. I said, 'I think the doctor did a Caesarean, and put the baby back in.' "

Olive Ann was in and out of the hospital throughout 1987, and back on chemotherapy. At length the cancer went into remission—or she "got well"—once again. In the aftermath, however, confined to bed with an overtaxed heart, she began to feel that her illness would never end. She had planned another novel to be called *Time, Dirt and Money* which would take up the *Cold Sassy* characters at a point ten years later and would focus on Will Tweedie and the young schoolteacher he marries. But her doctor forbade any exertion at all until her heart was stronger. Her spirits sank when she realized this command spelled an end to her writing.

Then, with her usual gumption, Olive Ann came up with a plan. The fact that she couldn't get out of bed didn't have to mean she couldn't write, did it? So what if she couldn't use the typewriter or her new word processor? Heir of the front-porch oral tradition of storytellers, offspring of a family of talkers, a pretty good talker herself, Olive Ann knew she could always talk. So why not dictate the sequel to *Cold Sassy Tree* into a tape recorder and have the tapes transcribed? "Wish me luck," her last letter said.

I do wish her luck, of course. But I think she's got something better than luck going for her. What she says of Grandpa Blakeslee is true also for his creator. Olive Ann, too, lives with courage and gusto and knows how to look death in the face. As I scan again her last brief letter, reading between the lines for the volumes it speaks of her indomitable spirit, I think of a story she told me during that long afternoon in her Atlanta parlor.

"When my father was fifty-five," she says, "he had cigar ash burns all over his suit. 'Daddy,' we said, 'you ought to get a new suit.'

"I wouldn't live to wear it out," he told them.

"And he lived to be eighty," Olive Ann says.

So here's what she thinks. Here's what empowered her, in the face of death, to write a novel full of life. "Your life looks very different," Olive Ann says, "if you think in terms of living to be one hundred. If you're sixty and think you're going to die by seventy, there are a lot of things that you're not going to start. Of course, you *could* die at seventy, but you could really spend a lot of boring years if you ended up living to be a hundred and never did anything that you hadn't done the day before.

"But if you think, 'I may live to be a hundred,' that's forty years you give yourself. You have time to do almost anything you'd want to do."

What does Olive Ann Burns, recuperating from her second bout with cancer, want to do? She wants to get well. She wants to be able to write in the cabin called the "Write House" which she and Andy are building in the mountains. She wants to finish *Time, Dirt and Money*.

"Then," she says, "I would love to travel." She would like to go to a lot of places she hasn't been.

Choosing to Change

Not all crisis leads to change.
Positive change involves choice.
The innovator must choose the elements
of the reconsidered life.

6

Going Global

There are no second acts in American lives, Scott Fitzgerald said. He was dead wrong. If America is about anything, it is about second acts, third acts, and even—for this country is Shakespearean in scope—fourth and fifth acts. The central theme of America is starting over. If you have the gumption to choose to change your life, Americans believe, you can do it. The country will cooperate by providing a New World, a New Deal, a New Frontier, a New Beginning, a New Age.

And we have time-honored methods through which you can choose to change. One is moving on. You can write a second or a third act by changing location. The fountain of youth; go West, young man; Pikes Peak or bust; California, here I come; one

113

giant leap for mankind—Americans have always held to the view that the unfallen Eden, the land of perpetual renascence, is still around here somewhere, and certainly worth looking for.

Moving on doesn't always accomplish what it's originally meant to accomplish. "I want my life back," Betsy Williams says, a pathetic declaration, though Betsy sounds quite cheerful making it. She sounds just as cheerful, in fact, as she did two years earlier when she told me she was changing her life completely. Then, she had made up her mind to put some distance between herself and Sam, her married lover.

For sixteen years, Betsy and Sam had conducted an affair as stable and permanent as many marriages, but limited. Betsy became dissatisfied with the limitations of the relationship. She saw them as limitations in Sam. "Sam is wonderful," she told me then. "He's a power figure, respected, prestigious, irresistible. But he's afraid to make a change. I realize now that he will never leave his wife to marry me."

So Betsy left. "I don't think I could leave my lover without leaving New York," she said. After thirty-one years in Manhattan, fifteen of them in the same apartment, fifty-year-old Betsy flew off with high hopes to the eternal spring of California. She looked forward to having a new little car, a bright new apartment, and a new love. She might even find a husband.

Nine months later, at home in San Francisco, Betsy spoke of the move. "I think that I was absolutely right to do it, that it was a healthy, not a neurotic, flight." Sam was still in her life, although their "complex and tantalizing relationship" had lost its "negative intensity." "Sometimes," she wrote me a month or so later, "I even muse about whether I really moved to California in order to preserve the relationship, since being closer to Sam geographically made me so much more frustrated with him."

The next time Betsy called, she reported that Sam was flying out West frequently for short visits, and that she planned monthly trips back East. "I'm no longer dependent on him," she said. "I know he won't take care of me. I feel very much on my own, and I've completely lost interest in marriage. At this point, it's hard for me to understand why anybody wants to live all the time with anybody."

At times over the past two years in California, Betsy has contemplated a return to Manhattan, but knows that her feelings of independence might not survive the move. Her friends regret that Betsy's sojourn in California did not entirely end her affair with Sam. Betsy, however, says the break gave her the perspective she needs. Just leaving, moving into a new place, helped her to reach a new place in her thinking as well. Whether or not she decides to continue with Sam, Betsy's change upset the balance of power that had made her feel like a victim. "I don't feel powerless any more," she says.

For Kay Fanning, the New World was the forty-ninth state, Alaska, a frontier outpost in which to reinvent herself. In 1987, when we talked, Katherine Woodruff Fanning was the editor of *The Christian Science Monitor* and the first woman president, in its nearly seventy years, of the American Society of Newspaper Editors. Yet, born to wealth and wed to millions, Kay never worked on a newspaper until she was pushing forty, when she divorced her multimillionaire husband, Marshall Field, moved to Alaska with their three children, and took a low-level job on the *Anchorage Daily News*.

"I've always had a great sense of adventure," she says. "Somewhere within me I think I always had a desire to start over, to see if I could really make it on my own. I'd had all kinds of advantages as a child, and certainly my marriage had been full of privilege. So I wanted to be a real person, living in the real world, and I wanted my children to be real people."

Sitting behind the large, functional desk in her sunny but plain office in the *Monitor* building in Boston, Kay is strikingly attractive and very real indeed. Tall and erect, wearing a tailored gray gabardine suit and a red blouse which sets off her wavy shock of gray hair, Kay, at sixty, has the candid eyes of someone who trusts people and the warm smile of someone who likes them. I smile back. What does she mean by "living in the real world," I ask?

"In Chicago, for the thirteen years I was married to Marshall, I was what I suppose people would call a 'society wife,'" Kay answers. "I served on boards, I did volunteer work, I entertained, I was a wife and mother. When I divorced him in 1963, I left that kind of existence—as someone said, I went from the Junior League to the Urban League. I rejoined the real world, that's how I think of it.

"I think that people with great wealth tend to be isolated, insulated from other people. I wanted my children brought up on a block with a lot of other children from a wide variety of families, not living in a single stratum area. I wanted my children —and myself—to have some racial and economic diversity in our lives. I guess I wanted to be just like everyone else."

Kay was certainly not brought up "like everyone else." The only child of a banker in Joliet, Illinois, forty miles from Chicago, she grew up on a comfortable eighty-acre estate. Young Kay swam in a private, indoor swimming pool. For her first years of school, she was educated at home like a young princess. Ten friends her own age were brought in every day, and a trained teacher was hired. "I had very, very easy circumstances economically, in a very pleasant home, and a very happy family." But as she reached her teen years, Kay was also lonely. Her parents decided on boarding school, and sent her East to the exclusive Westover School in Connecticut.

At Westover, Kay was miserable for the first time in her life. "I didn't fit in. The other girls teased me, and I was unpopular. I didn't have any friends. I despaired that I would ever amount to anything."

In her unhappiness, Kay turned to religion for comfort, particularly to Mary Baker Eddy's *Science and Health with Key to the Scriptures,* the "textbook" of Christian Science, which her mother had given her before Kay left home. Mrs. Woodruff had been ill and, though the family was Presbyterian, had become interested in the Christian Science doctrine of healing. "I didn't become a Christian Scientist," Kay says, "but I sort of carried the book around with me. It just made a great deal of sense to me, and it inspired a tremendous interest in things philosophical."

In 1945, after making the debut in society that her parents expected of her, Kay entered Smith College. Successful and happy there, she augmented her continued interest in religion with a newly developing social consciousness. Kay studied Oriental religions, read philosophy and the Russian novelists, and became concerned with the lives of the less fortunate. "I was a person who was always asking, 'Why?' 'What is this thing called being?' Somehow, I still thought there were some answers in *Science and Health,* but I wasn't about to take it terribly seriously during those years."

116

Kay, who majored in English and took every writing course Smith offered, planned to work on a magazine in New York after graduation. "I thought, 'I'll have a career first and then I'll get married, phase marriage in,' " she says. But her parents wanted her at home for a while, so dutifully the pretty, well-bred, and well-read daughter came back to Illinois. Soon she became, as one society columnist called her, "the Grace Kelly of Chicago." On May 12, 1950, one year after she left Smith, Kay married Marshall Field IV, Chicago's most eligible bachelor. The princess had found her prince.

But the prince didn't want a career woman for a wife. Rich, powerful, and accustomed to getting his own way, Marshall Field owned a publishing empire which at various times included the *Chicago Sun-Times,* the *Chicago Daily News,* Simon & Schuster, and World Book Encyclopedia. In his opinion, Mrs. Marshall Field IV didn't hold paid employment. She stayed at home, available to talk over his problems with him, to entertain his associates, and to raise the children. If she needed other interests, she could travel with him or take her rightful place in Chicago society.

Kay wanted more. In part, she was motivated by *noblesse oblige.* "I don't mean to sound too idealistic, but I wanted to make something of my life. I had always felt, even as a child, that because I had a more privileged life than most, I ought to contribute something to the world." She also felt she might have talents which were not being used. As she listened to the discussions of newspaper work that went on over her dinner table, Kay sometimes thought, "That sounds like something I could do."

In 1963, the Field marriage fell apart. For some time, Marshall had sought release from his emotional problems with alcohol and drugs. In fact, he was to die from a combination of tranquilizers and alcohol at the age of forty-nine, two years after the divorce. Kay was not in great shape herself. She was smoking two or three packs of cigarettes a day, leaning on tranquilizers and sleeping pills, and "enjoying my wine a little bit more than I knew was good for me."

During the marital crisis and divorce, she moved with their three young children to a townhouse in Chicago's Old Town, deliberately separating herself from the Chicago "Gold Coast" and all that being Mrs. Marshall Field meant. Involved in the civil rights movement and the Council on Foreign Relations, she left the Junior League for the Urban League.

But Kay knew herself to be in transition. She looked back on a disappointing past, but she did not allow herself to feel resentment for the wrong turn her life had taken. "I'm not about to say," she tells me, as she reflects nearly a quarter of a century later on the experience of her first marriage, "that it wouldn't be absolutely wonderful to find the right career and the right husband right out of college and to go forward from there. But I do think that a certain amount of turmoil and trouble probably helps us grow a little. When things work too easily, maybe one doesn't grow as much."

At the time of the breakup, what she was heading toward concerned her more than what she was leaving behind. "I felt my life was like a runaway cable car on a San Francisco hill—out of control," she wrote later. Soon after she divorced her husband, Kay hit "a very deep low," so low that she even considered suicide. She remembers looking at herself in the mirror and thinking, "I don't like this person very much. I want to be somebody different."

Kay didn't do away with herself. Instead, she did herself over. The first step was to turn back to what she intuitively felt Christian Science offered her. She went to a professional Christian Science practitioner. Then, with "a certain amount of discipline, and a certain amount of study, and a certain amount of willingness to give up my old ways of thinking, I turned my life around completely." In a year's time, Kay threw out her cigarettes and gave up all her pills. Since 1965, she has not taken even an aspirin, nor had a drop of anything alcoholic. She joined the Christian Science Church.

The second step was the move to Alaska. Kay didn't know what she wanted to do with her life. "I was really working it out with prayer," she says. "I had tried everything, but I didn't have any answers. So I was praying for an answer as to where I could go and what I could do that would be a right move for me."

"Why Alaska?" I ask. "In the sixties, Anchorage must have seemed like the end of the world."

Kay laughs. "Oh, it did." Once again, she recalled, her intuition came to her aid. She describes a visit from Tay and Lowell

118

Thomas, who lived in Anchorage. Tay was a good friend from their Smith days. The Thomases showed Kay some films, and Kay remembers thinking, "Anchorage is such an ugly city. I wonder why I'm going to move there." Before she knew she was considering the move, she had intuitively already decided to give it a shot.

I am intrigued by Kay's repeated references to intuition and decisions made on the basis of it. "You seem the most practical, matter-of-fact, pragmatic person in the world," I tell her. "Yet intuition seems to have been instrumental in the biggest decisions of your life. How does your intuition work?"

"It isn't anything supernatural, not a voice or a flash of light, or anything like that," she says quickly. "I feel it's very natural, and I think that many Christian Scientists would tell you that they've had similar experiences. I suppose it is seeing a force that is much greater, much smarter than you are, working in your life.

"Christian Scientists are deeply Christian. But we don't see God as an old man with a beard sitting up on a throne somewhere. We see God as mind, as a great intelligence. If you are open to what that mind can unfold for you, the right thing to do seems very natural, very right."

For example, the love which she had developed at Smith for the Russian novelists, especially Tolstoy and Dostoevsky, probably influenced her instinctive movement toward Alaska, Kay thinks. "I loved reading about the winter. There was a sort of peace from the winter, from the snow. I love snow. I love the beauty of snow and mountains and stillness and peace." After the turmoil of the previous few years of her life, peace and stillness were welcome prospects.

The children, who were seven, ten, and twelve, were in school, but they all went up in March, over spring vacation—"not a very nice time of the year," Kay says. Tay told her, "If you like it now, you'll like it anytime." The kids didn't have an inkling that Kay was considering moving to Alaska. As far as they knew, it was just a visit to the Thomases, a vacation.

Kay and the children rented a car and drove around the unfamiliar, exotic countryside. They traveled way up above the Arctic Circle to Nome and Kotzebue. The children were enchanted. One day, Barbara, the youngest, said "just out of the blue as we were driving around," Kay recalls, "Mommy, why don't we move to Alaska?" The other two echoed her.

"This was what I had been waiting for," Kay says. "I said, 'Do you really want to?' "

"Yes," the children clamored.

"Okay," Kay said. "Let's look for a place to live." They found a tract house under construction in Anchorage. Kay bought it in its unfinished state. The skeletal house seemed the right metaphor for an unfinished woman. "I think I had a sense of who I was before the move to Alaska," she says, "but I hadn't summoned up the courage to be that person. Alaska was where I grew up psychologically, and started thinking for myself, not reacting to what someone else thought, not necessarily adopting the views of my parents or my husband, or anybody else." In the fall, when the house was ready for occupancy, Kay and the kids went back.

Then Kay took the third step in her personal makeover. For the first time in her life, she set out to look for a job. Kay didn't have a big divorce settlement, but she had support for the children. She "knew where the next meal was coming from," as she puts it. Thank heaven for that, because she and the children could hardly have made it financially on the two dollars an hour she was paid at first by the *Anchorage Daily News*. Her official title was "librarian," but she quickly learned there was no library.

"You've got to picture this: it was a tiny newspaper, housed in a warehouse. They hired me really as a file clerk, to try to put files together of photos and clippings. It was to be the beginning of a morgue—a newspaper library—but mostly it was just digging in old cardboard crates and sorting through clippings, photo prints, and negatives." She remembers it as "tedious work in a stuffy room next to the noisy Associated Press radio wire." Though ten years later the *Daily News* still didn't have much of a library, grubbing in the crates served Kay well as a quick course in Alaskan affairs and "who was making news."

Within a few months, she wrote her first story. She wrote it on her own time, and turned it in. It made the front page of the paper. "From then on I was a reporter." Ostensibly, she worked part time so that she could be at home when the children came from school. But, to find peace and quiet to write her stories, Kay would get up at three in the morning and work until seven, get the kids off, then go in to the paper until three in the afternoon. It was exhausting but exhilarating, like Alaska itself.

As for Alaska, Kay had fallen in love with it. "I loved it from the moment I got there. I just felt that I had arrived in my place. There was a grandeur about it, excitement in the air, a quality of energy, mental energy and physical energy.

"It wasn't an easy place to be—I mean, just physically it wasn't easy at that time. The street we lived on wasn't paved. We had to wait six weeks to get a telephone. There was one department store in town. But for someone interested in news, when the oil boom came soon afterward, it was a tremendously exciting place to be. It was a place to begin again.

"I loved the adventure, the frontier feeling, the closeness to my children. They could walk to school, and bring their friends home. And they were in a classless society. They had white friends and black friends and all kinds of friends—unfortunately, not many Eskimos, though I hoped that they would.

"I didn't know when I went there that I would stay for eighteen years. I thought I would stay at least a year, but I did feel—I guess the word is 'led' to go there, and that I had a place there."

That summer, she and the children returned to Chicago for a visit. Kay had been on her own then for three years, an important time in her development. "I didn't really like being alone with the children very much," she says, "but I think it was necessary. It was a time for growing and deepening." Before the Chicago visit was over, Kay knew her time alone was over. She had a new love to place alongside her love for Alaska.

Larry Fanning had worked for her former husband. Kay had not known Larry well, though she knew in what regard Marshall, who was now dead, had held him. Larry was a savvy and seasoned newspaperman. As editor of the *Chicago Sun-Times,* Fanning had given an inexperienced Ann Landers an advice column. He had hired Mike Royko, Joseph Kraft, and Nicholas von Hoffman. Later, Larry went on to edit the *Chicago Daily News.* Like Kay, Larry had liberal views and a sense of adventure. At the end of the summer, Katherine Field became Katherine Fanning.

The Fannings' plan was to pool their resources, "which were adequate but not tremendous," and try to buy a small newspa-

121

per somewhere. When Larry accompanied Kay to Anchorage to sell her house—"and then to bring me back to 'civilization,' " she says—what Kay had hoped might happen did happen. Larry, too, fell captive to the fascination of Alaska.

"Larry could see that there was a chance really to matter there. Although Alaska is a vast state geographically, in terms of people it's almost intimate. In the newspaper business, you could know everyone—the governor, the senators, the people who were making things happen. All the decisions that were going to affect Alaska for years were being made at that time. We could be involved with the evolution of a state." The small paper the Fannings bought, in the fall of 1967, was the still library-less *Anchorage Daily News*.

Everyone Kay and Larry knew in the newspaper business advised against the purchase. The *Daily News*, a morning paper with a circulation of eight thousand, was a pathetic number two paper in Anchorage. The afternoon paper, the *Anchorage Times*, had a circulation of thirty thousand. It was owned by the powerful Atwood family, who were at the center of the social and economic structure of Anchorage. "We had very, very hard times," Kay says. Kay and Larry had sunk all their money into buying the paper, and had none of the fall-back capital they needed.

Their operating budget was meager, too. The entire staff of reporters and editors never numbered more than fifteen. In spite of her lack of experience, Kay was Larry's assistant in everything. She wrote a column, edited the Sunday magazine, served a stint as an accountant, even sold advertising. "Advertising was our life blood," Kay says.

Selling ads was hard because the Fannings' liberal editorials didn't win friends for the paper in the very conservative Anchorage establishment. They took minority positions which angered the wealthy, Kay says. "We supported the Alaskan natives—the Eskimos, the Indians, and the Aleuts—in a native land claim settlement."

Other editorials angered everyone. "We wrote an editorial advocating gun control, which was almost enough to get us shot"—Kay laughs—"because everyone in Alaska had a gun."

During the oil boom, when the business community thought oil would be Alaska's economic salvation, the *Daily News* took an environmental stance. "We ran a thirty-two part series called 'Oil on Ice,' pointing out the possible environmental hazards of an Alaskan oil pipeline."

Larry and Kay, who decided together the editorial position the paper would take, tried to see every issue in terms of morality and justice. For their pains, Kay says, "We were seen as carpetbaggers, outsiders who didn't understand Alaska."

They also had idealistic notions about the way to run a paper. "We saw the *Daily News* as a sort of laboratory where we could take young people and train them, and try new things." Not the way to make money in the newspaper business, perhaps, but the *Daily News* was more than a business for Kay and Larry Fanning. It was "a crusade," Kay says, "a tiny paper, but a thing bigger than I was."

Kay has described herself as "raw as any of the kids we hired and I envied those with enough training to know what a pica was." Larry, a perfectionist, demanded her best. The two of them would sometimes go back to the newsroom after dinner, and stay until three or four in the morning, writing and rewriting headlines and cutlines—"occasionally to the point of tears," Kay has written.

All three of the children worked at the paper, too. Ted, the oldest, who had inherited half the voting stock of the $400-million-a-year Field Enterprises, bankrolled it as well. "It had become," Kay says fondly, "a real family operation."

This family operation went on for four years. Then, in 1971, Larry Fanning died at his desk of a massive coronary. Kay was devastated. "I was very deeply in love with Larry," she says. "We were quite wonderful together. He was everything to me."

"I know she was crushed," a former *News* reporter told *Boston* magazine in 1985. "But damn if she wasn't back in the newsroom three days later, tearless. This was the beginning of Kay Fanning and her relentless optimism, this total refusal to admit that failure could ever exist."

Kay doesn't agree; she thinks her optimism began much earlier, though it was sidetracked for a while during her marriage to Marshall Field. "I've never courted the idea of failure," she says. "I don't believe in failure, or that certain areas of life are closed to me because I'm a woman, or for any other reason."

She credits her father for the beginnings of this optimism.

"From the time I was five years old, I can remember his talking to me about the Soviet Five-Year Plan and things like that. It basically never occurred to me that there was anything I couldn't do."

Her religious faith was an even greater factor. "I felt I had a very strong power upon which to lean, much stronger than I. And I've never felt that the intelligence to do what needed to be done was mine personally. If it was mine, it would be limited. The ability to overcome limitation is based on being able to lean on that greater power."

Kay needed all the optimism and confidence she could muster after Larry's death. Several of her most valued reporters came to her, and asked her to keep the paper going. Kay was torn. Her greatest fear was of not being adequate to all the responsibilities she had. "I had been catapulted into the top position at the paper before I had held very many of the bottom positions.

"And I also felt that my children had lost a second father. They had been devoted to Larry, and they needed me. I'm very deeply committed to my family, and I was concerned with their emotional survival. But as time went on, the solution to that seemed to be bringing the children down to the paper rather than my going home to them."

Thus, in the aftermath of the loss of her husband, Kay set about learning newspapering "from the top down. I had done a little of everything, but I hadn't done it long enough. I was really forced into learning a great deal very quickly."

"I had been married to two editors," Kay wrote later. "Now I was the editor. At first I was uncomfortable behind Larry's big desk. Whenever a man came in to meet with me, I would sidle around the desk, pulling my chair to the side. I knew I was moving into a job usually held by a man but I had always enjoyed being a woman. I vowed to cherish my womanhood, to make it as effective and decisive as necessary but never to become like a man."

Womanly or not, she didn't like it when men assumed that a woman could not possibly want to continue in the manly job of editing a newspaper. In one instance, Dave Stein, Larry's general manager, presented Kay with a brand-new organizational chart that he had developed. Essentially, the chart phased Kay out. Kay rejected it. Dave knew she needed his help desperately in the transition, and he announced his plans to go into real estate.

"Some angel," Kay wrote later, "prompted me to smile and say, 'All right, Dave, if the real estate business is going to make you happy, I wouldn't dream of standing in your way.' " Dave stayed.

Another instance of male condescension came from Bob Atwood, the publisher of the opposition paper, the *Anchorage Times.* Chronically pressed financially, Kay signed a joint operating agreement with the *Times* to save money. She realized that Atwood clearly did not take her seriously, either as an ally or as a potential opponent, when he remarked, one supposes he thought gallantly, to the widow, "It's just a matter of time before some man on a white horse will gallop up and carry you away."

Kay did not want a knight on a white horse. She had already been a princess who married a prince, and she had other ideas now. She knew that a woman could succeed as an editor because of what she had learned from Larry Fanning's management style. "The way he handled people," she told me, "the way he nurtured his staff, the way he would always be available to talk to writers about their personal problems or anything else they needed to talk about—he *mothered* his staff, he really did mother them.

"I'm often asked whether women have a different management style from men. And I say, well, there is a different management style, but I learned it from a man."

How well Kay learned can be attested to by the fact that, under her leadership, in 1976 a series on the Teamsters union in Alaska won for the *Daily News* journalism's highest award, the Pulitzer Prize Gold Medal for Public Service. Alaska had never before won a Pulitzer.

"That same year," Kay says, "we went publicly broke. Four months after the Pulitzer, we came out on the front page saying that we were losing money and that it would soon not be possible to continue publication." Kay had sunk everything she had into the *Daily News,* and Ted, Field's heir, had spent $5 million of his own money with no prospect of repayment. Kay realized that something had to be done.

The *Daily News* limped along for two more years. When the Alaskan community understood that the paper was about to go under, a surprising number of people rallied to its support, and formed an organization called the Committee for Two Newspapers. The Committee sold subscriptions and advertising and solicited donations. "Every time we were down to not knowing where the next payroll was coming from, something would happen," Kay says.

Though she recognized that the hat-passing she and the Committee were doing was not a permanent solution to the financial problems of the paper, Kay did not give up easily. When Bob Atwood, acting out of the joint operating agreement Kay had signed with the *Times*, tried to shut the *Daily News* down, "We went for an injunction to stop him." With his talk of men on white horses, Atwood had not bargained for Kay's tenacity. He didn't much relish dealing with a stubborn woman.

The little *News* took the big *Times* to court. Kay describes what happened. "The *Times* lawyer made an impassioned plea before the judge, saying, 'This obsessed woman, and her little newspaper!' And bless the judge! The judge told him he was out of order. And eventually the court ruled for us."

The settlement from Atwood just gave Kay time to realize that she would have to shut the *Daily News* down or sell it. On January 3, 1978, two weeks before she planned to close the operation, she found a buyer, C. K. McClatchy Newspapers. Under the terms of the sale, Kay retained management of the paper, with complete editorial independence. With the infusion of McClatchy funds, circulation of the *Daily News* rose rapidly. By 1982, the "obsessed woman and her little newspaper" had fifty thousand weekday subscribers, and had surpassed Bob Atwood's *Times*.

A year later, in May 1983, Kay was offered the editorship of *The Christian Science Monitor*, in Boston. Her first reaction was "Oh, I'm not qualified for that job." But the board members who made the offer pointed out that she was uniquely qualified, because "the position combined my two great loves, the newspaper business and my religion. And when I realized that they felt there was something that I could contribute, the decision was made very quickly." Two weeks later, by the first of June, Kay's name was on the masthead of the *Monitor*.

She still had fears that she would be inadequate to the demands of the new job. Coming into Boston's Logan Airport, she joked with friends later, "I almost bailed out over Buffalo." But again she had that intuitive sense of "being led into something that would be a right idea, and that therefore I would be supported in what I needed to do. It was just a challenge that I couldn't turn away from."

Twelve years after Larry Fanning's death, Kay married Amos Mathews, who had helped to design the Alaska natural gas pipeline. "For the first years after Larry died," she says, "I couldn't imagine being with another man. I hardly wanted to walk down the street with a man. I had lots of male companionship in my work, but not in my personal life." For her "very happy remarriage," Kay intuitively—and we know what that means—chose a man who is very unlike Fanning and unlike Kay herself. Amos is not a newspaper person, not a Christian Scientist. He is just a "wonderfully supportive" human being, Kay says.

For example, Amos was glad to leave Alaska when Kay did. In their new life in Boston, he cheerfully took on the kind of chores that once belonged to Mrs. Marshall Field IV, planning and shopping for meals and tending to the details of running their apartment. In the *Monitor* offices nearby, Kay often arrived at her desk by eight o'clock in the morning and seldom left it before six or seven in the evening.

As a global newspaper with a worldwide staff of only one hundred and sixty people, the *Monitor* was a formidable challenge. But Kay succeeded in bringing her own sense of moral urgency to an institution which, before her coming, was, in the opinion of another Boston editor, "respectable, but a little tired."

"Isn't there a vital public service to be performed," she wrote of the challenge she took up, "in determining what the public is going to read each morning and evening? Doesn't the content of our newspapers establish the very thought structure of our community and our world? And if that is so, then it is a supreme privilege and responsibility to be an editor."

In 1988, Kay Fanning left the *Monitor*. But in 1987, on the summer afternoon of our conversation, she is still very much there. In fact, it is almost seven and the light outside Kay's office is fading fast as we conclude our interview. The editor of *The*

Christian Science Monitor bends, takes a pair of running shoes from a paper bag under her desk, and changes shoes. Extraordinary and innovative as she is, I think in amusement, in some ways Katherine Woodruff Fanning has certainly realized her ambition to be "just like everybody else."

Part Two

The Skills for Change

We are great fools. "He has spent his life in idleness," we say, and "I have done nothing today." What! have you not lived? That is not only the fundamental, but the most noble of your occupations.

—MONTAIGNE, "On Experience"

Accepting the Constancy of Change

Through such acceptance,
innovators become active
rather than passive
in their attitude
toward change.

7

Driving Toward the No-Goal

In Part One, we examined the process of change described by the innovators, the movement from discontent through provocation and crisis to choice. In Part Two, we shall examine the factors which make change possible for the innovator. These factors I have chosen to call skills in living, and I have identified four such skills: accepting the constancy of change, listening to the inner voice, recognizing the opposites of existence, and creating a strong ego.

Why skills in living rather than qualities of character? Because, though everyone is born with some natural ability for each of the four, that inborn ability can be honed until it becomes a skill. Honing those skills, practicing the art of living skillfully and well, is, as Montaigne said, "not only the fundamental, but the most noble of your occupations."

Take the first skill, accepting the constancy of change. Chemistry, biology, indeed all the sciences reveal that change is the first law of nature, yet human beings often dread change and are, in a sense, addicted to stability. Alcohol and drugs are not the only addictive substances which militate against our willingness to change. Any obsession which provides a temporary or false sense of security is an addiction. In order to accept the constancy of change optimistically, *Waldo Gurewich had to overcome one of the most common addictions in this overfed country of ours, an addiction to food. In Waldo's case, the addiction to food grew out of his relationship to his family.

"My family was always afraid of change," Waldo says. "They're overprotective. They gave all us kids the feeling that the world is unsafe, and that it's best to cushion yourself, to stay in the family. Even though my father made some big changes and did very well with them, we never talked about the good things that would come from a change, but always the trauma."

The family is Jewish. Waldo's father's parents came to Chicago's South Side from Russia after the Second World War; his mother's parents emigrated at the same time from Poland. In Chicago, the whole family—Waldo's grandparents, parents, aunts, and uncles—metaphorically pulled their wagons into a protective circle by buying houses within a few blocks of each other. There, huddled in the bosom of a self-made ghetto, they brought up Waldo, his sister and brother, and their cousins on a diet of death camp stories—stories of loss, of suffering, of starvation.

Waldo's father went into the construction business and did very well, financially. But, having lost everything once, the family feared that history would repeat itself and they became obsessed with security. Waldo's mother, a housewife, was determined that none of her children would ever go hungry if she could help it.

And help it she did, with a vengeance. Mr. Gurewich built a storage room in the basement and equipped it with a king-size pantry and a large freezer, and Mrs. Gurewich prepared for the dangerous future by filling both to the top with food. "One of her hobbies," says Waldo, "was bargain-shopping. If she got something on sale, she bought practically whole job lots—cases of tuna fish, two dozen packages of Yodels. So there was always something to eat."

If there was a shortage of food at home for some unfathomable reason, Waldo had only to walk two blocks in either direction to get to an aunt's or a grandmother's kitchen. Waldo was a champion eater. He had pneumonia when he was six months old, and a favorite family joke was that as soon as he got better he asked for a hamburger. "I was trained to be an eater," he says.

When Waldo was nine years old, the school doctor called him and his mother in for a conference. "He yelled at my mother, 'You're making your son fat,' then he yelled at both of us. But he didn't give my mother a diet for me. He sent us both home frustrated and miserable but still ignorant about what he expected us to do. So my mother yelled at me, and I cried. Then I went down to the basement and ate some Yodels.

"Food was always the main line of communication between me and my mother. Even now"—Waldo is thirty-four and has his own apartment in another section of Chicago—"when I call my mother, she'll say, 'What are you eating?' That's her way of saying, 'Are you doing okay?' or 'Are you taking care of yourself?' "

His whole personality, Waldo says, was "built around being fat. I was 'Wally,' the cute little fat boy.' Being fat kept me from having to be much of anything else." By the time Waldo had finished college, he had been fat as long as he could remember. He was sixty-five pounds over the top level on all the weight charts for his height and build, and, worst of all, he was gaining weight faster than ever before.

Waldo panicked. He wanted desperately to be "normal," but he found himself completely unable to control the eating habits of a lifetime. "When I ate chicken, I ate a whole chicken—that was my usual portion. When I ate cake, I finished the cake." A talented artist—"I was 'the fat guy who paints' "—Waldo decided to take a master's degree in art therapy. "I knew I needed therapy to get the fat off, and that before you actually became an art therapist, they made you go into therapy yourself.

"My parents would have done anything for me—they paid for my education with never a question or a complaint—but they were very unenlightened about psychotherapy, very suspicious of it. They would have been really uncomfortable with the idea that a child of theirs would need such a thing.

"But I could tell my parents I had to go into therapy because it was part of the art therapy program. And I told myself that, too, for a long time. I was going to be a therapist, set up a private practice, and work with disturbed kids." The chief disturbed kid, as he well knew in his heart, was cute little fat Wally Gurewich.

After he went into therapy, slowly and painfully Waldo lost sixty-five pounds. It was never easy. One morning, for example, after having joined a weight control group and adhered to the program diligently for several months, he woke up one morning "and all I wanted to do was binge. The control went away and I just wanted to eat constantly. I was living alone at last, which was a big break for me, but I didn't have Yodels and all that good stuff ready at hand.

"So I went to the supermarket. I couldn't *not* go to the supermarket. But I made up this game. I put all the things I was craving in the pushcart, and then one by one put them back on the shelf. The game was, that if I won, they would stay in the supermarket.

"I played the supermarket game many times before I lost the whole sixty-five pounds. Sometimes I would spend an hour and a half in the supermarket, putting food in the cart and then putting it back on the shelf, and I would leave with nothing. I wasn't going to give in to that craving without a battle."

There were times when he lost the game. Early in the supermarket battle, Waldo got all the way home with a frozen chocolate cheesecake, "one of my things. I ate half of it, and then I was so disgusted with myself that I threw the rest in the garbage.

"Two o'clock in the morning, I got up out of bed. Like a madman, I went into the garbage pail, and I dug that cake out and I ate it. That's really hitting bottom. I wasn't out in the street, or out of money, or a drunk, but I was out of control. I knew that I was sick."

His family didn't help in the least with his attempts to lose weight. Waldo remembers going to a family party where "everyone was wildly obese. I had lost all this weight, and the relatives were taking bets on how long it would take me to gain it all back."

Only one member of the family seemed to realize what Waldo had accomplished. An aunt came up to him and said, "You little bastard! I always wanted to be thin, and now you've done it. I hate you."

"She had tears in her eyes," Waldo says, "but she threw her arms around me and gave me a big hug. Knowing that someone in the family approved was nice."

That was ten years ago. "I guess my family is still waiting," Waldo says, "expecting me some day to blimp out, you know? But that's because they think of me as 'fat little Wally.' I've changed, but their image of me hasn't changed. They don't really know me now. That's not going to happen."

Waldo did not lose his addictive personality at the same time that he lost all those pounds. He redirected his cravings. During the first year of dieting, he munched raw carrots incessantly as a substitute for Yodels and cheesecake. He consumed mountains of carrots, so many carrots that finally he turned "as yellow as if I had jaundice" from carotene poisoning.

Forced to cut back on carrots, Waldo switched to diet drinks. At one point, when he was doing volunteer work in a hospital for troubled children, he took frequent advantage of his aide's uniform to race through the ward shouting "Emergency!" The only emergency was that Waldo needed a quick diet Coke fix.

Even today, Waldo realizes that he will never be able to relax his vigilance toward food. In order to reject what he shouldn't have, he habitually thinks of himself as a thin person, eating the way thin people do.

Nevertheless, if the new, thin Waldo is an unknown quantity to his family, that thin stranger took some getting used to for Waldo himself. "One day about four years after I lost my weight," Waldo told me, "I saw my reflection in a store window. I said, 'That's not you,' when I saw this thin person. And it really freaked me. I went home and had a good cry, if you can believe it. It just hit me that I would stay thin, that I would never be that fat person again. It was like I was mourning the fat, saying goodbye to the person I had lost."

Several years ago, Waldo left his work as an art therapist to become a counselor in a weight control clinic where he can put his experience to good use for the benefit of others. Today, however, food and weight are no longer the center of Waldo's personal life. Art is. Waldo has a new addiction, his painting. The passion that as a little boy Waldo poured into cushioning himself from the dangers of the world, the grownup Waldo pours into painting giant, boldly colored abstracts. Lush, over-blown, hyperbolic, they could almost be called fat person paint-ings. His art is fat, but Waldo isn't.

Overcoming his addiction to food has made Waldo comfort-able with the constancy of change, and he has completely changed his painting style several times. "For a while I was painting like the Impressionists, and I got a lot of praise at that point. Everything was 'lovely' and 'beautiful.' Then I started to change, and everyone said, 'Why are you changing? You were doing such wonderful things.'

"But the painting—*it* just starts to change. I don't say, I have to do this, or I have to do that, or I have to use another color. Something just starts to work in the painting—it's like being in a paper bag and you just start to punch your way out. At first it was a little scary, but now I don't mind it. I never mind the change." Waldo's art thrived on the transitions in his life.

Art generally thrives on change. Many of us have an idealized notion of the painter alone in his garret, or the writer in her ivory tower, but historically, the arts have flourished in places and periods of instability and transition. The great Greek dra-matists wrote during the most dynamic periods in Athenian history, as statehood became imperialism. Shakespeare came of literary age when Elizabeth I was on the throne of an England fighting for independence and a national identity. The Greek fight for independence energized the poetry of Byron and Shel-ley, while the French Revolution affected Wordsworth and Cole-ridge. No one has said better than Wordsworth what the artist needs to create: "emotion recollected in tranquillity." Emotion comes from change.

But art is not all recollection; it may anticipate a coming change. Chekhov, Dostoevsky, and Tolstoy, like seismographs, caught in their work the first faint tremors of the advancing Revolution. And, if the years after America's entrance into the First World War saw the destruction of our parochial innocence as a nation, those same years also produced the work of three writers—Hemingway, Faulkner, and Fitzgerald—who remain contemporary in spirit a half-century later. The point is that the most volatile periods of history call forth especially large numbers of creative, innovative people.

Change sharpens the wits and stirs the emotions of ordinary people as well as artists. "It is a law of nature we overlook," H. G. Wells writes in *The Time Machine,*

> that intellectual versatility is the compensation for change, danger and trouble. An animal perfectly in harmony with its environment is a perfect mechanism. Nature never appeals to intelligence until habit and instinct are useless. There is no intelligence where there is no change and no need of change. Only those animals partake of intelligence that have to meet a huge variety of needs and changes.

The dangers to all human creativity and intelligence lie not in instability and turbulence, but in constriction and boredom.

And creative, innovative people can tolerate more conflict, more tension and paradox, than others can. The test of a first-rate intelligence, Fitzgerald said, is the ability to hold two conflicting ideas in the mind at once. Think of those conflicting ideas as freedom and security: freedom implies mobility, security implies stasis. For complete security (as if there were ever such a thing), we must jettison complete freedom (which also doesn't exist). The innovator cultivates the skill of mediating between those two polarities in his own life. The ability to live with that kind of irresolution, and the conflict, tension, and paradox which it engenders, is central to the innovative life. Ed McCabe is in the process of working out such a life for himself.

While chubby little Wally Gurewich sat in a high chair in his mother's kitchen, just across the way in the bottom end of north Chicago, scrawny fourteen-year-old Ed McCabe was finishing his first day of work as a Good Humor man. Ed, who weighed one hundred pounds soaking wet, was, in fact, soaking wet. The day was hot the way a summer day can be in Chicago when there's no cooling breeze and the moisture in the air from the lake is palpable. All day long, sweat dripping down his stiff collar and puddling under his heavy black belt, Ed had had to pedal like hell just to move the heavy Good Humor bicycle wagon. When, back at the Good Humor place, Ed realized that after a hard day's work he had made exactly $3.70, he was in anything but a good humor.

The next morning, Ed used his brains instead of his legs. He filled the wagon again with Good Humor bars. When he got safely out of sight of the office, however, he dumped the ice cream bars. Then Ed went back to the apartment where he lived with his mother and stepfather, ordered in twenty quarts of beer "for a party we're having" and charged the beer, at fifteen cents a quart, to his parents' account at the liquor store. He loaded the beer into the Good Humor wagon and pedaled over to the local high school. In less than two hours, the summer school kids had cleaned out the beer at a dollar a quart, and Ed had paid off the liquor store and returned the wagon and the ice cream profits to Good Humor. The kids were happy, the liquor store was happy, and Good Humor was happy. Ed McCabe was happiest of all. He had pulled off his first marketing coup.

That good day, described by James Kaplan in *Manhattan,inc.*, has become part of the legend of Ed McCabe. Ed remembers plenty of bad days when he was growing up in Chicago. "My father died of cancer when I was eight," he tells me, "and my childhood was not a happy one. By the time I was ten or eleven I had three jobs. I was a delivery boy and I worked in a florist shop and I had a newsstand job. Weekends I had newspaper routes. I was frustrated because I felt like I was the breadwinner, and that I had a destiny, but I was not—" He breaks off and pushes his untidy black hair back with a gesture that says he would like to be reaching for a cigarette but won't.

"I was so frustrated," Ed continues. "I knew what needed to be done with our family, me and my mother, but I couldn't do it. I was an eight-year-old *kid*.

"And that kind of frustration has stuck with me through my whole life. I've played many musical instruments, but I would hear music that I couldn't get through the horn. My mind could compose it, but my fingers and mouth couldn't play it. And I have visions of paintings or sculptures, but I can't get them out through my hands."

That frustration and the energy that idealism generated made Ed McCabe an advertising genius. "An adman's adman" James Kaplan called him. Admen claim, for example, that McCabe's concepts for Volvo ("Fat Cars Die Young"), Frank Perdue the chicken king ("It takes a tough man to make a tender chicken"), Hertz, and Western Union, among others, are advertising classics. In his more than three decades in advertising, McCabe has become the top concept person in a business which is all concept, which is about peddling Good Humor in a form the public will buy.

And McCabe was rewarded for his brilliance. At the age of twenty-eight, he started his own Manhattan agency: Scali, Mc-Cabe, Sloves, Inc. At thirty-five, he was elected to the Copywriters' Hall of Fame, the youngest person ever to win the honor. "There are thousands of people out there," Kaplan wrote in 1986, "who would kill to be what and where Ed McCabe is." Yet I have come to talk to Ed because, at the age of forty-seven, the adman's adman decided to become his own something else.

What that "something else" is, is still, you might say, under construction. Squeezing around ladders and brushing by cans of paint to climb the narrow steps leading to the fourth floor office *cum* bedroom where McCabe is currently sequestered, I have met several bulky corporate types in suits coming down from a consultation with the advertising genius. But there is nothing corporate about McCabe himself, and he is anything but bulky. In fact, I think, as I study the short, lean man before me in his faded greenish chinos and blue sweater, rarely has the street kid been so visible in the adult. Even under the lines of Ed's craggy, handsome, but decidedly worn face, I can see the tough but tender little boy he must have been.

We are sitting, Ed on a short stool which makes him look even more like a dissolute child, I on a straightbacked chair like his teacher, in a large room which is the whole top floor of a building in TriBeCa which Ed recently purchased. He is now, with the help of carpenters, electricians, painters, his girlfriend, Carolyn Jones, and his secretary, Emily Feinberg, transforming the building to house his and Carolyn's living quarters on the top two floors, as well as the headquarters for his new McCabe Communications on the lower two. Emily moves around, dealing with the madly ringing phone, the workmen, and a young-looking black cat trying to slither out to the street. I take in lots of windows, white walls, a neatly made queen-size bed, an open closet with a tidy arrangement of jeans and jackets.

But mostly I take in McCabe. Ed is discussing his ultimate artistic vision, a vision not to play or paint or sculpt, but to live. The master of concepts has a new concept for his own life, a concept which involves only one plan: to plan nothing. He will do only what he wants to do, only when he wants to do it. McCabe Communications will communicate with one client at a time.

"What I will do," Ed tells me, "is conceive and focus a company's creative thrust, their core communication to the public. Companies, personalities in public affairs or entertainment, events, promotions, whatever needs structuring creatively so people can see what it is in its best light—I'll do that. I will charge them a fee for that, and that's it. I'll present my recommendations, but I won't do any advertising. I'll do my job, be paid, and be on my way.

"Then, if I decide that after doing that number on that particular day I want to go to Hollywood and make a movie, I'll go to Hollywood and make a movie. Then, if the Hollywood thing doesn't work, if I need money, I'll come back and do another thing for a client. But the goal here is not to make a lot of money —it's to allow myself the luxury of doing what I want. I'm purposely affiliating myself only with very limited timespan projects, because I'm still not sure what I want. I know that I want this more than I wanted what I was doing. But this is only a step.

"Of all the changes I've made in my life, I guess this is the biggest one—not knowing what's coming. My entire life, I always knew exactly what the next step was going to be, and now I don't."

But this being ready for constant change is the kind of behavior people expect of kids in their twenties, I argue, playing devil's advocate. Young people are supposed to jump jobs until they find one that suits them. "It's the old book jacket thing," I say. "You know, 'X has been a cabdriver in New York, a stevedore on a banana boat, a rumrunner from Panama,' and so on." Why would Ed give up the edge he's gained in the most competitive business in the country to try breaking into the movies, on whichever side of the camera? Or writing a book? Or driving a racing car? Isn't nearly fifty a little, well, old for such romantic shenanigans?

"Listen," Ed says, "I'm more youthful than the twenty-year-old of today ever dreamed of being. I've seen those people at work. They have every move in their career planned, every move in their lives. They are locked in to a pattern, just the way I was.

"I was an old man at eighteen. People didn't know if I was twenty or forty. They couldn't tell. I wore banker-like black suits. I had to succeed at what I was doing and nothing was going to stop me. I had been through a lot already at that age, and it showed in ways that I can't even describe.

"And people were quite disturbed by that. I was very intense. I mean, there wasn't enough air for another person in the same *city*. I took it all."

The city was Chicago, where his father was a traveling salesman who had just gone into real estate when he died in 1947. "Are you like your father?" I ask Ed, and the anger of the child whose father abandons him by dying is evident in his evasive "I don't know, I didn't know him." But then he answers the question.

"He took me to an amusement park once," Ed remembers. "I threw balls at those bottles and couldn't knock them down. So my father bought all the teddy bears in the stand. Yeah, I remember that.

"He was a very show-biz, huge kind of character. He would disappear for weeks and months at a time, and then come in with twenty skid-row bums on Christmas Eve, with no announcement to my mother, and ask her to feed them. I mean, always doing the big crazy things. I have that occasional overdramatic expansive craziness that my father had. And he was a drinker, and I have been that."

"Bigger than life" is the phrase Ed uses for his father. "The smallest person I know who's bigger than life," someone has called Ed McCabe.

Ed thinks he's a lot like his mother. "I have the same stubborn doggedness that she had, and the same kind of humor. She was the ultimate realist, totally irreverent, outrageously blunt. Most of my advertising slogans were words I heard from my mother."

In spite of her intrinsic toughness, Ed's mother was "very vulnerable after my father died. She needed help." Ed contributed toward the rent and groceries, for his own sake as well as hers—"I sensed this was independence." When Ed was eleven,

143

Mrs. McCabe married again, a move which wiseacre Ed considered bad judgment on her part. Ed began hanging out with the demimonde—the tough kids who spent their nights at roller rinks and pool halls and their days standing around in doorways looking for trouble. Ed wasn't really big enough or tough enough for the streets, but he was sneaky and he was smart, so he managed.

School began to seem irrelevant to his real life. When he was sixteen, he dropped out of high school, thus ending his formal education. Ed knew he had to have a job to keep the truant officer off his back. He filled out the forms with the state employment agency, lying about having finished high school. A perceptive agent sent the brash, fast-talking kid to a place where brashness and fast talk would do him no harm and might even help— an ad agency.

"I didn't choose to go into advertising," Ed says. "Before I walked into McCann-Erickson that first day, I didn't know that advertising agencies existed." But he landed a job in the mail room at McCann-Erickson. By the end of the first week Ed had figured out a plan for his life.

"How can I get to be a copywriter?" he asked a superior. "You have to have a college education," was the answer. "And I hadn't even finished high school," Ed says. So part of the plan included, not going to college—that would cost too much and take too long—but educating himself by reading. Over the next couple of years, Ed read. He started with the Harvard Classics, and to them he added, with great curiosity and liberality, whatever anyone suggested. "I didn't know what an education was," he says, "but I was determined to get one."

In the meantime, the teenaged autodidact was also working hard at McCann-Erickson. He moved out of the mailroom, into the art and traffic departments. When he saw a chance to volunteer for copywriting on the side, he took it. His ads, which were fresh and original "because I didn't know any better," won awards. Again he was sneaky and smart, and those qualities paid off just as they had on the streets. While most kids his age were sitting in a classroom, McCabe was racking up time in the trenches. At twenty, with four years of experience under his belt, he came to New York. Before he was thirty, he was the co-founder and creative mainspring of an advertising agency with his name on it.

At Scali, McCabe, and Sloves, Ed became a man possessed. He was addicted to advertising. "I'm a totally immoderate person in all things," he says, "and always have been. If one is good, a hundred is best, and a thousand is even better than the best. And it doesn't matter what it is. If it's peanuts, I have to have many peanuts." For the next twenty years as Scali, McCabe, and Sloves got on the road and then pulled ahead of the competition, it was memorable ads.

Ed especially enjoyed the early days of the agency. He liked being the underdog, the new kid on the block, liked "that undaunted jousting at windmills, you know. Give me an army to attack and I'll go after them. Fighting with one person is boring."

To create ads that would eventually give his agency a reputation as one of the most innovative and effective in the country, Ed worked around the clock. In a way, he never stopped working. His mind was always on the client, the concept, the ad, the next ad, and the next, ads infinitum. "I was frantic, and single-minded, and driven, trying all the time to do and move and create. Don't get me wrong—it's a strength. I definitely consider it a strength. But you have to know when to stop. I once started nine corporations in three months. I had to start cutting, or I would've had a hundred."

Ed McCabe became too good at what he was doing. Scali, McCabe, and Sloves attracted the attention of the giant corporation, Ogilvy and Mather. In 1977, Ogilvy and Mather made an offer the small, independent company couldn't refuse. Ed McCabe instantly became a richer man, but he soon found that life in the corporate zone didn't much suit his entrepreneurial spirit.

"This was a business that had been largely driven by the force of my personality and my way of doing things. It was a partnership, but, philosophically, in many ways I was the ascendant partner. And when we sold the company, it became something else, and that something was not what I wanted. My concept of business is intensely creative and personal, and this became everything I hate, have always hated."

For a while, Ed tried to make it work, because he regarded giving up as failure. After all, he had gotten where he was by never letting up for an instant. Carolyn Jones, his fiancée, called him to his senses because "she was able to articulate and identify what I was feeling. 'Look what you're doing, you fool, you,' she said. And I began to see that sometimes giving up is the greatest success. I could have stayed in the old place and been the guru and gotten paid for it, and I think I probably would have gradually died. My importance to me, my feeling about myself, would have died, while I balanced security against my dreams.

"Now what's real? I finally decided that the security is not real. The reality is the ability to dream and do the unexpected. So finally I just said, 'Stop! I'm getting out. I've had enough. I'm gonna take a gamble and invest in myself.' "

The first dream Ed brought into the light of day after leaving the company was indeed unexpected. In January 1987, he and Carolyn decided to compete in the toughest auto race in the world, the Paris–Dakar Rally across, as Ed was to write of it for *Esquire* later, "eight thousand miles of bad road," including a lengthy stretch in the Sahara Desert. Ed told an interviewer before the rally that he had the best possible reasons to do it. "It's incredibly punishing. And I have not been in very good condition lately." Also, though Ed had had some experience racing cars, Carolyn had not. "All of these things are good reasons for me wanting to do it. I mean, if I was perfectly fit, younger, and had my driving skills honed and a very experienced partner, I'd never do this."

"There were two things about that race," Ed tells me, "and they are a perfect example of the two sides of me and the forces at work in me. On the one hand, it was going into danger, a daring adventure, and all the romantic, wonderful, dream-the-impossible-dream things. On the other hand, it took the ability to organize a mountain of details into a given mission, to do a production like making *Ben-Hur*."

Ed commissioned a custom-built Mercedes for the rally. He and Carolyn trained for a year. They spent hours in the gym working out. They practiced yoga for the mental and spiritual control they would need through endless days and sleepless nights sealed in the equivalent of a space capsule hurtling across the sand. They did cross-country drives to condition themselves and to get used to being in such close quarters with each other.

146

They even studied French, "for me the most mind-numbing of all our endeavors," Ed wrote, because the route instructions would be in French. When they were tempted to give up, "the sheer magnitude and complexity of the project gave it a life of its own and swept us over the rough spots," Ed reflected afterward in *Esquire.*

Some spots were rough indeed. During the rally, Ed and Carolyn were lost for seven hours in Algeria. The Mercedes ran out of gas, stranding them in the desert for "fifty-three hours and twenty-seven minutes." Armed only with American dollars and T-shirts, they faced hostile brigands who found blond Carolyn very attractive. Even though after the eighth day they were officially out of the race, they tagged along with the rally until the end. Then Ed found that, in twenty-two days, he had lost fifteen pounds and had gained a startling new patch of gray hair.

"It was a mind-clearer," Ed says of the rally. "It gave me a new fix on what's important—feeling alive and excited and involved, putting everything you have to use. I worked for a year, single-mindedly, without allowing much else in, and went for it, and did it to the best of my ability. And that's what I want—that ultimate challenge. I figure I could handle one a year."

So that's why McCabe Communications will take on only one client at a time. Ed McCabe, an extremely tight, wound-up man, is trying to hang loose, to be ready for the next big challenge. "The problem with most people," Ed says, "is that when the big vision, the big opportunity, comes along, they're not in a position to act upon it. But I'm well placed. I have the security I need, but I also have the freedom of not being involved in anything small that's sapping my energy and attention. It's a wonderful, wonderful position to be in."

Nevertheless, he sometimes finds his freedom terrifying. "It's such a break with my past, because I always had to be doing something, and I had to be getting a paycheck." He's given up the concept of the paycheck for "the annual or biannual hit. It's a totally alien way of doing things, and yet all the happiest and most successful people I know operate that way."

Does he wish he'd done this years ago, I ask? Ed says that he isn't sure that he could have. "As I get older, I have more absolute belief in myself and what I'm capable of doing. I really believe that if I decided to, I could be the architect of a building,

147

make a feature film, and set a new world record in sports—and I could do all three of those in the same year if I wanted to."

Ed not only accepts the constancy of change; he welcomes the constant possibility of change as the best part of life. The goals that you set up in advance, Ed says, may simply be too small for the person you become. "It's always diminish, diminish, diminish your goal, because that makes it easier to accomplish. So I'm trying not to think of goals any more. I don't like to say I'm keeping my options open—I hate that yuppie phrase—and there are people who spend a lifetime keeping their options open and don't do anything. I can close all my options very quickly when I know what I want to do.

"Let's just say I'm driving toward the no-goal with as much dedication as I can."

Once the idea that, as E. B. White put it, "the only sense that is common in the long run is the sense of change," has been made a permanent part of the psyche, the innovator feels free to initiate change himself rather than to wait for change inevitably to catch up with him. He decides to become an active agent rather than a passive victim of change, to control and direct the way in which his life will change.

At that point, innovators have the willingness to respond to challenge which British novelist Margaret Drabble demonstrates. In an interview I did with her in 1986, that writer explained the many changes she has made in her career—actress, novelist, essayist, travel writer, biographer, teacher, lecturer, playwright—as what we might call an "automatic yes policy."

"I decided very early in my career," Margaret Drabble told me, "that when I was asked to do something I hadn't done before, I would just say yes." Accepting the constancy of change allows one to "just say yes" to the manifold opportunities of life.

8

To Continue
a People

Accepting the constancy of change means accepting the constant challenge to enlarge rather than to diminish goals. Throughout their lives, the two innovators whose stories await you in this chapter have constantly set higher personal ambitions. Beyond the personal, each has also come to be a pioneer of enlightened thinking and enlarged expectations for a race of people. Each is a kind of Moses, able to reveal the Promised Land to those bound by outgrown habits of thought.

But Moses saw to it that the Israelites took the Ark of the Covenant on their journey. This holy relic from their past symbolized that which endures, and must endure, in a constantly changing world. In all change, something or someone must not

149

be let go. Pioneers rarely travel empty-handed and alone. The immigrant Shimerda family in Willa Cather's *My Ántonia,* who traveled together to the raw Nebraska plains, brought with them two precious objects: a bag of dried mushrooms from some dark forest of their native Bohemia, and a violin. Food for the body, food for the soul. Stephen James and Emily Korzenik, too, have a proper respect, a reverence, for the past of their peoples.

But *il faut être de son temps,* as Baudelaire has it. You must be of your own time. As the world changes, so must the thinking of the races who inhabit it. That's where people like Stephen and Emily come in.

When Stephen James, a moral philosopher on a bicycle, arrives for our interview on a hot July afternoon in 1987, he is sharply quizzed by the doorman of the apartment building where I live. "Is this a delivery?" the doorman asks.

Stephen replies that it is not.

Dubious to hostile, the doorman reluctantly buzzes my apartment. "There's a man down here who says you are expecting him," the doorman says on the intercom. "But," the tone of his voice says, "he really plans to rape, murder, and rob you."

You see, Stephen, a high school dropout from the Bronx, is black. Or, as Stephen himself would say, with his usual semantic precision, he is a dark brown Black.

"Don't worry about it," Stephen tells me now in a soft musical voice, as I apologize for the doorman's distrust. Stephen folds his lanky frame into a chair and gratefully accepts a cold drink. His almond-shaped eyes are unguarded, his smile open. "I'm used to the assumption," he says, "that you are a certain thing because of your skin color. Certainly no one ever assumed that I would be a scholar." But here Stephen is, a Roads Scholar, as *People* called the ghetto-bred city bus driver who has just received a full six-year, $57,000 fellowship from Harvard for its Ph.D. program in American literature.

The Harvard fellowship is but the most recent of a series of academic honors for Stephen, who was born thirty-four years ago to a city clerk and an absentee father whom he hardly knows. A Lehman Foundation scholarship eased his just-completed senior year at Lehman College in his native Bronx, a Phi Beta Kappa key adorns his key ring, and his college diploma reads *summa cum laude.* Stephen, as "part-time student extraordinaire" and "an illustrious example of today's nontraditional student," has even been read into the *Congressional Record.*

Now that same "student extraordinaire" is moving with his family out of the Bronx. Stephen grew up in the South Bronx, one of New York's roughest ghettos, living in a small apartment over a storefront with his mother and grandparents. Through his two marriages and the birth of three children, he has stayed in the Bronx. But now he is leaving his hardscrabble existence as sometime security guard, carpenter, and, most recently, bus driver. Stephen the scholar is off to Cambridge with his second wife and young son. He will be nurtured by one of the most prestigious universities in the country. How does he feel on the eve of this phenomenal change in his life?

"Grateful," Stephen says. "The system gave me an opportunity, and rewarded me for taking it." Yet, grateful though he may be, Stephen James is also determined to change some things about the system. Stephen believes that all of life is a moral argument, and he decidedly knows the positions he wants to argue. Those positions, he says, will gain credibility when he has a Harvard Ph.D., which he calls "a union card in communications." The social change he wants to effect? To obliterate racism in America.

Since the sixties, civil rights morality for many black people has begun with the premise that "black is beautiful." Stephen agrees. He has spent a lot of time studying the contributions of mute, inglorious Miltons who, because they were black, are unremembered today. But Stephen argues further that, although black is beautiful, gray or plaid are not only more beautiful but are inevitable. He would like to see his people exchange black pride for pride in the universal family of man. He would like blacks and whites to recognize that any notion of "separate but equal" races in America is just that—a notion.

Stephen traces his racial consciousness back to 1962, when he was almost ten and read about James Meredith's struggle to get into the University of Mississippi. Never before that crucial day had his mother told him that some people are "black" and others are "white." He lacked, he insists, any sense of racial identity. "Why," he asked his teacher, "don't they want this man James Meredith to go to school?"

151

The other kids in his mostly black class laughed and poked each other as the teacher tried to explain the inexplicable in terms a child could grasp. She only confused Stephen, and that confusion bred his moral energy. "That question turned out to be definitive for my whole life," Stephen says. "At the time, I didn't know that there really was a 'they.' I thought when I grew up that I would look like Superman or Hercules."

The classroom debacle and other such episodes set Stephen apart from the other kids. Identified as a gifted child, he refused to leave his neighborhood to go to a special school. But with questions like the one about Meredith, he soon became odd boy out anyway. He learned not to ask questions, and compensated for his silence and frustration at school by creative activities at home. Luckily for him, the family television set went on the fritz, and there was no money to fix it. The fact that "I completely missed the Uncle Miltie era" further separated him from the television-obsessed generation in his ghetto school.

Instead of television, Stephen had books. His mother, who had completed two years of college, bought books compulsively. Stephen consumed whatever she bought. He recalls reading all the Sherlock Holmes stories, *Treasure Island,* and especially *The Three Musketeers,* which he read over and over. The slogan of the musketeers, "All for one and one for all," began to work its way deep into the psyche of the lonely little boy.

A single mother in the ghetto who brings books home by the armload is anything but stereotypical. "Do you get your smarts from your mother?" I ask the grownup Stephen.

"I don't think smarts are genetic," Stephen says. "The desire to learn might be genetic, but the ability to learn is not. I think I've *developed* that. But if people want to learn, I don't think it's possible to stop them. The ability will come. And I wanted to learn."

Yet this eager student dropped out of his mostly black high school in the middle of his junior year. "If school means going to classes," Stephen says, "I really 'dropped out' from almost the beginning." A talented musician who now plays the cello, organ, piano, and guitar, Stephen would go to his orchestra class and rehearsal, but he cut everything else, spending the rest of his class hours working out in the gym. "I was caught between the gangs and the bureaucracy," Stephen explains, "too much of a nerd for the hip kids who ran things and not regimented enough to please the teachers. I had *no* friends in high school. I didn't fit in anywhere, and I was very unhappy." Finally, he dropped out.

Unlike most black kids who don't make it through high school, Stephen went on immediately to get his Graduate Equivalency Diploma. He steered clear of drugs and ghetto crime. Instead, he got a job in 1970 as a security guard at Lehman College in the Bronx. There the tall, wiry, black boy, who had rarely been out of his own neighborhood, first experienced racial hostility. When he got on an elevator, he noticed, white people would get off. Stephen thought at first he smelled bad. He washed more carefully. That didn't help. He took more pains with his clothes. That didn't help. At length he had to recognize that the only thing left was something he couldn't change: the color of his skin.

In 1973, Stephen left Lehman and became a carpenter's apprentice, then worked as a carpenter until 1977. At nineteen, he married, and subsequently had two children; then he divorced, remarried, and had a third child. Carpentry was too seasonal for all these responsibilities, so in 1978 Stephen passed the test that enabled him to become a city bus driver. A bus driver's salary, which was half his carpenter's pay, was steady but insufficient— one hundred dollars a week, and he owed sixty a week in child support, fifty a week for housing. Stephen began to work seven days a week to provide for his family.

As a bus jockey, Stephen drove a split shift, which required him to work early in the morning and late in the day. Most people would not regard this punishing schedule as an advantage, but optimistic Stephen did. Every day from nine till four, he was free. He decided to go to college. Of course, he chose Lehman, where he had worked as a guard.

"Going back to school," the high-school dropout says, "I wasn't confident, but I was determined." He soon saw that, in a school where so many students were lackadaisical and unmotivated, determination was enough. Stephen got A's in his first two classes. Then a new bus run opened and he had to drop out. Two years later, he registered again for classes but couldn't find the tuition money. He decided to wait till the following year when he could use his vacation pay to go to school for two more

153

semesters. Then he had to drop out again. And so it went, in and out, in and out. "I finished college in nine semesters," he says, "but it took me nine years."

During the semesters when Stephen could afford tuition, his hours were grinding. He reported to work at six-thirty A.M., drove the bus into Manhattan and back, and was on campus by ten. At three, he left school for the afternoon bus run, which he completed at seven. After time with his family, he hit the books till two A.M. or later, and sometimes studied till time to go to work the following morning.

His "dark night of the soul" came one semester when he had the money to register for twenty-three credit hours, an enormous load for a part-time student. Soon after the semester began, Stephen caught pneumonia, his temperature climbing as high as 104°. He told his teachers he would be out a week, but even sick he had to keep on driving his route. Exhausted, he couldn't shake his illness. "I felt that nobody understood what school meant to me, that no one was helping." He dragged on through Thanksgiving, feeling fatally discouraged.

Then a miracle occurred. Bus company employees went on strike. Stephen could stay home from work, get well, and catch up in his classes. During this experience, Stephen realized how much those classes mattered to him. At school, Stephen felt that he had found his place in the world. He had people who wanted to talk about ideas with him. He had an excuse to study, to pursue the learning that was the need of his soul. Being bookish wasn't frowned upon; it paid off. In spite of all the adversity he had encountered, Stephen finished at Lehman with a nearly perfect record, 3.99 out of a possible 4.00.

No one expects much from blacks in the educational system, Stephen says. "It's not normal for black people to come out at the top of the class." Stephen's success shattered those prejudices, raised those low expectations. As a reward, Stephen received first a Javits Fellowship, with a stipend for graduate study, then the full scholarship to Harvard.

Yet Stephen is not an ivory tower intellectual. His years as a laborer and a bus driver took care of that. During his college career, Stephen was also getting another, nonbookish education. "I think I have a degree in psychology as well as in literature," he says, "from driving the bus and talking to the people I met." Stephen did not separate his experiences at school from those with his bus passengers. With his earnest, gentle, quizzical manner, the manner of a born teacher, he engaged all who seemed willing to talk in discussions of moral issues.

For example: When Reagan came into office, Stephen would often ask a busload of passengers, "Is Reagan smart enough to do the job? Is he the best-qualified person available?"

"I myself," he says, "don't have any illusions that we have a meritocracy in this country, but a lot of people do. I played up to this convention to draw other people into a discussion, to make them think. If you really want to say something to people, you can find a way and a place to say it."

Although Stephen "wanted to be a Renaissance man" and the breadth of his knowledge is impressive, his focus has always been literature. For Stephen, all literature expresses a view of right and wrong. Great literature provides a moral education for the serious reader. Thus, to him, *Anna Karenina* is neither just a story of human life nor a constructed artifice to be dryly deconstructed. It is a finely crafted piece of fiction which presents a moral truth, art which exemplifies significant lessons of love and fidelity. Stephen wants to reveal to others the insights about good and evil which he finds in literature.

"The great Chinese teachers," Stephen says, "believe you shouldn't die with knowledge. You should pass that knowledge on and empty yourself completely before you die. The strongest desire I have is to communicate my ideas to others."

What are these ideas? One has to do with what he calls "disexpectation" of blacks, even by other blacks, who pass on within the black community such discouragements as "keep your eyes level" and "don't aim too high." "Everything in our society we would automatically assume to be invented by a white," Stephen says, "never by a black." He remembers, for example, once reading a *National Geographic* article about African churches built in pits, an archeological find which was also an architectural marvel. The article argued stringently for the most obvious conclusion, that the churches were built by early Ethiopian Christians. "But why try so hard to prove what should have been self-evident?" Stephen asks. "Because of disexpectation—the widespread idea that nomadic whites must have built those churches because the native blacks couldn't possibly have done it."

Disexpectation creates an interior stumbling block for blacks as well as an obstacle in the world, Stephen says. "I went back to school in the second Nixon year. I was conscious of the bad things in society, but I was also conscious that people expected me to fail because I was black." Blacks themselves, Stephen claims, are thus socially conditioned to believe that they can't succeed.

For this reason, Stephen thinks his academic success can make him an example for young black people. But he insists that he didn't begin his own quest for knowledge for ideological reasons. "I went back to school to prove that I personally could do well, but I soon saw that my doing well would prove a larger point." He considers himself Kantian. "If I do things for other people, then I'm sure it's right. Do it for yourself alone, and it's probably selfishness or self-interest."

With the kind of optimism so typical of innovators, Stephen tells young blacks not to get discouraged and give up, that in a perverse way being black has actually been an asset for him in a racist society. "Being black is an exaggerator. If you're bad and you're black, you're despicable. But if you're good and you're black, you're great."

"Don't you want to save your race?" other blacks sometimes ask him. The answer is no. To Stephen, it's "important to dispel the myth of racial purity. Ethnic groups exist, all right, but in their country of origin. That's not what America is all about."

I remind Stephen of the line about the inevitable loss of racial purity at the end of William Faulkner's novel *Absalom, Absalom!* Shreve, a Canadian, and his Mississippi roommate, Quentin Compson, have talked through the night in a dorm room at the same Harvard toward which Stephen is bound. Quentin is obsessed with the necessity of keeping the white race "pure." Practical, progressive Shreve thinks racial purity is a nonsensical ambition, doomed to failure. In the darkest hours before dawn, a time when people really do face the truth, Shreve tells Quentin that "in a few thousand years, I who regard you will also have sprung from the loins of African kings."

"I'll bet Quentin doesn't believe it," Stephen says. But he is delighted with my example just the same. "Why don't you write a book," he asks me, "on the Federal Register? Part of that has to do with the crazy methods we've had to adopt in this country even to determine what race you are. You know, 'you're black if you have such and such a proportion of black to white blood.' " Stephen believes that notions of racial purity or racial pollution will die in time anyway, but that euthanasia for racism wouldn't be a bad idea.

"What is the *American* race anyway?" Stephen asks. "Whitman called it the race of races, or maybe the race of all races. Shreve is right. In a few thousand—say even one thousand—years, the whole question of race will be moot."

Then Stephen reminds me of something Mark Twain said, that those who would know the American mind should study the game of baseball. "We call it our 'national game,' " Stephen says, "but it's really an ideal for our society as courtly love was for the Middle Ages. And what's the most important rule? That every player has to be given his chance at bat. The game takes a moral position, you see. Some players will do extraordinarily well, others really bad. Look at Mickey Mantle; he struck out half the time. But nobody said, because Mantle struck out, that whites make lousy baseball players."

With ideas like this, I ask, why doesn't Stephen go into politics? "You can't be yourself in politics," he says. He would never turn down a chance to express his views, nor would he compromise those views in order to be elected. "One of the things I'm most afraid of is that I will die and no one will say these things, so I'm going to say them. That's the biggest reason that I want to stay alive."

You can teach any valid moral precept to anyone, even an eight-year-old, Stephen insists. "My children don't believe in race. They don't believe that Columbus 'discovered' America, any more than Koreans and Vietnamese are 'discovering' America now. I just teach them that in common sense you can't discover somebody's house. Look at the English here—discover: you're not uncovering it.

"I'm interested in words. Someone called me a genius. 'Genius'—that comes from the Greek, meaning belonging to the genes. I don't think learning is in my genes. I'm different from others only in the Socratic sense that I realize how similar we all are. The rest is serendipity."

157

"It seems to me that if you're concerned about preserving the Jewish people, then the very least you should do is reach out to those who want to be Jews," says Rabbi Emily Korzenik. Emily is explaining why she has made work with intermarriage of Jews and Gentiles, as well as conversion to Judaism, a significant part of her years as a rabbi. By a conservative estimate, 35 percent of Jews are intermarrying with non-Jews. Yet an Orthodox rabbi wouldn't think of performing an intermarriage ceremony. A Conservative rabbi might think of it, but he would be put out of his rabbinical organization if he did it. Both the Reform and the Reconstructionist rabbis also must function under guidelines that prohibit it.

But to Emily Korzenik, the edict against intermarriage stems from historical reasons which no longer apply. "When Christianity dominated Europe," she says, "everybody who wasn't Christian was a second-class citizen. The reaction of the Jews to that kind of persecution was 'You don't want me, I don't want you.' For a long time the social communities were almost totally separated."

In contemporary America, however, all races mingle. Blacks marry whites, Orientals marry WASPs, and Jews marry Gentiles. Miscegenation is the name of the game. So Emily, a Reconstructionist rabbi but a woman of today, takes an independent stance toward intermarriage and conversion in Judaism. She acknowledges that such independence may damage her standing with the hierarchy of the Jewish religious community, but she's willing to take that chance. Like Stephen James, she believes that you must be of your own time. Even a religion as traditional as Judaism must constantly accommodate changing social circumstances.

"If a Jewish person and a non-Jew want to have a Jewish wedding and create a Jewish family, I will perform an intermarriage. And I don't think I'm taking a liberal position."

It's a rainy day in April and I have taken the train to Scarsdale, New York, a bastion of upper-middle-class prosperity and respectability, and then a cab to another such bastion, the home Emily Korzenik has shared for years with her husband and their four now grown children. Catching sight of Emily in the garage, I have come in with her through the back door, so we have landed at the kitchen table, to my pleasure. Surely this cheerful, ordinary, suburban kitchen must be one spot where the woman Emily Korzenik, neat in a tweed skirt and sweater, looking every inch the lawyer's wife she is, and "Rabbi Emily," as her congregation calls her, meet. Am I right, I ask?

Her dark eyes smiling but her manner brisk, Emily sets me straight. "One of the nice things about being a woman who became a rabbi late in life is that I don't feel myself divided or set apart," she says, "as young male rabbis often do. And my people don't approach me as something different. I'm a friend who can perform particular functions in their life." Ordinary human life fifty-seven-year-old Emily knows about because she has lived it. Ten days after Emily was graduated from Vassar College in 1949, she was married. Ten days after her marriage, she turned twenty, and "proceeded immediately to have four children."

Yet Emily Korzenik is a woman who is definitely "having it all." Even as a very busy young mother, Emily had a private agenda. "I was just so busy with four little people that there wasn't too much time to worry about it, but in the back of my mind I knew that some day I would be doing something else."

Very early, that "something else" became political activism. Emily remembers driving around to collect money for Adlai Stevenson's run for the presidency, with one baby in a basket and another in a car seat. Then she served on the Scarsdale Democratic Town Committee. When the committee discussed sending her as a delegate to the regional convention, another member jokingly objected, "We can't send Emily. She won't do what she's told."

"Doing what you were told was what the woman's role in politics was supposed to be then," Emily muses now. She set that role on its ear, and all Scarsdale as well, when she and a political science professor from Bard College ran for office against the establishment choices in a local Scarsdale election. Emily wanted to shake up smug Scarsdale, which she describes as "socioeconomically a single community with very little variety. There are no poor, no 'other side of the tracks.' "

Predictably, she took some flak in local politics, but that did not deter Emily from running as a reform candidate for the New York State Assembly in 1974. She won the primary, in which she spent one hundred dollars against her opponent's maximum, but lost in the general election to the Republican nominee. "It wasn't a gentle situation," she says, "but I did well and people seemed to respect what I did. That gave me a great sense of strength."

Meanwhile, Emily had also involved herself in education. While "the baby was still crawling around on the floor," she began leading Brandeis study groups in everything from American diplomatic history to classical civilization to "the new Africa" to the Far East. Emily approached the groups she led with a characteristic seriousness. "We don't eat anything here," she told them, "and we don't talk about our families. And if you don't want to read seventy-five to one hundred pages for each meeting, don't join the group." When her children were older, Emily took a master's at Sarah Lawrence, and then taught history and social studies at exclusive schools such as Horace Mann and Fieldston.

Emily was also very much involved in Jewish religious, communal, and philanthropic life, especially through the synagogue in White Plains to which the family at that time belonged. "I had every role I guess you could play in the synagogue," she says. At various times she served as synagogue president, chaired the temple school board, and directed the adult education program. Emily also chaired the ritual committee, "an even bigger thing for a woman" because of this committee's responsibility for Jewish tradition. "That synagogue," she says, "is one of the few institutions that I have ever been a part of in which women really are peers—and that includes academic and political organizations, in which women really aren't quite peers, for all we say about it."

And Emily has a good bit to say about it. Feminism is an important fact in her life. During her teaching days in the seventies, Emily taught a course called Women in the Labor Movement in the extension program for Cornell University. The group consisted of fourteen women, seven black and seven white, from all walks of life—hospital union workers, clerical workers, middle- and lower-management personnel, even an older woman who had demonstrated in the labor marches during the Depression. "These were very honest women, people who came from work at six o'clock with a sandwich in their hands, people who cared very much," Emily says. "And we had the attitude that 'we're going to change the world and fulfill ourselves in all the ways that we want.' I think that's what gave me this great women's bond."

Unlike Katherine Fanning, who is skeptical about any real influence the Women's Movement *per se* had on her becoming editor of *The Christian Science Monitor*, Emily doubts that she would have become a rabbi without the Movement. "To say that change comes just out of yourself—well, I couldn't say that. The presence of the Women's Movement and the opportunities burgeoning out of it were tremendously influential for me. I would say I was responsive to the changes that were out there. And then, you know, you become a part of the changes and help to create them for somebody else."

But why a rabbi? Why not a lawyer or politician? What motivated the teacher, Emily Korzenik, a forty-seven-year-old Scarsdale matron with four children, to take the daring step of applying for admission to rabbinical school? First and foremost were her family background and her ethnic consciousness.

The daughter of a manufacturer, Emily Korzenik née Faust comes from a prosperous, upper-middle-class, New York Jewish family. In 1883, her maternal grandfather, an architect, was graduated from City College of New York, "which was then the poor man's Harvard," Emily says. Emily's own parents, fourth-generation Americans, lived in a spacious apartment on West End Avenue, traveled, went to the opera and the theater, and though not rich, "certainly had ease in the world. Life was very comfortable." They sent their bright daughter and her older brother to private schools, to summer camp, and on to good colleges, in Emily's case Vassar.

Out of that ease and privilege, Emily gained "a certain kind of confidence and routedness. Stability is a great advantage to change. If you feel secure within yourself, you can make changes."

Her family also gave Emily a sense of pride in herself as a Jew. The architect grandfather founded a synagogue in New York. Emily's mother served as president of both the women's organization and the parents' organization in the synagogue. Emily and her brother had a Jewish upbringing. "I felt my Jewishness very strongly," she says, "and I was happy with it. Not everybody of my generation was. Some of my friends, in fact, were very eager to be WASPs, but I never had that feeling."

Both the stability and the Jewish pride continued in Emily's marriage to Sidney Korzenik, her mate for thirty-six years at the time of the interview. The son of immigrants, Sidney Korzenik is, his wife says, a very traditional, philosophical, intellectual Jew. His parents came to America, leaving behind in their Polish village a little dirt-floored hut and a few chickens. Though Sidney's father had only an elementary school education, he knew Hebrew and had had his bar mitzvah. In the United States, he grubbed along in the clothing business, but "it wasn't for him," Emily says. "He should have been a scholar." The household was Orthodox.

Emily's husband Sidney became the scholar in the family, and like Stephen James entered Harvard on a scholarship. Sidney majored in philosophy, and then went on to get a master's and to do all the course work for a Ph.D. in philosophy. In law school, though he worked full time, Sidney was graduated as salutatorian of his class.

And Sidney "cares very much about being Jewish," his wife says. "With my liberalism and his traditionalism, we had a hard time getting our act together. But our Jewishness was important to both of us; it is the center of our lives." Over nearly four decades, Emily has learned more about tradition and Sidney has had "to deal with a little more liberalism."

Emily admits that Sidney has not always been altogether at ease with his wife's activities. Her teaching, a traditional female role, pleased him, her participation in politics less so. Her next change he found even more startling. When her teaching job at Scarsdale High School was phased out, Emily decided to become a rabbi.

"Crisis absolutely forces change," Emily claims. "You have to deal with things that you wouldn't deal with if you could help it." The loss of her teaching position at Scarsdale High was a real blow to Emily. Though she lined up another job in teaching, the effort provoked her to question her goals. "What am I doing?" she asked herself. "Is teaching in high school what I really want to do for the rest of my life?" The candid answer was no. She wanted work in which all the parts of herself could come together. Emily wanted to become a rabbi.

162

The director of one rabbinical college refused even to talk to her about the possibility. "Please don't apply," he told her, "because I'll turn you down." In 1976, Emily was accepted elsewhere, and, in turn, she dedicated the next five years to study. Having already gotten a master's from Sarah Lawrence as an older student helped. Her family helped even more. "Mother," her second son told her, "you've been a teacher. As a rabbi, you'll still be a teacher. You have a sense of adventure. Go for it."

No member of the family was more helpful than her conservative husband. When Sidney saw Emily struggling with Heidegger and Spinoza, he brought his own experience in studying philosophy to her aid. "I had a scholar in residence, you might say, to deal with these tough subjects," Emily laughs. She also had Sidney's financial support, an advantage which, as she repeatedly and gratefully recognizes, gives her a certain independence as a rabbi.

In 1978, in her second year of rabbinical training, Emily was interviewed by the small congregation in Stamford, Connecticut, which she still serves. After a deluge of applications for the position of rabbi, the selection committee had narrowed the choice down to six men and Emily. In her second interview, the committee asked Emily if a woman had anything in particular to offer as a rabbi. The question roused her feminist blood. She insisted that there were no distinctions between men and women. A good rabbi needs three qualities, she told the committee: compassion for all human beings; a thorough knowledge of Judaism; and the desire to impart that knowledge to others. Men and women alike can have these qualities.

In spite of her feminist answer, Emily jokes that her sex turned the trick for her. "After a while you really get confused when you talk to six men. But they knew who I was."

Today, Rabbi Emily knows better herself who she is. Her feminism, like her character, has continued to evolve. Being an older woman is an important part of who she is, and of who she is as a rabbi. No longer does she make the claim that there are no distinctions between men and women. She has come to see that an older woman rabbi does have special understanding and skills. "When you've cared for a dying person in your own family, as older women usually have, you are more able to help people with a death in theirs. When you've seen four of your own children through a bar mitzvah, as I have, you know the tensions that can occur. And during the rituals for a new baby, you know how tired the new mother is because you've been in that situation. There are just things women think of that the average male rabbi doesn't.

"Being a rabbi actually is very congenial with traditional feminine roles. It's involved with families, nurturing, being sensitive to individual needs. Life experience, particularly female life experience, is valuable in my work."

Here's the kind of rabbi Emily Korzenik is. After a wedding at which she officiated in 1986, one of the guests, a prosperous businessman, told Emily that he had just come back from Poland. In Kraków, he had visited a soup kitchen and place of worship for elderly Jews. "The young people have all left for Israel or somewhere," he told Emily, "but these old ones are the last leaves upon the tree. They survived the Holocaust, and have come back to Kraków, who knows why—because once upon a time it was their home, I guess."

Touched by their situation, as the man was leaving Kraków he asked the director of the soup kitchen, Mrs. Jakobovich, a woman in her seventies, what he could send the group from America. He expected her to say food, warm clothes, blankets, all of which would clearly be welcome.

Instead she said, looking at him with her wise, faded old eyes, "Bring us some life, bring us some youth, bring us a bar mitzvah."

Back in America, the man tried to interest various Jewish agencies in the poignant wish of these old Jews of Poland, but nothing had come of his letters and calls. "Rabbi Emily," he said, "can you do anything about this? If you will take a bar mitzvah to Kraków, I will pay all the expenses."

"Many things in life come through just such chance encounters," Emily says. "But you have to respond to the opportunity." Emily responded.

First she telephoned thirteen-year-old Eric Strom of Stamford, Connecticut, who was studying for his bar mitzvah, and whose forebears on both sides came from Poland. "Eric," Emily asked, "how would you like to have your bar mitzvah in Poland, in an all-expense-paid trip?"

"Wow!" Eric said. "Sure, Rabbi Emily. But will you talk to Mom? If I tell her, she'll think I've been watching too much television."

After she "talked to Mom," Emily set to work. With her empathy for others and her sense of decorum, Emily knew that the old Kraków Jews would not cotton to the idea of a female rabbi leading the service. So she enlisted the aid of an Orthodox male rabbi who was himself a survivor of the Holocaust. A Pole with a great deal of verve and vitality, the rabbi had testified at war crimes trials. He has, Emily says, a message he wants to express, which is "the vitality of the Jewish people to survive." Nothing could be better for the occasion Emily intended to create.

Then there was the red tape to cut through. The Polish government invited them, tried to disinvite them, and then invited them again. When news of the upcoming trip got out around the United States, the press was interested and Emily had to field those queries. She was also besieged with requests like "I have an old cousin there. Could you take a box of things for her?" So Emily was very busy for the weeks leading up to the scheduled departure time.

At length, after all the preparations were complete, the little party set out for Kraków: the male rabbi and his two daughters, eager to see their father's homeland; Eric, the bar mitzvah candidate, his little sister, his parents, and three of his grandparents; Rabbi Emily with her husband Sidney, who was visiting the land from which his parents had come in poverty and hope; and two photographers to record the historic homecoming.

Eric's great-grandmother, a sturdy old lady in her eighties, was invited to come also. She declined firmly. "Why," the old lady asked, "would I ever want to go back to that terrible place I ran away from?"

In some ways the trip was indeed very difficult for them all. "It's hard for caring Jews to go to a place like Poland," says Emily, "where three million out of the three and a half million Jews who lived there were killed in the death camps." But they went. The bar mitzvah was beautiful and the party afterward very special. Mrs. Jakobovich had saved her food stamps and had cooked for weeks. The guests and their hosts feasted on potato soup, small portions of sweet and sour fish, bits of cold meat, potato and carrot salad, rice pudding, and strudel.

"Good food, but it stuck in my mouth," Emily says. "I knew how poor they were, and what they were having to give up to serve us. I thought, 'Oh, please, you keep it. We don't need it.' But I didn't say anything. I ate, and I said how good it was." Rabbi Emily knows how to bend to the occasion.

Indeed, Emily defines living well as "bending yourself" to fulfill the purpose of life, rather than sticking to a death-dealing abstraction. After all, the Nazis exterminated six million people in the interest of "racial purity." Life itself counts.

But life must have purpose, and Emily believes that purpose, especially after the Holocaust, has to be expressed in moral and ethical terms. "Because," she says, "there's no other way for life to have purpose."

Like Stephen James, Emily Korzenik has the optimism to see possible handicaps as advantages. Others might use Stephen's skin color, Emily's age and sex, to excuse failure or lack of ambition. With a kind of grace, Stephen and Emily skillfully treat those possibly negative qualities as positive attributes. Thus, each of these strong and dynamic leaders can influence others to accept the constancy of change even for an entire race. To continue, a people, like a person, must evolve, must be in its own time.

Still, as both Stephen and Emily recognize, the past has treasures that should not be lost. Even Holden Caulfield, that consummate young American, maintained that "certain things, they should stay the way they are." In America, especially in the enormous potentiality of America, the past must be preserved, revitalized, and used. Throughout the constancy of change, we carry the past with us like a bag of dried mushrooms from some vanished forest of human experience. Add water or wine, and those mushrooms will replenish the stew of life.

Listening to the Inner Voice

Innovators use hunches, feelings,
dreams, "signs," and intuitions,
as well as intellect,
in deciding what they want
for their lives.

9

Satisfying the Soul

Innovative people allow themselves to unfold. They look inward. Innovators watch for signs, study the stars, wake in the middle of the night prepared to record dreams. Their dedication may remain firm—an art, a religious belief, a beloved person, something permanent in the midst of constant change. But more than most people, innovators listen to the inner voice.

The inner voice is the intuitive side of the psyche that sends off signals when we are in the presence of something important to our lives. We all receive these signals of fear, love, passion, awe, warning. Common as they are, the signals are often disregarded by those who attempt to function on an entirely rational level. The innovator, however, tends to have a more finely tuned receiving apparatus. He cultivates the skill of interpreting the signals sensitively and imaginatively. Though he will probably not change his life dramatically on the basis of such signals alone, on the whole he trusts them to clue him in to something missing or awry in his life.

A chance remark made by a casual acquaintance voiced Victoria Boothby's inner anguish. "You remind me of a plant that's been put in the wrong soil," a young man told Victoria, who was married to an alcoholic minister and who for years had been desperately "keeping up appearances" in the small New England town of their birth. The words fell like rain on Victoria's parched spirit, and desires dormant in her came to life. "I recognized the truth," she says. "I needed to be transplanted." On the rational level, then, she faced the hopelessness of her marriage. Victoria divorced her husband, moved to Manhattan, and in 1986 appeared in *Stepping Out* on Broadway.

Katherine Fanning saw films of Anchorage, Alaska. "That's such an ugly city," she thought to herself. "I wonder why I'm going to move there." Notice the faith in intuition, which in Kay's case was followed by a pragmatic, on-the-spot check of the advantages Anchorage offered her and her children. Her intuition proved to be sound. As owner and editor of an Anchorage newspaper, Katherine was responsible for Alaska's first Pulitzer Prize.

One enchanted evening, Nancy Schwartz saw a stranger across a crowded room. "It was Steve. And he came over and said his little lines and I said mine. And I said to myself, 'Self, he's the one.' " Nancy and Steve have been married eight years. The inner voice spoke, and like the other innovators, above, Nancy paid attention.

Can the inner voice give us the wrong instructions? It can. Not every inner voice saying "he's the one" turns out to be right when "the one" is examined rationally. Nothing destructive was at work in any of the examples I have given, but that doesn't mean the inner voice cannot wreak havoc from time to time. These signals from within need to be checked and balanced by observation of the world without. Just the same, they are important because they help us to know ourselves.

For the ancient Greeks, urgings from the depths of the psyche came from powerful but amoral gods who took human life very lightly and were mostly unconcerned about the consequences of the commands they issued to mortals. The Greeks created their gods in order to describe the complexities of mortal existence. Because the gods live forever, they think that any mistake can be rectified in another millennium. But human life is pathetically short. We rarely have time to live down truly enormous errors. The primary human task, to Homer and to the Greek tragedians, is learning to honor the whimsical and often contradictory commands of the gods.

In his Nobel speech, William Faulkner spoke of "the human heart in conflict with itself." The Greeks externalized that conflict by imagining rival deities contending for primacy in a single human being. Pity the poor mortal who is claimed simultaneously by Athena, the goddess of wisdom, and by Aphrodite, the goddess of sexual attraction! Nevertheless, however disruptive their commands, *all* the gods must be heard. You can't avoid trouble by refusing to listen. A jealous, devious god, an inner voice not given proper respect, may sneak in the back door, as with Lois Grant's arthritis or Brad Warner's nightmares. "The soul wants what it wants," Saul Bellow's Mr. Sammler says. Innovators cultivate the ability to strike a balance between the dark cravings of the soul and the clear light of principle, rationality, and common sense.

Such a man is Gilbert Kaplan, who fell in love with a piece of music on his way to becoming a multimillionaire publisher. When Gil was in his early twenties, a friend gave him a pass to hear the American Symphony Orchestra rehearse Mahler's Second Symphony, with Leopold Stokowski conducting. Gil was no musician—his musical training had begun and ended with three years of compulsory piano lessons as a child—but he was profoundly impressed by the symphony, which he had never heard before.

The ninety minutes of sound in the highly complex work, subtitled *Resurrection,* into which Mahler had poured all his metaphysical yearnings, touched some deep chord in Gil Kaplan. The night after the rehearsal, Gil tossed restlessly in bed. The music, with its questions and its answers, kept coming back into his head. The next afternoon Gil went to the concert to hear the

THE SKILLS FOR CHANGE

Resurrection again. "By the time the fireworks erupted in the last movement," he has said, "I was completely broken up."

From that day on, Mahler's Second became Gil's obsession. Because the ambitious work requires a full orchestra and a choir of two hundred, New York performances of it were rare, but Gil attended them all. In addition, he read everything he could find about the symphony and listened over and over, hundreds of times, to every available recording. Gil Kaplan's own inner voice spoke to him through Mahler's music.

If he pursued the meaning in the music, Gil believes that in some curious way the symphony pursued him too. On a holiday, Gil met Lena, the Swedish girl he was later to marry, and they arranged to meet again in London. On their first night together in England, the two impulsively attended a concert at the Royal Festival Hall. And the program? Mahler's Second.

Meanwhile, on another front entirely, Gil was pursuing a separate and seemingly much more rewarding dream. In 1967, Gil, who was making $15,000 a year as an economist at the New York Stock Exchange, came up with the idea of investing his life savings of $6,000 and whatever capital he could raise from other sources into founding a business magazine for professional investors, to be called *Institutional Investor*. The magazine was not to be sold at newsstands but distributed free of charge to top investment executives. It would make its profit, if any, from advertising.

The idea was audacious, but from the beginning *Institutional Investor* specialized in audacity and urged its readers to follow suit. The long-term investor, Gil wrote at the end of his first editorial, "should be eccentric, unconventional and rash in the eyes of average opinion." Knowingly or not, the twenty-five-year-old fledgling publisher and editor was describing himself. With this venture, Gil was taking a big chance. He could be completely wiped out, could lose all $144,000 in borrowed money and every last penny of his own meager savings.

His risk paid off. The magazine quickly found its market. By the time *Institutional Investor* was two years old, its audacious young founder was a millionaire. Ten years later, the success of the magazine turned another, earlier dream into a genuine possibility. Gil began contemplating an audacity which would be guaranteed to make him seem even more "eccentric, unconventional and rash in the eyes of average opinion." He had the money to do it, so he decided to try to conduct Mahler's Second himself in front of a full orchestra. That was the only way, he became convinced, that he could express the special feelings the music aroused in him.

Some millionaires spend their money on making more money, others on wine, women, and song, others on polo teams and condominiums. I don't know of another Gil Kaplan, who spent his money (or some of his money, because he has plenty) on learning to conduct a symphony. He approached his ambition logically. After reading several books on conducting and waving his arms around a lot while he listened to records, Gil hired a young conductor as a coach. The two spent the month of August 1981 working, measure by measure, on a single movement of the *Resurrection* Symphony. In September, for only slightly less than his original investment in *Institutional Investor,* a terrified but determined Gil hired Carnegie Hall and the American Symphony Orchestra for a private rehearsal. "It worked," he said later, "but barely."

Six months later, with the same measured effort, Gil had learned another movement of the symphony. Once again, he engaged hall and orchestra. This time, he conducted both movements. His success was more marked than before. When Gil put down his baton, the musicians applauded.

Gil made up his mind to conduct the entire work, which has been the Waterloo of many a professional conductor, in front of an audience. For the next year, he flew all over the world, from New York to London to Melbourne to Missouri to Holland, to hear concerts, to talk to conductors and musicians, and even to study Mahler's original manuscript of the music. He memorized the entire score, a prodigious feat. He engaged orchestra and hall for twelve rehearsals, five of them with choir and soloists. When he felt close to being ready, Gil sent out nearly three thousand invitations to a private concert at Avery Fisher Hall in Lincoln Center. At this point, he had spent at least $200,000, maybe more, to prepare for the event.

But, you say, he had money to burn, so why not? Jack Coleman risked bankruptcy to open his inn, Lois Grant laid her marriage on the line to become an architect, Ed McCabe risked life and limb to drive the Paris–Dakar Rally. But what, after all, did Gil Kaplan risk on his private eccentricity?

Gil risked his considerable reputation as a man of good sense, as an editor whose publication could be trusted by those invited to the concert: international bankers, financial ministers of governments, corporation chiefs, and others powerful in the financial community. If Gil failed to pull the concert off, he would lose face—and face, authority, and credibility are precious commodities in the world of high finance. Gil could become a laughing-stock. Who takes financial advice from a joke?

As the time of the concert neared and word of it got about, people did laugh at Gil's hubris. In some circles, Gil Kaplan, the millionaire who can conduct only one symphony, is still considered laughable. But Gil never set out to be a conductor; he set out to conduct Mahler's Second. A private urgency, an inner voice, moved him to change his life, and on September 9, 1982, Gilbert Kaplan exchanged his banker's gray suit for a maestro's flamboyant tails and white tie. Then he stepped to the podium, and raised his baton. Why should we care what happened next?

Gil himself has answered that question. "I had the feeling," he told a reporter after the concert, "that people in the audience were urging me to fulfill my dream because each of them had a secret ambition they had not attained. So they were up with me on the podium that night, playing baseball for the Yankees, writing the book they never wrote, or getting the girl they never got. If I had failed, they would have as well. I could feel their nervousness."

Neither Gil nor the orchestra—nor the audience—failed. The orchestra played beyond itself, and, "since I don't consider myself a great conductor," Gil said afterward, "I have to conclude that something was at work here. Looking back on it, I do not believe it was possible to do what I have done."

Gil is purposely vague about the nature of the "something" at work. "I don't want to talk about the supernatural," he has said, "but I do believe there is something going on between me and this piece of music." From the beginning, over twenty years ago, his inner voice told him so. Since that first performance, Gil has gone on to conduct Mahler's Second, by invitation, with orchestras all over the world, and his reviews have been generally favorable.

Why did Gil set himself an impossible task? Faith is involved—faith in oneself, faith in the meaning of life. On the subject, Gil has sometimes quoted Mahler, who himself questioned the value of life. "Is it all nothing but a huge, frightful joke?" Mahler asked. The *Resurrection* Symphony was Mahler's answer to that perennial human question. The symphony has come to be Gilbert Kaplan's answer as well.

Brother Job had been a monk for eleven years when the inner voice spoke to him and told him to leave the monastery. The scene was a Monday morning class for the whole monastic community. Brother Job had incurred the wrath of the superior teaching the class, and was getting an especially severe tongue-lashing for the sin of pride. The public reprimand was embarrassing. In the middle of it, Brother Job heard the inner voice speak.

"Now don't misunderstand me," Job Michael Evans tells me during our conversation five years later. "I am a very logical, rational person. Nothing like this ever happened to me before or since, and probably never will again.

"But I had a kind of out-of-body experience during this class, while my superior was ragging me on my various faults. I was sitting in a chair. At the same time I literally felt myself up above in the corner of the room, looking down on me as I sat there squirming, waiting for the monologue to finish.

"Then I heard the voice. It was a real voice. It said, very quietly, 'This is not a good place for you to be anymore. You are going to get hurt if you stay here. When this is over, go up to your room, get your belongings, and get out of here.'

"And it said again, 'This is not a good place for you to be.' The voice kept repeating that: 'This is not a good place for you to be.'

"I was surprised and disturbed that I was having this experience, and yet I absolutely trusted it. And I did just exactly what the voice told me to do."

When Michael Evans went into the monastery and became Brother Job at barely twenty-one, he was searching for several things. First of all, he wanted a family. The oldest son of the eleven children of a Catholic psychologist and his wife, Michael loved the intimacy and hurly-burly of life in his big family. The six sisters and five brothers were close. Parents in a big family

175

have only so much attention to go around, so the kids learned early to befriend each other. "A creepy sense of humor" was the family trademark.

But for the Evans children, this marvelous life ended immediately after high school. "We were told the summer we graduated that we had to leave. No lack of love or anything like that," Job Michael says, "but we were raised to be very independent. Like the Kennedys, but with a lot less money."

Every summer, growing up, Michael and his brothers and sisters were packed off to various camps and or to relatives. For example, several summers Michael left the comfortable family home in Ann Arbor, Michigan, to pick strawberries on an Amish farm in Pennsylvania. Life on the farm was simple, with no electricity and no indoor plumbing. For the first few days each summer, Michael could hardly even understand what his hosts were saying to him. Rough, but from such experiences he learned to be resourceful and independent. "You look at your self-pity," he says, "and you say, 'That's enough of that. Now let's get going.' "

At thirty-six, the Job Michael Evans sitting across from me is a living testimonial to the success of his parents' methods and perhaps to the profit of his years in the monastery. The geniality of his bearded face, the intelligence and humor in his brown eyes, the composure of his manner, speak of a man at home with himself. Nevertheless, when young Michael Evans had worked his way through college and graduated at twenty, he really wanted to go back home. Instead, after six months as a Trappist, he joined New Skete monastery, a quiet retreat in the hills outside Cambridge, New York.

His family had some reservations about their young son's decision. Job's father wanted his oldest boy to follow the original plan to go into anthropology, Job's major in college, and do field work in a science related to his own. Both Job's parents felt "cut off" by their young son's monastic isolation, but, strong Catholics, "they accepted it pretty well." Job's next-younger sister, Beverly, was not nearly so accepting. "Lonely, forsaken, and unhappy," Beverly thought her outgoing brother was making a mistake.

At New Skete, however, Brother Job found a monastic family similar to his biological family. There were eleven monks, as there had been eleven Evans children, under the direction of a strong, authoritarian head or "father." There was even a sister group of nuns to provide the feminine influence. "An *American* monastic group," Job wrote for the monastery journal, *Gleanings,* in his first idyllic years at New Skete, "will take its cue from the *American* family, which is robust, mobile, and noisy"—read the Evans family—"though obviously there remains a basic respect for silence, consideration of others, and for the different levels of growth in the family." The new young "brother" basked in the perfection of his new family. He meant never to leave home again.

Perhaps I should have begun Job's story with another reason for his going into the monastery, his religious devotion. A cradle Catholic, Job had felt his Christianity primed for the monastic life when he fell under the spell of the autobiography, poetry, and theological meditations of the Trappist monk Thomas Merton. An original mind with a brilliant prose style, Merton was something of a cult writer with enormous impact on the serious, searching young of the decades following the Second World War.

"Merton was a real mentor for me," Job remembers. Although Merton wrote quite freely of his own problems within the monastery, Job felt that the right choice of monastery could do away with those difficulties. And he was convinced that New Skete was the right choice for him.

His love of nature was another powerful reason for Job to enter the monastery. During a college summer, he had rented a cabin in the mountains of Vermont, and spent three months in blessed isolation and silence. That time among the pines made Job pine for more. The hilly, wooded acreage of New Skete seemed an answer to prayer. At the monastery, Job studied the night sky in order to learn the names of the heavenly bodies. And, as he wrote in another issue of *Gleanings,* he learned to see not only the extensive view from a high spot on the New Skete land, but the intensive view, "the birch leaf at my feet. Soon I began to experience concretely, on a day-to-day basis, what I had formerly only intuited: that a tiny birch leaf, crumpled and dry, can be as beautiful and important as the larger and more encompassing view of fields and mountains."

If Job had been a pagan Greek, we might have thought him

directed by Artemis, the goddess of wild things. As it was, he felt a thrill of identification with lines from the book of Job, the Old Testament hero from whom his monastic name came:

But ask now the beasts, and they shall teach thee; and the fowls of the air, and they shall tell thee:

Or speak to the earth, and it shall teach thee: and the fishes of the sea shall declare unto thee.

Who knoweth not in all these that the hand of the LORD hath wrought this?

In whose hand is the soul of every living thing, and the breath of all mankind.

—Job 12:7–10

Job had always intuited that the natural earth had much to teach him. Here was gospel proof that the beasts, the birds, and the fish, as well, could set lessons for him to learn.

The chief beast at New Skete was the dog. The monks of New Skete support themselves by breeding and raising German shepherds, and by training all breeds. The training and breeding dogs, never more than twenty or so, are divided among the monks. Thus each dog has his own personal master and handler, and is given a lot of individual attention in a quiet, contemplative atmosphere. For the New Skete brothers, the dogs are far more than a way to make money. Philosophically, the monks believe not only that they have much to teach the dogs in their care, but that the dogs teach the monks valuable lessons in behavior and responsibility.

When Job first entered the monastery, though he vaguely realized the place of the dogs in the society, he took very little interest in them. For him, the big attractions at New Skete were the natural setting, the family atmosphere, and the beauty of the Eastern rite liturgy based on Greek and Russian chants. As a boy, he had never had a dog and really knew nothing about dogs.

At New Skete, however, Job found that dogs were a genuine part of the monastic environment, "an absolute part of your life as a monk." All the dogs lived in a house, but each monk cared for his own special dog, brought the dog inside the dining hall to

178

lie beside him at mealtime, trained the dog, and was responsible for the dog's manners and personality.

"I openly confess that I ruined my first dog," Job says. When he entered the monastery, Job was given a six-month-old German shepherd puppy to train. Job adored the puppy and "spoiled it rotten." Because Job didn't obey the monastery rules on the training of dogs, the dog didn't learn to obey either. The dog became shy, wouldn't listen to anybody, and rejected the advances of anyone other than Job. "I thought love was enough," Job says, "so I didn't train my dog correctly. I was so bad with it that they had to take it away from me."

Job was ashamed and embarrassed. "I didn't have a personal dog and everybody else in the monastery did." Then, to his eternal amazement, Brother Thomas, the head of the dog training program, asked Job to become his apprentice.

"Why?" Job responded, flabbergasted. "Why me? Everybody knows I am the worst handler of dogs in the monastery."

"I've been watching you," Brother Thomas told him kindly. "You have some good points. I think you will be a good trainer. You tend to get emotionally involved with the dogs, but you won't have that temptation with the training dogs because you will know that they are going to be leaving soon."

So, with the abbot's permission, Job joined Brother Thomas in his work with the dogs. Twice every weekday for the next year, Job took out fifteen or twenty dogs, one at a time, for twenty-minute lessons. Over and over and over, Job went through the mechanics of obedience training: heel, sit, stay, down, come. At length, "I learned to get the whole sequence right with every breed and personality of dog you can think of."

Brother Thomas was always there to help Job, "sometimes literally right behind me with his body pressed to mine and his hand over my hand, saying, 'No, *snap* it, this fast, *snap.*' Even when Job worked alone, Brother Thomas was near at hand, available if Job got stuck on some problem. "It was a real apprenticeship in the medieval sense," Job says. Though at first Job had seen the apprenticeship merely as a way to get his own dog "by proving I wouldn't be so lovey-dovey again," he soon became entranced with the training process and with the psychology of canine obedience. Then Brother Thomas was killed in an automobile accident, and without his beloved master Job discovered that he had some obedience problems of his own.

At the age of twenty-two, Job was handed the entire responsibility for the training program, and, at the same time, the boarding program, which meant running "a Holiday Inn for dogs." Even with a staff of three under him, Job found the organizational detail endless. The job meant counseling dog owners, which he came to like but which at first was difficult and time-consuming.

As if the dog program weren't enough, the monastery superiors also "asked" Job (no refusal was possible) to take on the role of guestmaster, which meant overseeing and making welcome the constant flow of guests to the retreat house on the monastery grounds. Some of the guests were troubled, which meant trouble for Job as well. In addition, as guestmaster, Job also served as liaison between New Skete and the press.

Job held these jobs for ten of his eleven years in the monastery. Between 1975 and 1978, he published six major articles on dog training. He became assistant editor of *Gleanings.* Job also set to work on a book, *How to Be Your Dog's Best Friend,* which was published by "the monks of New Skete" in 1978 and is now in its twelfth printing. The book was largely the work of Brother Job, but, Job says, "we were not allowed to take credit for what we did individually."

Job found that he liked writing, and, moreover, that he "had a need to write." "Who do you think you are, Ernest Hemingway?" his superiors asked. "Of course you want to be good," Job says, "but if you have that thing where you have to sit in front of a typewriter, it doesn't matter if what you write is good or trash —the need is the same." Thinking back to his mentor, Thomas Merton, and the reason he had joined New Skete in the first place, Job requested relief from his guestmaster duties so that he could be more creative.

The request was refused. Then a ban was placed on his publishing anything at all, even in theological journals. Writing, the official word came down, was a distraction from Job's duties to the monastery. The ban hurt. Overloaded with work, his creativity frustrated, Job attempted to comply with orders. But underneath, as he wrote in *Gleanings,* he felt like a spirited dog chafing under the wrong methods in obedience training.

Then, in his last year at the monastery, something happened which made the already "prodigal dog," as he called himself, feel even more prodigal. Job's parents divorced, after eleven children and thirty-three years of marriage. Distraught, suffering from his separation from his family in this crisis, Job was unable to sleep. When he did fall asleep, he dreamed awful dreams about his broken family. Finally, in exhaustion, he asked permission to see a psychotherapist in the neighboring town.

Permission was refused. "I am your counselor," his superior told him. "You don't need anyone else. Just forget about this thing with your parents. Grow up. It has nothing to do with your life."

Job was desperate enough to sneak off to see the therapist illicitly. The therapist was helpful but didn't want to be part of Job's disobedience. He refused to see Job again without monastery approval. Permission was again denied. Then came the day when Job was sitting quietly in a community class, listening to a lecture on his faults, and the inner voice told him to leave New Skete.

Job left. He went to his room and sorted his meager possessions into three piles: must-takes, must-leaves, and maybes. Within an hour, he had packed, had written a brief note explaining his departure, and had called a former monk to pick him up at the bottom of the hill on which the monastery sat. Soon Job was on his way into freedom. "I didn't know where to go, and I had no money," Job says, "but I had to leave."

After the divorce, Job's mother had gone to Florida, so Job joined her there. Legal entanglements surrounding the divorce prevented either parent from being able to help him much financially, but his mother, who was living alone, gave him a temporary refuge. At first, Job tried his hand at freelance magazine articles, dealing with the frustrations of slow acceptance and even slower payment. With no overhead, he was able to stash away a little money, but he soon saw that freelancing was no way to make a living.

Then one night, after he had been in Florida about three weeks, his mother took him out for a beautiful, candlelit dinner. As they were finishing up with a nightcap, his mother said, "Well, Mike, this has been a major change for you, a big passage, returning to secular life after all those years. As someone who has just gone through a big passage myself, I realize how difficult things must be for you. I have really enjoyed having you with me again. And I just want you to know one thing."

"What is it, Mom?" Job asked—"thinking she was going to say, 'I love you,' or something like that."

"You've got one more month here," his mother said.

"Don't get me wrong," Job tells me. "My mother does love me, but this is how I was raised—to be independent. And it was exactly what I needed at that point."

Job began to move fast. He called Howell Book House, the largest publisher of animal books in the United States, perhaps in the world, and to his surprise received a real welcome from Howell himself. "Everybody in the dog business knows you wrote *How to Be Your Dog's Best Friend,*" Howell told Job. "I wish our house had published it."

Howell commissioned a second book, with a six months' deadline, and Job got to work. Within a month, he had finished *The Evans Guide for Counseling Dog Owners,* and had collected a small advance against publication. His new life had begun. "The world was wide open," he says. "I could go anyplace I wanted."

After eleven years of *not* being able to go any place he wanted, Job was keen to explore what the country had to offer before he settled down. "Why don't I take a month and just travel," he asked himself, "see all my brothers and sisters?" The day he received the check from his publisher, Job walked by a travel agency. "Six hundred dollars!" shrieked an ad in the window. "Thirty days' unlimited mileage! Fly as often as you want!" Without another thought, Job turned into the agency and bought the ticket.

The next month couldn't have been better. Job went to twenty-nine cities in thirty days. Some days he went to two cities in order to do job interviews. The airline punched a hole for every city he visited, and when his travel time was up, there was literally no place left to punch. "We don't have an award for ticket use," the agent told Job, "but if we did, you'd get it."

Everywhere he went, Job found that the reputation he had made at New Skete, a reputation he had not known he had, preceded him. He would fly into a city and call on the editor of an animal magazine. "I'm Job Evans," he'd say, and the same response would come every time. "Oh, I know who *you* are—you wrote the monks' book." Job lined up columns with three animal magazines, *Dog Fancy, Cat Fancy,* and *Horse Illustrated.*

Job had a number of job offers as well, but intuitively he backed off. The taste of freedom after the extremely structured monastic life made him realize that he wanted to be his own boss for a change. So he decided to start a dog counseling service for owners. After contemplating several possible locations, he fixed on the toughest but most challenging spot in the country, New York City. His family thought Job had gone berserk to move from the quiet of the New Skete hills to the heart of the urban wilderness.

Job had a lot to learn in his new life. "I considered myself a businessman," he says. "In the monastery, I had been in charge of fund-raising, and I had handled a budget. The only difference was that now I had no budget." He was also a businessman who had never written a check and for whom, after a cloistered decade, America was a strange and unfriendly place. The street noise bothered him, the traffic, the confusion. The first meal that Job ate alone, he panicked. "I started to cry during it, because I hadn't eaten by myself in eleven years."

Nevertheless, with only the money left from his book advance, now less than $2,000, Job moved into an Italian neighborhood in Bay Ridge.

Then he began to try to drum up trade. Like his father before him, Job was now a psychologist, working with the behavior of dogs and their people. Job had business cards printed which read "Patience of Job: training for dogs and people." Over the next two years, Job was going to need all the patience he could muster.

He began to canvas the offices of veterinarians, hoping to get referral business from those vets he managed to impress. In his days at New Skete, his name and a mention of the monastery immediately opened doors. "Come right over," the vet would say. "I would love to hear more about the monastery's training techniques."

But "Brother Job" had done a lot better than plain Job Michael Evans was doing, especially in snobbish New York. As often as not, when Job called, he would get some gum-popping receptionist on the line. "You're who?" she would say. "The doctor doesn't see salesmen during office hours."

"I'm not a salesman," Job would protest. "I'm a dog trainer."

"Well, you can come to the office and wait; maybe I can work you in for a couple of minutes." And hours would go by while Job sat in some anteroom and waited, watching the receptionist file her nails.

"I lost a lot of status," Job says. "I paid my dues all over again. I remember in one veterinary office I sat for three hours and as soon as I stepped in, the vet told me, 'I'm not interested. Take your material. I don't work with dog trainers. But thank you for coming in.' After three hours!"

On one occasion, trying to see an Upper East Side vet with a dragon of a receptionist, Job actually made an appointment as plain Michael Evans and pretended he had a sick pet. "Where's your dog?" inquired the receptionist when Job showed up *sans* animal. "Oh, I just want a consultation," he told her. The receptionist looked at him suspiciously, but she took him into the examination room.

"Doctor," Job said, when the man in the white coat came in, "please don't be mad at me. I've been trying to see you for a month. I'm willing to pay for the time to explain my services to you."

The doctor went for Job's program. "People constantly ask me animal behavior questions," he told Job. "I'm in desperate need of a referral."

"Veterinarians are asked tons of questions," Job says, "and they are not grounded in animal behavior. Someone says, 'Well, the only thing is, Doctor, the dog bit someone last week.' And meanwhile there's a patient in this room, and someone in that room, and you are already two clients behind, and the waiting room is full.

"So it's a benefit for a doctor to be able to say, 'Animal behavior interests me, but it is not my specialty. Here's someone for whom it is. He's affiliated with our hospital. Call him, and let me know what he says.' And the client leaves with my card."

After two years in Bay Ridge, Patience of Job moved to the Upper East Side. Not long after the move, Job was mugged and slashed when he walked in on someone breaking into the mailbox in his apartment building. Job walked to New York

Hospital, holding his bleeding face. The beasts were still teaching him, he thought bitterly, but on the whole he preferred a
four-legged beast to the two-legged beast he had just encountered. Job felt a long way from the wooded hills, the blessed
peace, the order of New Skete monastery.

Then his parents' training came back. Job talked tough to
himself then, and he continues to talk tough to himself when he
needs to. "You're the one who did it to yourself, Job," he said.
"You chose to come here. Yes, the city is dangerous, dirty, a lot
trashier than the monastery. So take a look at the danger and the
trash. It's there. It's not going to go away, today or tomorrow.
You'd better get used to it. You chose to do this. Now get going."

Would Job go back to the safety of the monastery, to the
structured world he knew before that inner voice commanded
him to get out? He would not. But Job is slow to recommend
change to other people. "Not everybody can pull off a big
change without causing immeasurable, pointless misery for
themselves or for other people. Change is really not for everyone. If I had received more understanding and sympathy at New
Skete, I would probably still be there.

"But I agreed to do this interview," he tells me, "because
every society, monastic or not, is always so eager to keep people
in line. Once in a while, somebody should say, 'You can change.
Go ahead!' "

Change is possible. Take it from the original prodigal dog.

10

The Reasons of the Heart

When I first met Nancy Schwartz, she was Nancy Sanders, a college junior in a year-long American novel class I was teaching. Nancy sat in the front row of the large class, fixing me with an intense blue-eyed gaze. In a college where coeds got up at six to apply their makeup, where they dressed to kill for their class appearances, Nancy stood out. As far as I could tell, she wore no makeup, and her usual costume consisted of T-shirts over jeans in cold weather, over shorts in warm. After spring break, Nancy told me, with a touching youthful bravado, that she and her boyfriend had spent the holiday living in a car on a deserted beach, subsisting on bananas and peanut butter. Shades of the

186

sixties, I thought, smiling at the carefree and, in that environment, totally unexpected bohemianism of it.

I found Nancy charming. One day, just before finals, as she pranced out of class, the word for Nancy's charm came to me. "Nancy," I said, "you know what you have? You have chic."

She flushed with pleasure. From then on, even after her graduation a year later, we were friends. I got long, chatty, funny letters from Nancy several times a year. And when, years later, in a return note, I mentioned that I was working on this book, Nancy eagerly volunteered her own story, whose turbulence I had never suspected as she sat before me in that neat classroom row.

Just twenty-eight at the time of our interview, Nancy Schwartz is the youngest innovator in this book, but she has packed a lot of living and feeling into those twenty-eight years. Nancy insisted that I use her real name to tell her story. "I want to be me, not an anonymous nobody," she wrote me. "My life does spill onto the lives of others. But it's a wonderful, colorful Nancy life. How can it hurt anyone?" Just the same, I have changed the names of some of those others.

The interview took place on a hot August day in Dallas in the beautiful, luxurious home, complete with pool, Jacuzzi, spa, wet bar, fireplaces, you name it, that Nancy shares with her husband Steve and their two children, Jordan, then almost four, and Rachel, almost two. The white walls of the house are hung with colorful canvases done by Nancy herself. Nancy, small and curvy, with a pretty, heart-shaped face and long gold-brown hair, is a young lady who knows she has everything.

At last. Because for most of the years of her life her inner voice told Nancy that she was missing what she really wanted most. What Nancy wanted was her mother, her "real mother." In spite of the fact that Nancy had a perfectly good, kind, loving "mother mother," for her the term "real mother" meant the mysterious and unknown woman whose child she "really" was.

"The heart has its reasons which reason does not know," Pascal said. From the beginning, little Nancy Sanders, an adopted child, was tugged around by the reasons of her heart. She dreamed of finding her real mother—in her mind, Nancy never saw that phrase in quotation marks, but as a simple statement of fact. For Nancy, the woman who had given birth to her *was* the secret to Nancy's own identity. How could Nancy know herself, she wondered, if she didn't know her real mother?

"I felt like a piece of cookie dough that I had to cut into a shape all by myself," she says. "I didn't have an obese mother, or an artistic mother, or any mother to look at and say, 'Well, I'm going to be like that.' So I had to make my own mother." Nancy made what she called "the mother in the sky."

Many children have an imaginary playmate, a little friend who can be counted on never to disappoint. Nancy had an imaginary mother. The mother in the sky was a strong person who helped Nancy through things. If Nancy was afraid to go somewhere, she would ask, "Will you take me?" and the mother in the sky would. If Nancy needed someone to talk to, she would go outside and look at the sky. "I knew my real mother shared the same sky and that she might be looking at the moon at the same time and then we could talk, somehow."

Birthdays were both the best and the worst. On the fourth day of June, as far back as she could remember, Nancy would look at the sky and feel stronger "because my mother was thinking of me and knowing that she had had a baby on that day." But then Nancy would miss that wonderful mother most dreadfully. Often the little girl would come in crying, but she could not tell her adoptive parents, who loved her dearly, what was wrong. "They were raising me to be theirs, so I knew I should be grateful to them and try to be all they wanted me to be."

Nancy did try. She was a good girl. She made mostly all A's in school. In high school, she became a cheerleader and a prizewinning gymnast to please her parents, and spent long hours practicing, jogging, and doing weight training. Yet, in spite of her efforts to please them, and though her adoptive parents "were in every way the best people," Nancy didn't feel at home in her family. She felt alienated from her younger sister, who was also adopted; from her conscientious, protective mother; and most of all from her father. "When I was little, I would close my eyes and pretend to be asleep so I wouldn't have to say goodbye when he went to work."

Nancy knows that her parents "did everything they could and gave me every opportunity to do what they wanted me to do," but she felt, growing up, that her real mother would have understood her much better. If the Sanderses did anything wrong at all as adoptive parents—and what parents don't make mistakes? —it was in telling their girls to keep the news that they were adopted to themselves. They also discouraged discussion of it even in the family. The adoption was a family secret. But both Nancy's mother and father were tall and big-boned, and Nancy's petite frame came in for some joking comments. "I felt like a mutation, and hated having to keep quiet about the reason for my size. Sometimes I wondered, 'Do I have to owe these people for the rest of my life because they did me the favor of adopting me?' "

Why Nancy was so concerned about being adopted, when many adopted children accept the fact easily, is a mystery. Another adopted child, a young man two years younger than Nancy, told me he has rarely given his status more than a passing thought and has never had any desire to meet his natural parents. "My parents—I mean my adopted parents—are not only my real parents to me," he says. "They are *four times over* my real parents. I even catch myself thinking things like, 'Well, I get my blue eyes from my grandmother, I guess,' even though I know it's not true, of course."

Nancy's parents told Nancy she was adopted when she was four. But even then, they told Nancy later, she just looked at them and said, "I know." As Nancy got older, they told her all they knew about her mother. Her mother had given Nancy up at birth, though Nancy was six weeks old when the Sanderses got her. Nancy worried about those six weeks. Regardless of what her parents said, Nancy agonized, what if she had been with her mother those six weeks and her mother didn't like her and that's why she gave her away? "And then I remember thinking that if my own mother didn't want me, how could I possibly be a wantable person to anybody else?"

By the time she was thirteen, Nancy had begun an earnest search for her real identity. Whenever her parents went out for an evening, Nancy would frantically and systematically go through all the closets. Her father was a banker, who kept records of everything. She just knew there were papers somewhere, hidden among old tax returns maybe, that would tell who she was and who her real mother was. And Nancy spent a lot of time, and, she says, eventually a lot of money from her generous allowance, secretly answering ads in the backs of magazines, ads that began, "Are you adopted? We'll find your real parents for you." The agencies she wrote to never responded with hard facts. When she was sixteen, Nancy wrote to the state for her birth certificate, but she never got that either. Nancy became tremendously frustrated. Knowing her real mother became more and more important.

As a freshman at small Washington College in Maryland, needing love and not knowing where to find it, Nancy immediately fell hard for *Jim, the good-looking, popular captain of the lacrosse team. He also happened to be, she says, "the king of drugs on campus." Nancy knew nothing about drugs. "I remember emptying his tray of 'dirt' in the trash, not knowing it was pot, and then feeling like a jerk when he told me. He got stoned as regularly as I changed my underwear." Before long, Nancy was changing her underwear less often than she was doing drugs. "Pot was the staple on campus that year, like rice in the Philippines."

The problems began when Jim, who became her first lover by promising to marry Nancy in the summer, referred to her healthy athletic body as "stocky." Then Nancy found out that Jim had also been sleeping with her roommate, "who slept with everyone." Nancy blamed herself for Jim's infidelity, which confirmed what she already deeply believed: that she, Nancy, was "unwantable."

Though Nancy officially quit "seeing" Jim, literally she could hardly help seeing him in a student body of eight hundred. So Nancy "decided to make him a sorry guy" by having "the body of the year" and letting Jim see what he was missing. She weighed one hundred thirty. By the Christmas holidays, Nancy had lost fifteen pounds; by Valentine's Day another fifteen. Then she weighed ninety.

When she dropped to seventy-eight pounds, Nancy was very ill, but she kept insisting that she wasn't. Hovering in the back of her mind was the image of her mother in the sky. Somehow, Nancy believed that if she could get all the flesh off, her bones would be just like her mother's bones "and I could see more what she looked like." By refusing to eat, Nancy also felt that she was resisting growing up. Her real mother had given away a baby. If, by the time Nancy located her, that baby had become a grown woman, her mother might be put off or disappointed. Her real mother might even reject her all over again. So Nancy wanted to stay young and babyish as long as she could.

Nancy was living on lettuce and water and one dab of cottage cheese at night. She ran ten miles a day, vowing she would never be "stocky" again. Every time she got hungry, Nancy would either go for a run, which gave her one kind of high, or smoke some dope, which gave her another. "I was just a walking high," she says. "I felt like Gandhi, pure and spiritual. It was wonderful. People were telling me that I was sick, but I felt just fine."

At length, alarmed by Nancy's highly visible state of near starvation, the college doctor sent for her parents. No one asked about drugs, and Nancy wasn't talking. But when they heard Nancy diagnosed as anorexic, her mother and father arranged visits to a psychologist, the first of many such visits to come in Nancy's short life. The psychologist did his best, but it wasn't good enough. He took her clothes away from her, and Nancy had to earn them back by gaining: one pound, her shirt; another pound, her shoes. "Basically, I just lived in rags while I was gaining," she says. Then she learned to cheat by putting quarters in her shoes.

The psychologist didn't confront either Nancy's increasing use of drugs, or her central emotional problem, which was the very real need to meet her mother. He and Nancy talked about the effects of being adopted, but "I didn't want to know reasons," Nancy says. "I wanted to know the physical person, my mother. I really needed her a lot. I kept being worried that she was going to maybe die the day before I got there. Because I knew eventually, somehow, some way, I would find her."

Through all this, in an odd way, Nancy was still trying to be a good daughter to her adoptive parents. She had enrolled in business courses to please her father, whose first question about every course was, "What use will it be?" But, as Nancy sneaked in the art, literature, and dance classes that she loved, she fantasized that her real mother would approve, that her mother might even be an artist of some kind. Nancy filled entire notebooks with letters to the mother in the sky. And the next year, Nancy transferred to Southern Methodist University in Dallas, which was a long way from her home in New York. She wanted to get

191

away because "I didn't understand my feelings, and I hated my family."

This is Nancy's story, and for her, in the beginning of it, her parents were the bad guys, as parents often are when the young talk. But put yourself in the Sanderses' place for a moment. They had loved Nancy, had brought her up as well as they knew how, had given her all that they had to give. To them, she was their daughter. What more could they do, they must have asked themselves? The bout with anorexia had terrified them. By refusing to eat, Nancy exercised control over her life in a way so fraught with peril that Mr. and Mrs. Sanders tried to ease up on their expectations of their troubled child.

Her friends at her new school did not for the most part suspect that something was terribly wrong under Nancy's ebullient, attractive surface. Once in a while, Nancy would tell someone about her ongoing search for her real mother, and the response was usually the same, "You have perfectly good parents! In fact, you have everything. Why would you even care about someone who didn't want you?"

But Nancy did care, so much that she became, as she says herself, "just a mess, really."

Shortly after coming to Dallas, Nancy met *Donald, a buyer for a women's clothing store. Older than Nancy, Don lived in an apartment in upscale North Dallas, and drove an Alfa Romeo. Nancy liked Don at first because he "ran all the time and he kept me very thin." Soon she moved out of the dorm and in with Donald. They ran every morning together, then afterward Nancy roller-skated to her classes.

Nancy had never gotten along with girls very well, and Don became her best friend. But, though she and Don were sleeping together, Nancy felt there was a part of Don that she couldn't get to. She suspects now that Don may have been bisexual. For whatever reason, Don was not the man Nancy wanted to marry. "I knew that in his mind he was trying out the bicycle before he bought it, but I wasn't. I was just riding for the fun of it."

Don went to New York on a buying trip, taking Nancy with him, and they asked Nancy's parents to meet them in the city. "What are your intentions toward my daughter?" Mr. Sanders asked Don sternly, as the four of them sat at dinner. Don looked at Nancy. She shrugged. "I don't know exactly," Don said.

After dinner, Nancy and Don went on alone to the Waldorf. "There was a wonderful piano player, and it was starlighty and lovely," Nancy says. "I was really drunk, and he asked me to marry him, and I said, 'Sure.' I knew I wasn't going to, but it just fit in fine with the evening."

It fit in fine, too, to go back to the hotel, wake up Nancy's parents, and say, "We're getting married!" Mr. and Mrs. Sanders, "who were pretty old-fashioned," were thrilled. "Not really, Mom," Nancy told her mother the next morning, but Mrs. Sanders put that demurral down to her young daughter's very natural wedding jitters. Mrs. Sanders insisted on taking Nancy shopping and buying her all new clothes for her "wonderful engagement period."

This period lasted six months before Nancy broke the engagement and moved out of Don's apartment. Nancy's parents, who had announced the engagement in their hometown paper, were bitterly disappointed. They made their disappointment felt sufficiently that Nancy, who had always had everything given to her, who hardly knew how to wash a plate or to make a bed, decided to support herself. She got a job working nights, waiting tables at a restaurant.

Things were tough for the lonely, confused, frightened girl, sleepless, half-starved, both younger and older than her twenty years. For a while, Nancy, the girl who had everything except the mother her inner voice demanded, even fell in with a man who was older than her adoptive father. During that time, Nancy washed her hands of her parents, who were still unhappy about the broken engagement. Nancy wrote some pretty nasty letters home. Suddenly everything her parents had ever done seemed heinous to her, and she finished college very much on the outs with her family.

Nancy went on to do graduate work in psychology. For the first time in her life, she got jobs that mattered to her. She worked for a time with a hospital program for disturbed children. Then she became head of the library for a boys' club designed to keep black teenagers off the street. As librarian, Nancy tried to get the boys to read, tried to enlighten them about the wonders of education, but they wanted to go to the gym and box. So Nancy compromised by filling the library with boxing books and attending all their boxing matches. She developed a new sense of responsibility for someone other than herself.

Meanwhile, "different men for different functions" was her social program. "I wanted to date a lot of people before my rose wilted," Nancy says. Though she slept with most of these "people," Nancy wanted a more serious relationship. If she couldn't find her real mother, she thought, maybe she could find a husband.

Sexually promiscuous, Nancy was also using drugs regularly. She liked "the speedy drugs because I was tired a lot and I didn't like to sleep." One day someone gave her some prescription diet pills, which were miraculous. "I had discovered what I needed," she says. "I wasn't tired, I wasn't sad, I didn't think about my real mother—I didn't think about anything much. I was always happy, I could do amazing things. And I wasn't hungry, so I was really thin."

At the time she discovered the "magic" pills, Nancy went to a party alone. She walked in and there across the room was a young man in a maroon velvet jacket. "He's the one," she told herself. The man was Steve. Six months later, Steve and Nancy were married. "And, God, I was lucky," Nancy says, "because I was high most of the time. But I think somehow I picked the right person for me."

Steve Schwartz knew what he was getting because Nancy told him. She told him about her search for her mother, about the drugs and the guys and the booze; she told him everything. Steve sent her to his psychiatrist for what Nancy calls a "tryout." The psychiatrist, *Dr. Wallace, taped Steve's call and played it for Nancy when she came in. Sitting demurely on a big leather chair in Wallace's office, Nancy heard Steve's earnest voice on the tape saying, "She doesn't like herself, Doctor. She doesn't think she's okay. But I want to marry her, so tell me what you think. Is she okay or not?"

Dr. Wallace shut off the tape and looked at Nancy. He smiled slightly. "Well, Nancy?" he said.

"I'm not okay," Nancy said, a little hysterically, "but tell him I am, please tell him I am. Tell him that he can marry me."

"Wait a minute," the doctor said. "I'm not going to tell him anything of the kind, because it's already obvious that you're going to get married. And I'm not in business to tell people what to do. If you want to see me for reasons of your own, that's a different issue altogether."

Nancy took a deep breath and burst out crying. "I really need to come here," she sobbed. "I really need help. I am not well."

Admitting you are sick is the first step toward getting well. Dr. Wallace called Steve. "Steve," he said, "your bride is going to be just fine."

Nancy got married on a handful of diet pills and four shots of Wild Turkey. "Thank goodness for pictures, because I don't remember a thing about it." Mostly, what she noticed later in the pictures were her adoptive parents' happy faces. Nancy had gotten a prize, they thought. Steve had money, looks, everything Don had and more—the Schwartz family was Jewish, like the Sanders family. "You knew what you were doing about Don after all," Mrs. Sanders told Nancy.

In some inexplicable way, Nancy had indeed known what she was doing when she decided to marry Steve Schwartz, as she knew what she was doing when she got pregnant six weeks after the newlyweds came back from their honeymoon. "I tricked myself into getting pregnant. After all this body abuse I wasn't having periods, and I told myself and Steve that I probably couldn't get pregnant. I figured if I could just slip into pregnancy 'accidentally,' it wouldn't be such a major decision. But because I was adopted, I think I really needed to prove to myself that I could have a baby."

For the first three months of her pregnancy with Jordan, Nancy explained her confusing physical symptoms by insisting to everyone, including herself, that she was dying of cancer. Steve demanded that she go back to Dr. Wallace for counseling. After she had had one therapy session, test results came back from a medical examination confirming that she was pregnant. Nancy breezed into Wallace's office and said, "That's all that's been wrong with me—I'm pregnant. Now that I know, I'm fine, so I won't be coming here ever again."

"You'll be back," Dr. Wallace told Nancy somberly.

Pregnancy suited Nancy. She could be sick and lie in bed, have ups and down, get fat, just do whatever she felt like. She weighed one hundred pounds when she got pregnant, and before Jordan's birth she gained fifty-six pounds. Steve told her she looked beautiful, so she quit looking in the mirror. All her attention turned to the baby in her belly. Nancy held up flash cards before her swollen abdomen and read to the child inside. She would turn the lights on and off, and say, "Baby! Do you see that?"

"I was into all of this better baby business before the guy was even born. And then out came this nine-pound child, this massive blond baby, so big he broke his collarbone being born. And I thought, this is it. I'm going to be happy from now on. We'd have a cute little family that fits in a picture—we even had a dog.

"But I wrote to my real mother all the time, and the night after Jordan was born I wrote him a letter in case somebody should come and steal him in the hospital. I'd get up at all hours and go to the nursery and look to make sure he was still there."

Nancy had been drug-free for the months of her pregnancy, but her anxiety about Jordan accelerated and soon she was back on speed. The baby was everything to her, but she literally ran circles around him. "I never left him with a sitter. When I ran, I put him in the center of the track and I'd jog around him. I read to him for a solid year. I didn't leave the house without him. He even went to the bathroom with me."

If her fears for Jordan were out of control, so was her need for speed. "I was such a speed freak that I was seeing three different doctors in order to get all I needed." Steve signed her up for a drug abuse program, which he attended with her. "He just knew I needed help, and that I wouldn't go without him. He told me, 'Look, you'd do it for me. This is what marriage is all about.' I mean, I was basically losing my mind."

Nancy got pregnant again. "I needed a break from drugs really, and I knew that I would be straight. I would just slide through withdrawal and pregnancy and morning sickness." So she cleaned up her act long enough to have Rachel, another nine-pound baby, in August 1984. But with the birth of her daughter, Nancy's fears doubled. Here were two babies for whom she was all in all, and she was not okay. She would never be okay, she knew she would never be okay, until she had found her real mother.

Though Nancy had still not been able to get her legal birth

certificate and thus find out her real mother's identity, a change in New York state law made it possible for her to get information about her genetic and biological background. On Valentine's Day, when Rachel was six months old, that information arrived. In the terse description on a single sheet of paper, Nancy learned that the woman who bore her was five feet two, Nancy's height exactly, and, like Nancy, she weighed about one hundred pounds. And she had blue eyes.

Nancy's mother was described as having many social and family problems. She had been institutionalized for a year. Nancy herself was the younger of two illegitimate daughters of this woman, and both girls had been given up at birth for adoption. Nancy remembers the pain of learning that "I wasn't even the first child. I was the second. How did I know she hadn't gone ahead to have four more after me, and to give those away too? Maybe giving babies away was even a business for her!"

Nancy had to know the truth, and now she had a powerful ally in her husband. "Let's find this person," Steve said. "I'm sick of this. We can't live like this. If that is what you need, let's do it. Let's just do whatever it takes to find this woman."

So they moved on it. First, Nancy went to Dr. Wallace and begged him to declare her mentally incompetent so that, as her physician, he could get her mother's complete records. Wallace refused. "You are a perfectly competent person, Nancy. I won't do that."

Next, Steve and Nancy approached a lawyer friend. "Can you subpoena the adoption records?" they asked. The lawyer suggested that they hire a private investigator instead. The investigator he recommended offered to do the search for free because one of his daughters had given a child up for adoption. "He had a vested interest, because he wanted his grandchild, if it ever wanted to come back and look, to have all the help it needed," Nancy says. "He really understood the problems."

With a certain viciousness, because "I wasn't allowed to talk about being adopted for so many years," Nancy told her adoptive parents about the search. To her surprise, they didn't object. In fact, her father offered to help. They signed up with all the search organizations in the country, including some Nancy had already contacted as a teenager. But still, nothing seemed to be happening.

Then one afternoon Nancy got a call from a woman who identified herself only as "Bobbie." "Do you want to go underground to find your mother?" Bobbie asked. "If you do, there's a man who searches but nobody knows him except by the voice. Somehow, he gets you what you want to know for cash through the mail. I can put you in touch with him for twenty-six hundred dollars."

Steve was skeptical. "They could hire you a mother," he said. "How are you going to know? It's not the money that's bothering me, Nancy. Can you handle it if they take your money and hang up on you?"

Nancy felt instinctively that Steve was wrong. "I'll hate you forever if you don't let me do this," she told him. "Tell him to call me," she blurted to Bobbie, still waiting on the other end of the line. Then Nancy hung up and sat looking at Steve with wide eyes, wondering what she had gotten herself into.

The mysterious searcher called the next afternoon. "He had a voice like Big Bird mixed with a little Burt Reynolds, you know, sexy but kind, and immediately I loved him. I knew he was okay," Nancy says.

"What do you want to know?" the Big Bird voice asked.

Nancy stopped short. "If she's fat or thin," she said.

"If she's fat—?"

"And if she ever does drugs. Why she gave me and my sister away. What she looks like. Where she is. And if I can see her."

"Okay," Big Bird said, and the phone went dead.

A month passed before, late one night, the phone rang. It was Big Bird. "I got her," he said. "I know your mother."

"And I just cried," Nancy says. "I just sat there crying, and I said, 'Tell me about her.' "

Nancy's real mother, Lilian, was the daughter of Russian immigrants who spoke no English. When Lilian went to school, she was kept back in grade after grade because she never understood what the teacher was saying to her. In the seventh grade, Lilian was sixteen. She dropped out of school to be with her boyfriend, whom she planned to marry as soon as she was old enough. But before she was old enough, she got pregnant.

Her parents were furious. They took Lilian to a home for unwed mothers in Buffalo, where she sat and cried and waited for her young man to come and marry her. Then Lilian had her baby. She loved the baby for a week, while she waited to get married. But her young man never came.

Her parents came instead and said he'd married someone else. They would take her home. And Lilian began to get the baby ready to leave, and her mother said no, not the baby. So Lilian left the baby there, and she went home with her parents. But after that, Lilian was not quite right—she'd never been so very right—and she would get on buses and go around looking for this baby, and she was going to find the baby and bring the baby home with her.

But Lilian's parents said she should work, because they worked. So Lilian got a job working in a restaurant. One night a man with blond hair and blue eyes came in to the restaurant where she worked, and very soon Lilian was pregnant again. This time her parents didn't take her to Buffalo. You must have loved it in Buffalo, they told her. So you will stay at home, here. But you will not go out during the day, only at night, so you will not disgrace us to these neighbors.

So, for the next seven or six or eight months—who knew or cared how long?—Lilian sat inside and cried, with the blinds drawn and the windows closed, and only went out at night. And on the night of June 4, 1958, Lilian went to the hospital by herself while her parents were working. At ten o'clock she had her baby, and by eleven o'clock she was gone.

"And that was me," Nancy said, through her sobs.

"That was you," Big Bird said. "She never touched you, never. Because she didn't want to be hurt the way she was hurt the first time. She didn't want to hold you and have to leave. But when she got home, something snapped. She'd walk for miles and miles looking for her babies. And finally they put her in a mental hospital in Syracuse, and gave her electroshock therapy to make her forget her life.

"Later, she married and had more children, but she lost them too. Lilian has been called a schizophrenic. She is not well. If you want to see her, put the money in the mail, and I'll call you with the address."

Nancy put the money in the mail, and Big Bird called with an address and phone number in Syracuse. "Until you went to college in Maryland and then in Dallas," he told Nancy, "you never in your life lived more than five miles from your real mother."

Big Bird tried to brace Nancy for the conversation with her mother. Somehow he even got Lilian's psychological file from Syracuse Psychiatric Hospital, and read Nancy things Lilian had said to her psychiatrist. "She's strange," he told Nancy. "Be prepared. This lady is strange." Then he hung up.

Nancy sat looking at the number she had written down. Steve went off to bed, but Nancy drank some wine, and listened to music, and looked at herself in the mirror as she practiced saying "hi" to her mother. After an hour and a half of this, she dialed the number. "Hi," Nancy said to the woman's voice that answered. "Hi," she said again. "I think you're my mother."

"And we talked and we talked and we talked," Nancy said. "She was willing to talk all night."

"I've always felt that I had a dark cloud following me everywhere," Lilian told Nancy, "and I was glad that you got out from underneath it. I love you and I didn't want to hurt you at all and I had no way to get you. And why would I want to drag you into my miserable life?"

Lilian was afraid to come to Dallas, so the next morning Steve made Nancy get an airline ticket to Syracuse. He had to make her. Here Nancy had waited all her life, but when the time came to meet her mother she was almost as afraid as Lilian. She just couldn't make a decision, so Steve said, "Go. I'll take off a week and stay with the kids. Go."

Nancy went, with nothing but the jeans and shirt she was wearing. She'd lost twelve pounds between Big Bird's call and her arrival in Syracuse, and she was a wreck. Lilian had told Nancy to come to a Pizza Hut in Shop City, wherever that was. Nancy rented a car and drove around Syracuse till she found it. "I fly into the place, see a woman on a bench in the outer area, and fling myself upon her," she says. "And this freaked-out woman jumps up, and says, 'You weirdo,' and runs to her car. Can you imagine what she went home to tell about her experience at a Pizza Hut?"

In the back of the restaurant, Nancy found Lilian cowering in a booth. Lilian's hair was black, but her eyes were indeed blue, "the scary movie type that are clear blue, that you can see back into a long way. And she was dirty. She had a dirty coat and dirty shoes and I didn't know if her skin was that color or if she was dirty. She looked like a bag lady." At forty-nine, Lilian was exactly the same size as her daughter, but, "Sweetie," Lilian said to Nancy, "you're a bit too thin." "In some ways," Nancy says, laughing, "all mothers are exactly the same."

Together, they went back to the room where Lilian lived, which was about the size of Nancy's guest bathroom. Lilian's room, however, was filthy; it smelled like old clothes, rotting food, unwashed bodies. In its tiny confines were crammed eight tables, ten lamps which were not plugged in because Lilian is afraid of electricity, Lilian's clothes piled everywhere because Lilian thinks that closets eat whatever goes into them, Lilian's wigs. It was the room of a madwoman. Nancy's real mother is a schizophrenic manic-depressive on lithium and Thorazine, when she remembers to take them.

Nancy, the English major, has a real mother who cannot coherently complete a sentence. Nancy, the anorexic and exercise fanatic, has a real mother who lives on candy and sits passively waiting for her own mother, who has been dead for eight years, to come make her dinner. And Nancy, who yearned all her life for her real mother, has a mother who, until Nancy telephoned, had forgotten her second daughter's existence. "Every fourth of June," Nancy says, "when I'd look to the sky, feeling stronger on that birthday because my mother looked at the same sky and was thinking of me, knowing that she had a baby on that day—that was simply not true. Lilian doesn't know my birthday and had even forgotten that she had ever had me. She had me confused with her first baby."

Nancy saw Lilian's doctors, from whom she learned that Lilian's first baby, Nancy's half-sister, had been in a mental institution for years, a hopeless case. Next, Nancy arranged to meet Lilian's youngest daughter, Donna, one of the three children from Lilian's marriage who had been removed from their mother by the court. All three live in Syracuse, but only Donna was willing to talk with Nancy. "Go home," Donna told her coldly. "Sisters are people who grow up together. You're the lucky one. You got away."

Before leaving Syracuse, Nancy arranged for additional care for Lilian, and promised to call her once or twice a week. On the plane back to Dallas, as she tried to record the experience in a notebook letter—this one to Steve rather than to her real mother—Nancy realized the significance of the encounter with Lilian. "The mother whom I had loved," Nancy wrote, "who had made me strong during the shakiest moments of my life, whom I had been looking for as long as I could remember—that mother was me, Nancy Sanders Schwartz. I flew to Syracuse to find me.

"I suddenly felt as if I'd been running around in a panic, looking for my car keys, late for something unknown and urgent, when I had my keys in my hand the whole time. And the only place I wanted to go was home."

Back in Dallas, Nancy had what she calls "the Scrooge experience," after Ebenezer Scrooge in Charles Dickens's *A Christmas Carol.* Like Scrooge, who is visited by the ghosts of his life and thus learns what really matters, Nancy felt what she calls "rushes of happy." She saw the whole world differently. "My kids looked different. My husband felt different. I tasted food, I liked people, and I wanted friends terribly. I just wanted to go park in the grocery store and ask every person who came in, 'Will you be my friend?' And then I went to all the people that I'd been hateful to and said, 'I'm sorry. I don't hate you really.' "

Chief among those people were her adoptive parents. She called her parents a lot, and they were always there to listen. Nancy knew then that if Lilian had said, "Go to hell, lady. Get away from me," her parents would have been there to pick her up. "So I called them a million times," she says, "saying 'I'm sorry, I'm sorry.' " And they said, 'Don't be sorry. You've made our lives so rich and we love you.' "

Let Steve have the last word, good Steve Schwartz who realized that, for reasons of her heart, Nancy had to listen to the inner voice that directed her to find her mother. Steve would have had a lot less trouble married to one of those coeds who got up at six to put on makeup and dress to kill for class, but he knew what he was doing. Steve chose Nancy, "okay" or not. Steve used to joke that he liked coming home to Nancy because he never knew what to expect. Nancy might be up or down or mean or miserable or happy or hating or loving. "Why have another woman?" Steve would say. "I have six in my house as it is."

At the height of Nancy's Scrooge experience, Steve came home one night, took a look at Nancy's yet again smiling face,

202

and said, totally exasperated, "When is this flower child nonsense going to stop? It's so thick and sweet and juicy around here that I can't stand it."

So Nancy is working on leveling off, going at it with the combination of intuition and rationality that she brought to the sixteen-year search for her real mother. For years, her inner voice told Nancy that her real mother guided her life from afar. All future happiness depended on finding in the flesh that strong mother in the sky. That mother, Nancy's real mother, her inner voice insisted, was the key to Nancy's own identity.

At last, after years of dogged pursuit of that chimera, Nancy found a broken, pitiable, deluded woman, and learned the extent to which she herself had been deluded. Apparently Nancy's inner voice had been wrong. The dream mother had never existed. What would Nancy choose to do with that knowledge? How would the loss of her illusions affect her?

Nancy decided that the inner voice was right in its urgings, but that its discoveries needed to be interpreted by her reason. She had placed herself in a position where the illusion of the hovering, protective, maternal presence was shattered. Thus, for the first time, Nancy came to know her own strength. She, Nancy Schwartz, had the strength she had attributed to her real mother. "I hugged myself a lot, because I was the strong mother, myself," Nancy remembers. Through the revelations that came out of that self-induced crisis, Nancy has changed her life.

Recognizing and Exploring Opposites

For innovators,
everything has a recognizable
and intriguing opposite.
Thus they are open
to the complex possibilities
of the world.

11

What Now? or What Else?

Many opposites in life offer themselves to our incessantly creative imaginations. The truth is, we all want to contain multitudes. We all hate to knuckle under to the limitations that humanity itself imposes. Declare for one value, and its opposite will strike you in the face. Decide to live in the country, and you will crave the charms of the city; move to town, and you're likely to pine for the pastoral. Commit yourself to one man, one woman, one profession, and on a restless Friday afternoon or a dark Monday morning, you will suddenly yearn toward the enormous attractions of the opposite. As Saul Bellow's Mr. Sammler put it, "The opposite makes the opposite."

When we long for what we lack in our lives, there are two

questions we can ask: "What now?" or "What else?" These questions signal two distinct approaches to filling the gap. Those who ask "What now?" subtract. They leave what they have, to opt for a completely new life, as different in every detail as possible from the life which preceded it. Those who ask, "What else?," add. They increase the satisfactions of their present life by bringing into it whatever they construe to be missing.

As an example of the "What now?" approach, consider the actress Stockard Channing, who told a reporter for the *New York Times,* "I've lived many different kinds of lives with different kinds of people. It's a source of renewal, and it's a source of disruption. I have a sense of the explorer in me; I wander off and follow my nose. I've slept on floors and been a bohemian, I've been a Park Avenue matron, I've lived in Hollywood, and I wouldn't deny any of it; I'm all of these people. I'm a chameleon."

Almost everyone has Gauguin fantasies of running away from home, escaping to the South Seas, and becoming someone completely different. But few people are actually willing to forsake all the fidelities of the past in order to embrace the future, nor do they need to. I found in these interviews that the most successful changes occur when strong connections are maintained with the past, when lives are innovated rather than entirely re-created, when "What else?" is answered, rather than "What now?"

*Dominique LeClerq asked "What now?" when, after more than twenty years as a nun, she left the convent with her lesbian lover. Six weeks later, Dominique and her lover split up. Dominique, who had no money and no job, was also alienated from members of her staunchly Catholic family by her precipitous move into the secular world. Dominique gave up almost everything to start over. The next several years were incredibly difficult for the former nun. In fact, in her unhappiness Dominique tried several times to return to the convent but was rejected.

Dominique began our interview by announcing firmly that she was happier than she had ever been in her life. Then she started talking—and crying. The longer Dominique talked, the harder she cried. She went through a giant box of tissues in three hours on a Sunday afternoon. In the course of this tearful interview, Dominique unconsciously revealed in a most dramatic fashion

208

her still raw longing for the convent life she had forsaken for the ephemera of passion and the illusion of lasting love.

At last, her face red and swollen but her sorrow temporarily assuaged, Dominique confessed that she had recently found a modicum of peace. Though she had not been allowed to return to the convent, in the middle of the secular city Dominique was living by her convent vow of celibacy and, to the extent she could practicably manage, the vows of poverty and obedience as well. She had tried to create an entirely new life for herself, and, in spite of all her protestations, it seemed to me that she was miserable in it. Only by returning in spirit to the allegiances of the past had she been able to cope with her self-imposed trauma. "What now?" had almost destroyed Dominique's chances for happiness.

But the "What now?" approach can work more successfully. Take the fascinating metamorphosis of Duncan Aswell. Even more deliberately than Dominique, Duncan set out to alter the course of his life, to answer "What now?" with the most radical change he could imagine. What he realized, nearly twenty years later, was that, in spite of his intentions, some elements of continuity persevered: his love for books and some friends, his desire to write, his political and social convictions, even his family feeling. Striving for an opposite existence ended by confirming certain verities that endured the change. Without his conscious effort, even in a new city, in a different job, under a new name, in some important ways he was the same person.

Outside the modest frame house in a predominantly black neighborhood in Atlanta, the sun is shining and the neighbors are planning a potluck supper for later in the week. Inside, sitting next to me on the sofa in a shabbily comfortable, book-lined living room, the man talking is slight and pale, dressed in faded jeans and a short-sleeved shirt. Though he is white, as we came into the house he agreed, in response to the urgent invitation of a black woman down the block, to contribute a dish and his presence to the supper. A man living with opposites, I think to myself. My impulsive judgment is confirmed as he talks. Commanding eyes peer at me intently over a full brown beard, but his voice is soft and hesitant as he describes what he calls his "perfect getaway."

209

"What I did," the man says, "was to simply drop everything I had been doing, including my name, without any prior notice to anybody, including myself. I didn't know myself that it was going to happen until it happened, so I didn't leave any clues. I think it must have been what religious people call 'grace,' when something happens, and all the molecules change.

"I left everything that I owned, including all my identity papers, and just lit out for a new life. I had been Duncan Aswell, a university teacher. I became someone totally different: Bill Cutler, a wine salesman, and then a freelance writer." Bill Cutler is a prime example of someone who took a step others will probably only fantasize about. He did away with himself without dying, metamorphosed into his own opposite, took up habitation in a self-constructed new ego.

Bill began life as Duncan Aswell, the son of two prominent figures in New York publishing in the forties. His mother, Mary Louise Aswell, was a fiction editor at *Harper's Bazaar* and an early editor of Eudora Welty. His father, Edward Aswell, as an editor at Scribners, worked on the last manuscripts of Thomas Wolfe. Successful at work, the Aswells, who are both dead now, were failures at home, according to their son, and were especially failures as parents. Mrs. Aswell was loving but neurotic, Edward Aswell distant and forbidding. And the marriage itself was a failure. Just before the two divorced, when Duncan was a teenager, Edward Aswell even had his wife "captured" on the street and committed involuntarily to a mental hospital.

Matters were no better after the divorce. Duncan was placed in the custody of his alcoholic father. Having always shut himself off from his family, Edward Aswell spent the last ten years of his life literally shutting himself away from the rest of the world also. All around the family home, he built an elaborate structure of walls, flanked by a thick screen of trees. "He was like a mole," Duncan says. "He was acting out of some atavistic impulse, like a cave man needing security and failing to find it in Westchester County."

Failure was the name of the family game. Duncan himself wanted to be a writer, but was too afraid of failure to announce his ambition to his parents. He felt sure, in the highly charged atmosphere of the household both before and after the divorce, that as a writer he would be held to, and would fail to achieve, the standard set by the likes of Welty and Wolfe, his parents' other "children." Instead, trying to avoid failure in his parents' eyes, Duncan became a college English professor. When his father died, his mother softened in her rigidly high standards. But Duncan still felt himself to be a failure for having chosen a lower path than the high road of pure artistic effort.

The psychological problems Duncan had were accentuated, and he was thrown into a state of almost suicidal alienation, by being denied tenure in his fifth year of teaching at Wellesley College. Duncan was thirty-four, by all accounts an excellent teacher who had also published the requisite number of academic articles. He fully expected and believed he deserved a favorable tenure decision from the school. Tenure at Wellesley would mean a lot to him. It would be a tangible mark of success in his chosen life; it would also guarantee him till death or retirement the kind of security he had missed growing up.

Unexpectedly, his tenure was denied. Duncan had been a vocal opponent on campus of the Vietnam War and of racism. Wellesley students saw the negative decision as a political statement by the college. The all-female student body, normally so well mannered and obedient to authority, went on strike to have the negative decision regarding a favorite teacher reversed.

The students were successful, and Duncan's tenure decision was overturned. Belatedly, he was granted tenure at Wellesley. But by that time, Duncan was profoundly depressed. Failure, for whatever reason, to be approved for tenure brought back all the inadequacies of a childhood when nothing he could do seemed good enough. The tenure decision reversal came too late to restore Duncan Aswell's peace of mind. Despite being tenured, Duncan decided to leave Wellesley.

As the center of a collegiate *cause célèbre,* Duncan received numerous job offers. He accepted a position at Haverford College, moving from all-female Wellesley to all-male Haverford. Haverford turned out to be absolutely the wrong choice for him. Missing his friends and students at Wellesley, more and more unhappy with his teaching, Duncan made several suicide attempts and once even committed himself briefly to a mental institution. Then, the last suicide attempt, which nearly succeeded, put him "in touch with the part of me that wanted to stay alive."

One day, spontaneously, in the middle of a class, Duncan came up with a plan for "the perfect getaway." The class, full of white middle-class kids who were being asked to comment on *The Souls of Black Folk* by W. E. B. Du Bois, was going very badly. Duncan edged the discussion along, in a halfhearted attempt at Socratic dialogue, asking and then wearily answering most of the questions himself. It was uphill work, and very dispiriting for a dedicated teacher. Suddenly, in the middle of an exchange between Duncan and Duncan, he had an insight. "I don't have to do this anymore," he told himself.

"I wouldn't Joan of Arc it," Bill Cutler says, grinning at me. "I didn't hear voices. But I suddenly realized that the world was larger than this classroom I'd been circumscribed in. I could almost see myself moving off toward the horizon."

Without missing a beat in his teaching, Duncan began to work out the details of the perfect getaway in his head. As he continued to try to draw the surly, unresponsive students into engagement with Du Bois's book, he planned the moves he would make after class. He wouldn't go back to his house, wouldn't so much as pack a toothbrush. He wouldn't go to the bank or do any of the things that you do when you plan a trip. He had an appointment with his therapist that afternoon. He'd keep that, he thought. That would really throw them off.

Who was "them"? His mother perhaps, the university administration, certainly his therapist, who kept insisting to Duncan, "Your sense of self-worth depends on your going right on with the work you've always done; otherwise your life will fall apart." "Them" was all the repressive forces that all his life Duncan Aswell had outwardly obeyed and inwardly resented. Now he planned to escape from "them."

As a child, Duncan had loved the Hardy Boys books, with all the clever escapes which that enterprising team planned and carried out. Little Duncan used to sneak out of the unhappy house, go off in the woods, and pretend "that I would never go home again." As a grownup, he began to feel the excitement of fulfilling that childhood dream. After the counseling session, "where I did a big act for the shrink just as I had for the students," Duncan got in his car, with about fifty dollars in his wallet, and drove off toward the horizon.

In an unpublished book, *Into Thin Air,* Bill Cutler, once

Duncan Aswell, has described the adventures that he discovered on the horizon of a new life. The first was the name change itself. In a gay bathhouse in Camden, New Jersey—his homosexuality was another way in which he felt he had "failed"—Duncan tried on new names for fit. Very quickly he came up with "William" from the black writer William Edward Burghardt Du Bois, whose work he had been so fruitlessly trying to teach at Haverford. "Duncan Aswell" was a consummate WASP name. To lose it would be to go to his opposite, to "the soul of black folk." The surname was more difficult, but he relaxed and at length it came: "Cutler." After all, he was cutting loose, cutting the ties. He christened himself "William Cutler." "It sounded fine to me," he says.

After selling his Volkswagen—at a considerable loss, but he was in a hurry—Bill took out his wallet and destroyed all traces of his old identity. Driver's license, Social Security card, library card, birth certificate, credit cards, cards attesting to the health insurance, draft registration, eyeglass prescription, and voter registration of the citizen named Duncan Aswell were all demolished and stuffed into a trashcan. Getting rid of the detritus of his old life, Bill felt remarkably free. "I didn't know what I was going to do. All I knew was that I had no more obligations, that I wasn't any more tied to the earth. I could do anything I wanted to, go anywhere I liked."

The new Bill Cutler bought a bus ticket for Atlanta. He wanted to get away from his WASP roots and connections, and Atlanta seemed a plausible destination. At a five-and-dime across the street from the bus station, he bought a small suitcase to hold everything he now owned—toilet articles, a shirt, some underwear and socks, a notebook, fountain pen, paperback copy of *The French Lieutenant's Woman,* and a new thin red address book, embossed in gold leaf. Then he climbed on the bus to Atlanta. As the bus jostled him southward, Bill took out the paperback of *The French Lieutenant's Woman* and in the flyleaf of John Fowles's novel about the ambiguity of identity wrote his new name for the first time. "You own, therefore you are," the smudgy, shaky letters said to him. "You cast a shadow, thanks to us."

Next, in the new address book, Bill created a circle of imaginary friends, complete with phone numbers, addresses, and accurate zip codes. Then came a family. "Who is this 'William Cutler,' anyway?" he asked himself. "How does he happen to be riding this bus toward the South? What's his story? Who are his parents?" Before long, he had worked out a satisfactory—and satisfying—tale. Both parents dead, but alive in memory. A brawny, jovial, businessman father, an outgoing man with a hearty laugh. A retiring, gentle, steadfast mother, whose only arena was the home. Out of that happy marriage of opposites had come a wealth of love and indulgence for Bill, the only child, the apple of their connubial eye.

Bill now named his father—Tom Stewart Cutler. Tom and his wife—What was her name? He'd get to that—had so unswervingly believed that their son was a writer of genius that they had supported him financially until they died. That's why Bill had no Social Security number. He had never worked; his parents didn't want him to waste his talent and energy on a mundane job. "Not as long as I'm alive," his father had often said. But now Tom Cutler was dead, and his son, history-less, record-less, was on his way into an independent life.

But what about the lack of a draft card? Even indulged only sons of comfortable businessmen have to register for the draft. But not after they are thirty-five! So Bill Cutler established his birthday as February 2, Ground-Hog Day. Thus, he became a few months younger than Duncan Aswell had been. With the change of birthdays, another change took place. Instead of being a critical, studious Virgo like Duncan, Bill was an ingenious, unpredictable Aquarius. The dawning of a new age, the Age of Aquarius! Bill liked it. He sat back in his bus seat and closed his eyes. Giving birth to himself was an exhausting business.

"WELCOME TO GEORGIA, STATE OF ADVENTURE," a billboard on the side of the road declared when Bill opened his eyes again. Arriving in Atlanta, he set about giving the shadows in his mind and in the red address book some substance. First came temporary quarters, the local YMCA. Then came a bank account to house the proceeds from the sale of his car. Next came, appropriately for a writer, a library card. "How proud I felt as I walked out of the library!" Bill wrote. "I was a citizen of a town. My body cast a shadow. I had a home."

Then he acquired other things as well. He had become moderately knowledgeable about wine, so he landed a job in a liquor

214

store as the wine expert. Without a driver's license, Bill decided in the pleasant Atlanta spring that a bike would be a nice change from a car. Duncan Aswell had been a sedentary, isolated person. Bill Cutler, who bicycled everywhere, was much more gregarious, much more active physically. He joined a bicyclists' club. Through this group, he made friends. He felt more alive as Bill Cutler than he had ever felt as Duncan Aswell.

Duncan's father was dead, but in the four months before Duncan surfaced again as Bill Cutler by impulsively telephoning an old friend, Mary Louise Aswell became so concerned about the abrupt disappearance of her son that she put private detectives to work on the case. Bill Cutler came to recognize that Duncan Aswell was psychologically a very sick man. His lack of consideration for his family and friends stemmed directly from his illness. "I was intellectually conscious of the fact that they really cared for me, but I simply couldn't feel anything. I had no contact whatsoever with my emotions or with anybody else's emotions. I certainly wasn't thinking of them or of the grief I would cause them, any more than I had when I attempted suicide. And I didn't think of them for months."

One reason for his absence of conscience during the break was his previously overactive conscience. "I'd always been Mr. Conscientious. If I was sick, I would just shoulder-to-the-wheel it, and still meet class. I had drawn my own limits much too tightly. When those limits went, everything went." If he had held his own reins a little more loosely, he might not have had to make such a dramatic move to an entirely opposite kind of existence.

But what's in a name, after all? Call him what you will, Duncan Aswell or Bill Cutler, the quiet man who told me this story still has the same psyche he had when he ran away from home nearly twenty years ago. "Bill Cutler" has become a respected name among freelance journalists, and Bill has a New York literary agent and a fat, fascinating, though unpublished, manuscript about his life. But in some crucial areas of his emotional makeup, Bill is still Duncan, the fearful child competing with Thomas Wolfe for his father's attention. "The big getaway" has not changed that.

Just the same, Bill knows that he is envied by other people for making such a complete break with his past. When he wrote a very short version of his story for a local publication, the response from readers was so excited and tumultuous that Bill realized he had "really tapped into something. A lot of other people wanted to do the same thing, but they just didn't dare."

Bill doesn't recommend the virtues of becoming a Cutler to the world at large. Not everyone should "cut loose" and try to escape from his or her identity, as he did. Bill is, in fact, very much aware that his running away was, like suicide, the act of a desperate man. "I don't want to talk about it as, 'Hey, kids. This is the answer to your problems,'" he says. "It wasn't really mature. But it saved my life."

If Bill doesn't recommend a change of the kind he made, neither does he personally regret having made it. Nor does he harbor any lingering nostalgia for his former life as an academic. "So much that is good and healthy and healing has happened to me as Bill Cutler in this new environment that I certainly wouldn't choose to go back into the old world I had been in."

Less than a year after this interview, Bill Cutler died. Duncan Aswell died with him, of course. I didn't know he was ill when, during our last phone conversation, Bill told me that the longer he lived as Bill Cutler, the smaller the differences between him and Duncan Aswell seemed to be. "It's like a parallax," he said, reverting for a moment to the college professor. "The farther away you get from that moment of rupture, the more the two angles of vision come together."

"What are you talking about?" I asked. "I haven't the faintest idea what a parallax is."

He laughed and explained that as "Bill Cutler," he did not feel much more stable or substantial than he did as "Duncan Aswell." As he writes in *Into Thin Air*,

> People have a tendency to assume that the act of disappearing itself was some kind of watershed in my life—all uphill (or downhill, depending on their perspective) before I lit out, all the opposite after. I keep coming back to the idea that my life is woven out of a single fabric, and it keeps ripping and getting sewn back together. . . . I live—we all live—from moment to moment. Our characters and our behaviors are not set in concrete. It's been the genius of America to reveal that universal truth to the world and set people free to experience it, for bad as well as good.

216

Some, like Dominique and Bill, are able to survive in the heady freedom of nothing left to lose. But, as Bill came to realize, a life is a single fabric. By and large, innovators do better when they are wise enough to ask, at the first stirrings of discontent, not "What now?" but "What else?"

"What else?" *Rachel Weissman asked herself. It was 1970 and she was twenty-six years old, an unmarried, white teacher in an all-black college in Alabama. A large, warm, outgoing Jewish woman from New Jersey, Rachel liked her work, her students, her friends, her life. Since leaving home at sixteen for college, she had treasured her independence. But as the years passed, the opposite of independence had nagged at Rachel increasingly for attention. Rachel wanted responsibility. What would it be like to be responsible for a child?

"I envisioned reading bedtime stories, baking cookies, blowing soap bubbles in the park, and the occasional heroics of staying up all night with a sick child," she wrote twenty years later. "I imagined grasping a small hand in my own and waking to comfort bad dreams in the night." So, trusting her own intuition, Rachel reached out for that opposite of independence in a fashion that other people were to label as "odd."

She didn't look for a husband. She never thought of leaving her position in the black school. Rather than abandon the useful life which she enjoyed and had so arduously constructed, Rachel decided instead to add a new dimension to it: she would adopt a child. Why not a biracial child? It was hard to find homes for children who fell in the cracks between ethnic groups. Why not adopt an "unadoptable," older child? If she could save such a child from an orphanage or a succession of foster homes, Rachel figured, she would do both herself and the child a favor.

This kind of adoption, which has grown increasingly common over the last two decades, was uncommon enough in 1970 to be highly suspect. "I don't know," waffled the county social worker who had to approve Rachel's plan. "It's just plain odd. It's odd that she's a woman teaching math in a university. It's odd that she's a white teaching blacks, and that she's a Jew from up North teaching down here. It's odd that she's not married but wants to adopt a child, and a biracial child at that."

When this response was reported to her, Rachel felt for a

moment "as if I ought to join the circus." This feeling of being "a conglomeration of random oddities" she resisted by recognizing that hers was the unconventional personality of the innovator colliding head-on with the full force of social convention. Rachel persisted, and eventually adopted Amos, a bright, healthy three-year-old who was the natural child of a black father and a white mother.

To adopt Amos, Rachel had to deal with the incomprehension of others, of whom the social worker was only the first. Rachel's motives for her unconventional act were misconstrued over and over again. "I suppose you think you are a fine Christian by adopting that little colored boy," ran one letter after a story on the unusual adoption appeared in the local paper. "Well I can tell you I do not think it is the nobel thing to do. . . . If god had wanted the races mixed he would nt have made some one color and some another. . . . Redbirds and blackbirds dont mix." It set Rachel's teeth on edge to be lauded as noble, or condemned as "nobel." "That's just silly, and it's wrong," Rachel told a reporter. "I adopted Amos for selfish reasons, because I wanted him."

Well-meaning black friends questioned the advisability of the adoption on other grounds. "You'll raise him white," a black poet told Rachel, "but society will treat him black. And he needs to be ready for it. You're naïve. You've got your head full of white liberal clouds."

Clouds in her head or not, Rachel did a fine job with Amos. She managed to weather the struggles with babysitters, Halloween costumes, teenage insubordination, learners' permits, orthodontia, and homework that come with the territory for parents, and are harder for a single, working mother. When I interviewed her for this book, Amos was eighteen, a happy boy, a talented musician, and a good student. He had just completed his first year in college, and he was very proud of his new baby sister.

For I wanted to talk with Rachel not about Amos, whose adoption is past history, but about the newest change in her life. In 1987, at the age of forty-three, Rachel again asked herself, "What else?" Once again, she managed to answer the question not by giving up something but by adding something.

The newest addition lies sleeping on Rachel's lap as Rachel

and I talk. The answer this time to "What else?" is her newly adopted infant daughter, Sarah, who, like Amos, is a biracial child. Rachel, too, is not interested in talking about the similarities in the two adoptions but about the differences, and the difference that fifteen years of experience have made in Rachel herself. For Rachel, adopting Sarah has been a statement of confidence in her own femininity. "This time," Rachel says, "I really did want a girl."

In 1970, when she adopted Amos, though Rachel insisted that the sex of the child didn't matter to her, deep down she knew that she really preferred a boy. She felt comfortable with a boy because she had been working with men and was striving to succeed in what was largely a male world. As an academic, she had taught herself to "think like a man," to use the phrase women of her generation grew up with. Quite simply, she was afraid to take on a girl because Rachel had not come to terms, on the deepest level, with the opposite in herself, her womanhood. She felt confounded by the superficialities of femininity. She couldn't sew, knew very little about makeup or clothes, wouldn't know how to fix a little girl's hair, wouldn't have a clue about putting in hems. She was uncertain about the kind of female model she would provide for a daughter.

But being a mother to Amos brought Rachel into contact with the enormous depths, the strong secret pull, of her submerged female nature. Rachel has written that "having a child transforms the way you experience life, see the world." The women's movement also influenced Rachel's understanding of femininity and, to some extent, lessened the sexual discrimination in academic life. Rachel became a success in her own eyes both as a woman and as a professor.

Today, Rachel no longer believes that women are just like men, except less powerful. "I think that female persons are different from males," she says, "whether the difference is genetic or biological or sociological or whatever. Women are different in ways that I would like to say are good, and that's related to my wanting a girl." Comfortable with her new understanding of uniquely female power, Rachel has altered her perspective of herself and her femininity. Therefore, she feels different about the legacy she can offer a daughter. By adopting a girl child,

Rachel has embraced her own female depths, the opposite in herself of her calculating, rational, mathematician's intellect.

Not that Rachel expects to flesh out political or personal theories about feminism in little Sarah. If she ever had any such idea, she's learned better with Amos. Although Amos had lived with his mother's ardent pacifism all his life, as soon as he went to college he enrolled in R.O.T.C. And Rachel laughs at the frustration of another friend, a radical feminist and Marxist, whose teenage daughter recently insisted on going to a masquerade party disguised as a Playboy Bunny. You can't depend on your kids to act out your political agenda for you, Rachel says.

Or any intellectualized, abstract agenda, for that matter. In child-raising, Rachel believes, these philosophical and political positions are only relevant as they have sunk down into a deeper level of your being. But after forty-three years of living with herself as a woman, after fifteen years as a mother and at least that long as a conscious feminist, Rachel knows that she will be a fine model both of femininity and of feminism for her new baby daughter. "I still can't sew," Rachel says, "but I don't think that's so vital anymore."

Rachel explored the opposites of existence by using the "What else?" instead of the "What now?" approach. Her teaching, her friends, her devotion to the world of ideas and her place in that world were constants to which she added the life-fulfilling bonus of children. Thus she was able to build a bridge between the intellectual and emotional, the male and female, opposites in her own nature. Using the same approach, Kenny Schaffer was able to build a space-bridge between cultural opposites, the people of two massive world powers, the Soviet Union and the United States.

Kenny was thirty-six when stumbling upon Soviet television made him reassess what he calls his "media simplifications" about Russia. Having grown up with the newspaper image of Khrushchev pounding with his shoe on the table at the United Nations and of headlines blaring, "Khrushchev says, 'We will bury you,' " like others of his generation Ken was ready to bomb Moscow on signal. "My attitude was," Ken tells me, "everyone knows the Russians are under the couch, coming for our daughters."

Two television sets (both playing, on different channels), a stereo, computer, printer, electric typewriter, radio, and other electronic equipment dominate the cramped space in the funky penthouse where Ken has lived for nearly twenty years in a rent-controlled building just east of New York's Plaza Hotel. Ken laughs as I look for a free electrical outlet for my tape recorder, then relents and unplugs one of the television sets. "I'm a signal freak," he says. "Ham radio when I was a kid, and up and up. I crave signal, all the time."

The "signal freak" is a taut, slim man with a twinkle in his dark eyes and the brushy mustache of a barbershop quartet lead singer. At noon, his black hair still sticks up in morning spikes. Barefoot, wearing jeans and a T-shirt, he tells me that his craving for signal led him to the discovery which changed his life, which turned him from a hedonistic rock and roller to a passionate pacifist and advocate of world unity. Watching Russian television, Ken discovered that, as his friend Sting had put it in a song several years earlier, "the Russians love their children too."

Sting has been a friend since the old days when Kenny Schaffer was a rock and roll publicist, promoting stars like Alice Cooper and Jimi Hendrix to the great American public. An electronics prodigy as well as a fast mouth, in 1977 Kenny invented the wireless guitar and then the wireless microphone. These inventions revolutionized the staging of live shows by freeing performers to bop and shake around the stage. Thus Ken made a mark on rock and roll, and on broadcasting in general. "Every time I turn on the TV, there stands someone like Phil Donahue with my mike," he says. "That's a nice little buzz."

There were other buzzes that went with the rock life—the dope, the booze, the money, and especially the girls. Following groups around the country, Ken found "lots and lots of girls, all delightful and wonderful. It was more, more, more experience, and education too. I love learning about things, and that applies to every part of your life, including your nighttime affinities."

But after a while—"your hormones change, or something"—the pleasures of rock life palled. In his discontent, Ken returned full time to his West Side penthouse. Bored, he didn't know exactly what he wanted. As always, however, he craved signal, so he installed a satellite dish on the roof. Then Ken was chagrined to discover that he couldn't pick up American stations like HBO or Playboy with his satellite, because Rockefeller Center was in the way. In fact, there was only one television-transmitting communication satellite in the world that Ken could get from his roof. Periodically, it was straight over New York, but it was Russian.

So Kenny, the signal freak, began watching a lot of Russian television. "I would leave it on while I was making my phone calls, and I would just see things on the screen that were very contrary to perceived Dan Rather renditions." For example, very early in his Soviet spying, Ken was watching a Russian movie. During a highway scene in the film, it started to rain and all the Russian drivers pulled off the side of the road, took their windshield wipers out of the glove compartment, then went out into the downpour and put the wipers on the windshield. Kenny found himself roaring with laughter at the funny Russians. Were these klutzes installing their windshield wipers in the rain the criminals who were going to bury us?

In another scene on Soviet television, Ken saw a group of doctors operating in an emergency room. They were all wearing hospital gowns and surgical masks, all very proper "except that their noses were sticking out of the masks." Once again Kenny found himself "on the floor" with laughter. Before long, almost unconsciously, his idle watching led to his beginning to be curious and then informed about Russian society. A rubber shortage and the resulting vandalism, he learned, had led to the windshield wiper ritual, for example. But was the Russian custom of protecting the precious wipers any more absurd, when you got right down to it, than the American custom he observed in his rock and roll friends of removing an expensive car stereo and bringing it into the house for protection during an evening visit?

Gradually Kenny dropped his black/white simplifications and began to see that the Russians were just people, both good and bad, just as Americans are good and bad. Then he had another idea—that a satellite picking up Russian television would be a powerful educational device for people who were studying Russian culture or language. "Imagine learning Russian," Ken jokes, "by watching 'The Million Ruble Movie,' 'Laverne and Trotsky,' 'I Dream of Lenin,' or 'Mikhail's Navy.' What a blast!"

Over the next several years, Ken developed such a system, which he called Orbita after the Soviet Union's television network distributor. When I talked with him, he had installed his terminals in a dozen top-ranking American universities. Columbia University was the first to buy in, then the University of Virginia, where Soviet television was sent through the campus cable system so that students could watch "Good Morning, Siberia," or whatever in their own dorm rooms. Others include Penn State, Ohio State, the University of Indiana, the University of Michigan, and the University of Texas at Austin.

The Soviet government, which might have made an international fuss about Kenny "stealing" their TV signal, responded sympathetically to the American Orbita. "They were so surprised that for the first time Americans had gone to so much trouble to learn about their people and their culture," Ken says. In 1986, Ken Schaffer received a contract from the Soviet Union, giving his company exclusive rights to Soviet TV for educational use in America.

Ken has also been instrumental in setting up space-bridges, an arrangement via two-way large-screen video and translators, where groups of ordinary American and Soviet citizens can talk informally with each other. He can't understand why his little company has been the leader, or why some big outfit like AT&T doesn't "reach out and see someone," as he puts it. "I'd like all the people around the world to look at each other," he says, "with AT&T equipment. I don't feel selfish about it. If a wonderful idea is done, I don't care who gets paid what."

For Ken Schaffer, former rock and roll hedonist transformed into an enthusiast for world peace, money is not the object. In that respect, he's the same guy he always was, out for sensation rather than security. He still despises boredom and craves constant challenge.

But where he finds those sensations and gets that challenge has changed. Today he's serious about Marina, the woman in his life (only one, please notice, and she's a woman, not a girl), who is a specialist in Russian studies. And the current challenge that matters most to Ken is the enormous task of creating, bit by bit, universal, international sympathy among people on opposite sides of the globe. Space-bridges change the feelings of people about each other, Kenny says. Audiences in Moscow and in San

Francisco can cry together and laugh together, and "that little microsecond exchange is more important than all the books. Let the hawks in America, let the Joint Chiefs of Staff, look at the children dancing in Russia. Then they'll think twice about what they're doing, maybe."

"We're all bozos on this bus," Ken says, warming to his theme. "Moscow's fucked up, and Washington's fucked up. And if we would just all meet each other on that premise and shake hands: 'Hello, I'm a bozo.' 'Hello, I'm a bozo, too.' I mean, the most important thing we can do, after all, is to keep the species going."

Innovators like Rachel and Kenny often adopt and perfect a bifocal vision. They are able to pull together the demands of personal satisfaction and the headier rewards that come with making a contribution to the species. The ordinary person has a single vision at a time, a narrow view of life's opportunities. The bifocal vision of the innovator casts new light on dim, gray areas in life that an ordinary person might overlook or find uninteresting. The innovator brings those areas into sharper focus, drenches them in vibrant color, and *voilà!* they become possibilities for the "what else." Addition rather than subtraction, restoration rather than demolition, "both-and" rather than "either-or" distinguish the innovator. By asking "What else?," innovators attempt to reconcile their opposites in the elegant confines of a single existence. The opposite makes the opposite.

12

A Patchwork Life

If other innovators have bifocal vision, Martha Ritter's vision is at least trifocal. A potent social conscience commands her to work to make the world better. An energetic creativity enjoins her to write and to act. A healthy common sense bids her to support herself along the way. Reconciling these opposite urges has led Martha to adopt an ingenious and surprising plan of action for her life. To use her own metaphor, Martha is busily and deliberately making "a patchwork life."

Like a quilt, Martha's career consists of colorful but apparently random pieces. So filled with opposites is the vibrant patchwork of her life that it's hard to believe that one woman, still short of her fortieth birthday, can have done all the things

225

that Martha has done. At nineteen, she wrote and published an eyewitness account of the Soviet invasion of Czechoslovakia. Subsequently, she studied poetry with Robert Lowell and drama with Uta Hagen. Later, Martha served as a drama therapist for long-term psychiatric patients. In Peking during the Cultural Revolution, she helped train Chinese workers, peasants, and soldiers to be teachers of English.

More recently, she was at various times a writer for the Vera Institute of Justice and the Ford Foundation. In burned-out buildings in U.S. cities, Martha has interviewed scores of welfare women. In the halls of Congress, she has talked to Indians, Eskimos, and legislators about land issues in Alaska. Now a city planning executive in Manhattan, Martha has also written a novel, turned down a role on Broadway, and appeared on television as a prudish librarian swept off her feet by pimiento loaf.

"Pimiento loaf?" I ask, trying not to raise my eyebrows.

"I act in commercials to support myself," Martha says. "But, I know, it does lead to bizarre juxtapositions." A glowing American beauty with rich brown hair and a happy, open face, Martha, in a linen suit, a silk blouse, and pumps, is smartly dressed for this warm April day. She laughs heartily as she explains that while she was gathering material for her important study, *Alaska: A Last Great First Chance,* a lawmaker asked, "Tell me, why are you also selling deodorant on television?"

"That's when it comes home to you," Martha says, "that you are living two or three incredibly different lives at the same time. And whom do you disclose what to, and when, about what you are actually doing with the rest of your time?"

Sometimes Martha is daring in her revelations. Once, when three men were interviewing her for a writing job, one of them asked about her acting career. Responding to his interest, Martha told the interviewers that she had just come from an audition for a horror movie in which worms take over the world. The three were enthralled.

"Worms! How did you handle your queasiness about doing scenes with worms?" one of the men asked.

So Martha passed on the director's tip. "Martha," the director had advised her, "just think spaghetti, and keep thinking spaghetti." The interviewers were highly amused. Martha got the writing job.

In this case, Martha's variety was a plus. Some people like to know that "not everybody's living in a box," Martha says—that they are hiring a person with "a little bit of perspective and a little imagination and a little experience. Sometimes they want to welcome somebody like that aboard their ship." With other people, Martha feels she has to conceal part of herself so that her expertise as a writer in the field of social change or as an actress in legitimate theater will get a serious reception.

In her flexibility and her chameleon-like talent for negotiating change, Martha is very much her parents' daughter. Change is "really a fixture" in her family. Both parents are Quakers. They met at Yale, where Martha's mother was studying in the Divinity School and her father in the Law School. The idealistic young couple married and decided to make their home in Hartford, Connecticut, a smallish city where they thought they could make a difference in the quality of community life. Martha, the only girl, is the oldest of their five children.

Even before marriage, each of Martha's parents was already intent on bettering society. As a teenager, Martha's mother had traveled around the country speaking out for pacificism and against America's involvement in World War II. A sociologist and teacher, in the decades to follow she became a Freedom Rider and a member of the first Civil Rights Commission in Connecticut. Martha's father, a lawyer, was a vigorous opponent of McCarthyism and a labor sympathizer who organized some of the first municipal unions in Connecticut. During the McCarthy era, he was almost denied admission to the bar on grounds of character because of his and his wife's liberal leanings.

Thus, Martha grew up in a volatile household, peopled with her parents' causes. One night the Hartford firemen would be on hand, arguing vigorously about union strategy. The next night would turn up a group of homeless German refugees, half of whom would take up temporary residence under the Ritter roof. Mr. Ritter was in elective office, first in the city council, then in the state legislature. Every two years, the family braced itself for another election, and political aides and supporters were always in and out of the house.

When Martha was in high school, her parents picked a single, important, civil rights issue that they could devote their time to: housing. Together, they organized a nonprofit housing organization to help minority people find homes in some of the most exclusive suburbs in the country, some of which had never had a black or a Jew living in their environs. Mr. Ritter solicited contributions from anonymous donors for down payments on homes. Meanwhile, Mrs. Ritter got a real estate broker's license and started buying up houses.

"This was a time," Martha says, "when if you showed up with a black, the seller had a right not to sell you the house." Mrs. Ritter would take a "beard," a white friend pretending to be an ordinary home buyer. As Mrs. Ritter became better known, she would disguise herself with wigs, costumes, and fake accents. Even so, on a couple of occasions homeowners waved her and her "client" away with guns. So Martha grew up with people calling in the middle of the night and threatening to kill her radical father for his progressive politics, with people pulling guns on her mother, and, always, with a great parade of diverse people coming through the family home.

Martha describes herself as a very good political daughter, lively and talkative. "Perhaps because I was the only girl, perhaps because I'm the oldest, I took it upon myself to be a gracious hostess person even at a very young age," she says. Yet, privately, Martha suffered from some ambivalence about her role. Her feeling of being overloaded with the concerns of others often spurred the little girl to withdraw into a private, creative part of herself. Almost from the time she could write, she began composing stories and poems for her own amusement; soon she began acting, as well. She needed this personal antidote to her parents' overweening social involvement.

Her family encouraged Martha's activities, whatever they were; they urged her to "follow her own star." Mr. and Mrs. Ritter were loving, liberal, permissive parents. In their house, for example, what would have been the dining room "for more civilized people," as Martha says, was turned into a children's hangout. The Ritters replaced the built-in china closet with a ladder and a platform. They had the walls covered with a special surface so the children could write all over them. Bikes and pets were allowed, and so were friends, lots of friends; all the kids in the neighborhood congregated in the Ritters' big dining room.

On the other hand, Martha longed for a lawn like other families had. The Ritters' front yard was so worn down from the constant bombardment of people coming and going that it was actually lower than the sidewalk and had no grass. "That front yard really bothered me after a while," Martha says. "I knew it was an emblem of some kind of wonderful tolerance and individuality, but I also knew that other people might see it as negligence even though it was really just the opposite. Resolving that confusion was difficult for me." Often Martha had the same kind of double feeling about her parents, that they were "amazing, unique, crazy people who reached out to everyone"—and that they could be completely misunderstood by others.

How do you rebel against a rebel family, a family which itself turns convention on its ear? Unlike most of the innovators I interviewed, in being a maverick herself Martha is following a well-established family tradition. Her brothers, too, have followed their parents' pattern. Two are politicians, and two are writers, but all have tried to incorporate a diversity in their lives. One went to divinity school, then became a lawyer. Another, who is a writer, is also clerk of the Connecticut House of Representatives. A brother who is a playwright is getting a doctorate in English, but hopes to teach in Japan. Other innovators describe their family backgrounds as safe, secure, stable, even (the most common complaint) boring. Martha's family is never boring.

Even today, approaching seventy, her parents continue to make radical changes in their lives. After serving as a presidential appointee on the National Housing Partnership and as chairman of a real estate investment trust in New York City, Mrs. Ritter turned her attention to China, and has started a foundation to bring Chinese citizens to this country for study. Mr. Ritter spent three years trying to start a newspaper in Hartford. When his efforts failed, undaunted, he created an alternate energy corporation to try to cut down on energy consumption and costs. Neither of Martha's parents is doing what he or she was doing ten years ago, or most likely will be doing ten years from now.

"It's just amazing," Martha says. "Every time I go home there's a whole different set of books around. In order to rebel, I would have to be the most defined, integrated, conventional person that ever lived." There was a time, soon after college, when Martha made up her mind to be just that kind of person.

First, however, came a succession of changes more typical of her family pattern. After graduating with honors from Radcliffe in the class of 1970, Martha took the money she had saved working as a waitress, a reporter, and a camp counselor and went to England. There she studied poetry for a while with Robert Lowell, who had been one of her teachers in college. During this period, she was also taking acting lessons in London, and sending articles about her experiences abroad to a newspaper back in the States. For the next two years, she traveled and wrote, drifting into a series of adventures. "I didn't know what I wanted," she says. "I was on a search."

At length, "my whole body revolted against this kind of extended adolescence." Her periods stopped. She had terrible gastric pains, which sent her into hospitals in two different countries. At Oxford, while she was being interviewed for an advanced degree program—another of her big plans—her eye suddenly started bleeding. "Several dons were interviewing me," she says, "with, you know, 'Well, my dear, tell us about Dickens's grandmother,' and a tear of blood started rolling down my cheek." She was rushed to the hospital, where the diagnosis was uncertain. Needless to say, the tears of blood ended all thought of an advanced degree.

Next, Martha went to Israel. She had signed up to participate in an archeological dig. In Israel, excruciating headaches sent her again into a hospital. There she was, surrounded by youthful Israeli soldiers wounded in battle, and once again the diagnosis for her own illness was inconclusive. Martha began to believe that her numerous physical ailments, while very real, were also psychosomatic. Her body, she decided, was trying to send her a message of some kind. But what was the message?

In a very confused state of mind, she came out of the hospital and clambered back into the hole where she and the others were chipping away at the accumulated centuries of rock and dirt. "But, you know," Martha tells me, laughing that infectious laugh of hers again, "when you work on one of those digs you almost never find anything. I didn't find a damn thing. And it was hot and dusty, and you just take off one little layer of sand every ten days.

"And one day I looked up and I said to myself, 'What the hell am I doing in this hole? I'm twenty-two years old, and I haven't even begun my life yet." She had suddenly gotten the message, she felt sure. It was a message that required her to break with the family pattern of constant change and to limit herself to a single occupation. "I can't be an archeologist and a journalist and a poet and an actress," she told herself. "I have to choose one life."

Martha climbed out of the hole, came back to America, and began professional training as an actress. She could always write poetry on her own, she knew, but if she really wanted to act, it was now or never. So, for the next several years, she studied dance and voice and acting with a variety of teachers, including Uta Hagen. As she worked to perfect what theater people call "the instrument," her physical problems subsided, perhaps because "just having a home base" in a profession stabilized her.

At the same time, however, she could not bring herself to relinquish the involvement in social issues that was part of her family history. She could not, at any rate, support herself as an actress, so she made a living by turning her pen to good causes. Martha worked as a writer and general editor for the Vera Institute of Justice in New York, then as a staff writer at the Ford Foundation. Next came a stint as a consultant and writer for the Manpower Demonstration Research Corporation. At MDRC, Martha interviewed welfare mothers across the country. Her findings, which culminated in a study called *After Supported Work: Conversations with Former AFDC Participants,* led Martha to believe strongly in the possibility of deliberate and positive change for almost any life. "Given the opportunity to work at a job where the first day they didn't have to be perfect, these women started to flower," Martha says, beaming at the recollection of the "monumental transitions in the inner lives of these women" which she recorded for posterity.

Meanwhile, Martha was learning more about her own inner life through psychoanalysis, which she began at the age of twenty-three. In spite of her devotion to acting, she was still spreading herself thin between the theater and her social work. Although the two fed into each other to some extent, as a consequence of her analysis, Martha decided to make an effort to unify her life and her activities. "You can't continue living life on electric roller skates," her analyst told her. "The human vessel can take only so much."

So Martha took off her roller skates. Though she continued to work on the MDRC project, she applied herself even more diligently to moving up in the ranks of the theater. She had begun with a "dilettante's delight" in acting. The discipline required of a serious actor, however, seemed to her "the best kind of training you could get to live a generalist's life." Learning to read both a text and a person, to consider both individual motivation and social interaction, Martha saw acting as a center that would lend itself to pursuits in the world beyond the stage. She liked her work, and she became accomplished and successful in off-Broadway and television productions.

Then, in 1979, against heavy competition, Martha auditioned for a role in a Broadway play. The part was small and involved some nudity, but if she got it she would be working with Maggie Smith, an actress whose work Martha admired very much. After an anxious time of waiting for the results of the auditions, Martha learned that the role was hers if she wanted it.

That same afternoon, the postman brought an invitation for Martha to teach English in Peking. Her job: to make college English teachers out of the peasants, workers, and soldiers who were being brought up from their rice fields and military barracks and educated to replace what Mao had termed the "decadent intellectuals" as the new leaders of China. Martha's family training came to the fore. "I grew up with a feeling," she says, "that the grandest and most fulfilling thing you can do with your life is to try to help out, to fill in the cracks in the mortar of humanity." But—Maggie Smith! Broadway!

For twenty-four soul-searching hours, Martha contemplated the choice before her. She called her theatrical agent for advice. "You'd be crazy to turn this Broadway part down," he said. "Look, no one's going to know what you did in this play, but that doesn't matter. What matters is that you've got that credit—on Broadway, with Maggie Smith. You've got to go through the motions and get that on your résumé."

"But I can't live my life for the next line on my résumé," Martha thought. At that moment, she knew she had already decided to go to China. "I realized that in turning down the Broadway role I wasn't being true to that organizing, integrating impulse that a grownup was supposed to have, and which I had tried so hard to cultivate. In a way, I felt defeated by my own impulsiveness in making that decision.

"Yet how could I resist going to China where I could experience the opposite side of the world, and a totally different way of life, at the same time that I was helping some of these people who were starting to go down the drain after the Cultural Revolution?" Peking, with the appeal of the opposite, the double seduction of adventure and usefulness, was irresistible. Martha was, she decided ruefully, in spite of everything, her parents' child.

The intuitive desire to go to China brought home to Martha the realization that, regardless of what others thought, she would consider herself a failure if, as her analyst advised, she lived only the integrated, "beeline life" of the professional actress. She realized that the analyst was right, that she couldn't have a thousand lives, or a hundred lives, or even ten lives. But Martha also believed that, if she were to be "very careful and very discriminating, I could lead more than one life. I could take off my electric roller skates, but keep on my running shoes."

She needs those running shoes. Martha Ritter refers to her life today as one of more or less constant transitions. "It's not so much that my life was on a continuum and suddenly there was a blip on the screen, as that it is one big quilt. The changes I've made in the past are pieces in the quilt. Now, as I get older, I can go from one patch to another without losing any of them."

In this respect, Martha is not only the child of her innovative and pioneering parents, but also of her time, influenced by the spirit of her generation. In an article, "Echoes from the Age of Relevance," which she wrote for *Harvard Magazine* in 1981, Martha describes the members of her own class of 1970 as leading postgraduate lives of "an awesome fluidity." Reading through the autobiographical reports mailed back to Harvard, she discovered that her classmates "weave in and out of drastically disparate worlds with ease" and "blur the borders of vocation and avocation, pleasure and obligation." She attributes this "searching quality" and "mobility of Odyssean proportions" to the enormous social changes that took place in America as her generation stepped into adulthood.

"When we first got to college," she tells me, "people were still having candlelit dinners and wearing high heels. At Harvard, we women weren't allowed into the library to study—only men were. By the time we left, four years later, everything had changed. That loosening of the underpinnings of tradition affected us, and still affects us. A lot of people my age have felt free to do things that if they had been born five years earlier would not have been part of the picture."

The whole generation refuses, whenever possible, to leave anything out of their lives. They famously want to have it all. As Martha puts it, "When I was very socially involved with welfare reform or something, I would be aware that something having to do with my own creativity was not being used. And yet it's also not enough for me to sit alone and commune with my computer or to act in a play once in a while. After a time, I miss contact with other human beings and the feeling of being socially useful."

For Martha, the desire to have it all was heightened by an accident which she suffered in 1983. Walking down Broadway, she was hit on the head by a brick that fell twenty-one stories from a building undergoing repair. Her spine was compressed and the pain in her back was excruciating. She lost part of the skeletal support system so that, for a time, she was unable to hold her head up. Martha wore a neck brace for six months, and had to undergo more than two years of intensive physical therapy. "It took all of my discipline for a while," she says, "just to make my head stand up right."

Even more frightening was the fact that she lost pockets of her visual memory, an awful loss for a writer or an actor. Martha could read words, for example, but "they made no sense to me. I was absolutely terrified that something irreversible had happened to my brain." Though she has since recovered, the accident inevitably highlighted her sense of mortality, which in turn made her less inclined than ever to miss out on what life offers. So Martha is constantly moving from project to project in her patchwork life, refusing to leave anything out or any talent unexplored.

The transitions from one patch to another can be difficult. For example, beginning in 1984, Martha worked as Director of Public Affairs for the New York City Department of City Planning. She was up at six every morning, leaving home before daylight

234

and returning after dark, to fall into bed exhausted. With all her systems on "Go" and all of her adrenaline running, Martha was on five phones at once, talking to cronies at the water cooler or coffee machine, caught up in the issues of the day, reading every city paper.

But the job had wonderful compensations. "Exhausted as you are, there is a feeling that every part of you is being used to the hilt—your ability to make quick decisions, to analyze something politically, to zero in on an issue, to put a reporter in his place, to decipher a complicated city contract, whatever."

The one thing that wasn't being used was her own creativity. So after two years in City Planning, Martha decided to leave, "to honor my creative juices" by writing a novel. In her new life, which she supported by acting in television commercials, there were problems and adjustments. "Everything looks and feels different; the whole day is a different kind of experience." Living alone, she had to learn to get up, go to her computer, get her own juices flowing.

What was even harder was learning to stop at a reasonable time every day. When we talked, Martha had just spent four days writing nearly nonstop, pausing only long enough to eat and sleep. "When I stopped writing to come for this interview," she says, "I went outside and it was like I was on the moon. The person who less than a year ago was in touch with every heartbeat of the city was suddenly on the moon."

So it's not the lack of discipline that is most difficult for her in her transitions. "It's somehow finding the most integrated way of living each one of these lives," Martha says, "finding a balance. When these bridges from one state to another are continually part of your life, there's always a period when it's like learning to walk again."

Often, she needs a month or two to make the transition. As she "decompressed" from the job at City Planning, Martha felt an extreme relief—"like coming home, like coming back to a place where I could look at things more closely, and hear voices in a different way. But I missed the community that develops over a job, where you know everybody's moods and it's a kind of family. I do love that, and I missed it terribly. At first, I thought I'd made a mistake in gauging my flexibility at this point in my life.

"But as the gears began to shift, a part of me that had been totally dead for two years started to open up. And I thought, 'Oh, yes, I knew I had to do this.' Then I started to feel why."

Another difficulty Martha has with the transitions from opposite to opposite is the loss of status which often occurs. When she was in the Department of City Planning, people would sit by the phone waiting for her to return their call. As an unpublished novelist making her living selling products on television, she may be one of a hundred people to audition to sell cat food. There's also a certain confusion about her identity. For a while, when the phone rang she had no idea who would be on the line —"a reporter asking about city politics, my television agent telling me about a cereal commercial, my literary agent saying, 'How's the writing going?' It could have been anybody."

A third difficulty is the loss of success in the eyes of the world. People often don't understand why Martha doesn't want to climb one ladder or another, in city politics or into the Broadway sky. But, to live as Martha does, you have to be willing to give up that kind of verticality for a breadth of experience. Martha doesn't mind, she says, that such people don't consider her a success. "I know I'm disciplined and compulsive enough to get up a few rungs on most ladders, so it doesn't bother me when somebody says, 'Isn't it a pity that she's not mayor yet?' I've gotten beyond that. But for some reason I do mind if somebody thinks I'm a flake."

She consoles herself by recalling her parents' reaction to a concern she had once in college. In the beginning of her Radcliffe years, Martha was studying government and had plans eventually to run for Congress. Then at a certain point, as she puts it, "this political, government-studying person began to write poetry and to act." With real dismay, Martha went to her parents and said, "Look what's happening to me—I may not be socially useful!"

"Sweetheart," her parents told her, "look at Morris Cohen in the state legislature. He's a dentist. It's just a *part* of his life to be socially useful, and it can be just a *part* of *your* life. You don't have to be changing the world every minute of the day."

"But I still have not reached the point where I don't feel I have to explain why the hell I'm doing what I'm doing," Martha says.

"Because I'm a serious person, and I want to be taken seriously."

Serious, yes. Inquisitive. Flexible. Resourceful. A curious contradiction, Martha is an organized, disciplined risk-taker, "an incredible gambler," she calls herself, forcing herself to climb out on one narrow ledge after another in her ongoing determination to lead what she calls "a hyphenated life."

Does such a life include a husband and a family? Martha had not found her mate for life when we talked. "I want a traditional family," she says, "but I don't really know what I will do if I am not madly in love and married when my last eggs are screaming to be employed creatively." But Martha has a legion of friends—actors, writers, journalists, political friends, and all-purpose friends. Somewhere in that circle of connections there's sure to be the friend of a friend.

In the meantime, her life goes well because Martha wills it to. "I have a working relation with my life. If you're marching to a different drummer or if you're your own drummer, as I am, you may not be able to keep the drum in perfect shape, but you damn well better make sure you don't drop it in quicksand. I do seem to lead a life of extremes; exhilaration and terror are both a part of it."

Martha bears both the exhilaration and the terror with a kind of fortitude learned from her Quaker parents. "Quakers use the term 'inner light.' That notion has given meaning to 'following my own star,' but has also reinforced my feeling that every person on this earth has some worth. So I have a sense of responsibility for others, and I think I've developed a fortitude for meeting life head-on."

If her parents are perhaps the single greatest influence on her life, Martha also cites her former teacher, the poet Robert Lowell. "I was very close to him. He encouraged me to honor my own creativity, to listen to my own drumbeat. He had done that. He had been a conscientious objector, trying to change things in the world. And yet he also was the most incredibly private person, living in his imagination to an extraordinary extent. He taught me that in following my own star, I didn't have to lose touch with the planet Earth."

The randomness of Martha's patchwork life is more apparent than real. Martha knows what she's doing, and it is one of the primary tasks of humankind. All human beings must, like Martha, learn to bring opposites into cohesion. Men and women are not things, to be identified, as they often reductively are, by a single social function: "He's a doctor." "She's a lawyer." A person can change functions—"She's a lawyer, she's Jim's wife, she's Tommy's mother, and she's my best friend"—without sacrificing that essential essence, the self.

> We are things thrown in the air
> alive in flight . . .
> our rust the color of the chameleon.

Robert Lowell wrote those lines from *Day by Day* during the years Martha studied with him. Martha Ritter is living them. When Martha, "alive in flight," moves from writer to actress to urban planner, she defies the rust of disuse with her chameleon color. Deliberately, she forces herself to bring opposite skills and sides of her personality into play.

We define our humanity by the spontaneity and ingenuity with which we integrate our opposites as we fly high in the creative process of living. By that definition, Martha is supremely human.

Developing an Independent Ego

With imagination and courage,
innovators break with convention
and overcome obstacles
in order to follow
their dreams.

13

Getting Off Your Herculon

All the skills which we've been talking about so far in Part Two—accepting the constancy of change, listening to the inner voice, recognizing and exploring opposites—begin internally, in the psyche of the innovator. None of these skills would be sufficient for an external change in an innovator's way of life without a fourth skill. In order to "follow your own star" in the way you actually live, you must forge a strong, independent ego.

Can an ego be developed? Can you create an identity, a sense of yourself, which is sufficient to defy convention, inertia, even your own past? The innovators I talked to believe you can. This is not to say that genes, fortune, the unconscious, the *Zeitgeist*, and other unseen forces have not helped to shape the life and the personality that you have today. But an innovator sees "today" as just one stage in the continual process of becoming. You can exert some control over that process by taking charge of yourself. You can earn the life you want by being the person who deserves such a life, by creating yourself anew in an image you admire.

The trick lies, some say, in a consciously cultivated optimism. Hope to change yourself and the world, and change will come. After the disaster of the 1987 space shuttle explosion, Mark Jacobson, who writes a column on ethics for *Esquire,* chose to become an optimist instead of a cynic. Seeing that capsule in flames, he said, "knocks the swagger right out of you." Jacobson felt he could no longer afford his attitude of fashionable cynicism. In defiance of the image of failure looming triumphant on television screens across America, Jacobson voted to support hopefulness instead.

"Truthfully, I feel a little sheepish," he wrote in his July 1987 column, "sitting here telling you 'that's when I stopped being a cynic.' Nevertheless, I believe it." He simply gave up cynicism, a longtime habit of mind which he came to see as destructive.

A personality shift, Jacobson went on to say, like any other change, occurs in stages, and his shift from cynicism to optimism is not entirely complete. "I'm not contemplating embroidering a sampler that says LIFE IS TOO SHORT TO LIVE IT AS A CYNIC. In my dream of myself, I'm still striking all the *noir* poses. In fact, I've got plenty of skepticism left over to distrust a light too easily seen."

Nevertheless, using obvious, seventies consciousness-raising methods at which, in his cynical days, he would certainly have sneered, Jacobson admits that he is working at shedding his cynicism. To imagine a happy ending for the human race and for your own life, he says, "If you've got to con yourself, substitute the word *hope* for *death* in a made-up equation, you do it." In just such ways, the innovator creates an ego strong and independent enough to brook opposition.

Often opposition even helps create a strong, independent ego. Prynn Kaplan, a former dancer who supported herself for years by waiting tables in a restaurant, told me that when she began her own construction company in 1978, her mother's voice spurred her on. "How sweet," I said. Not exactly sweet, it turned out. What Prynn kept hearing her mother say was "When are you going to admit that you're in way over your head?"

"Well, if you ask me that," Prynn says, "I'm not going to admit I'm in over my head *ever*. My mother probably helped me more than anything else by always being negative."

Prynn's mother, who is dead now, was a housewife. She thought of jobs for women in terms of a forties movie. The heroine gets dressed up, goes in to "the office" wearing white gloves and looking pretty. She goes out for lunch with the boss, whom she marries in the last frame of the film. She never really has to work. But her new company had Prynn bossing a construction crew, heading off to a building site at 6 A.M. in a hardhat and coveralls, and spending the day and most of the night surrounded by male carpenters, electricians, and plumbers. Surely, Prynn's mother reasoned, a construction company was a man's business.

Prynn's friends, the other members of her family, and most of the rest of the country would have agreed. "Everyone thinks it's such a big deal I'm in construction," Prynn says. "If I were a man, no one would pay any attention. But I knew I had to do my job right, or admit I was just another dabbling female. Their opposition created a situation where I really had to come through."

Prynn has come through. When I interviewed her in 1987, her North River Construction Company in Manhattan had grossed well over $500,000 for the previous year. Prynn herself has earned respect with her "man's business." "I'm a lot more professional than most of the men I deal with," she says, "just because I don't want them to say, 'Well, what do you expect? She's a woman.' And some of them—the electricians, for example—were a little hostile to me in the beginning. But if you do your part—well, I'm their discovery now."

Yet Prynn did not set out to prove a feminist credo, and her path to success in a field regarded as almost exclusively male she describes as "circuitous." Prynn began a dance career at fifteen as a summertime Rockette, and danced professionally for the next ten years. But she was on her own financially at an early age, and "you can't make a living as a dancer." She started waitressing to pay her bills, working mostly in businessmen's lunch places. The hours were short—in by eleven, out by three—and with her long legs, her dancer's body, and her pretty face, Prynn made good tips.

When she was twenty-five and coming out of an unsuccessful marriage, Prynn had a twofold awakening. First, she realized that as a dancer she was "remarkably untalented. I got a lot of jobs but I think it was more because of my looks and because I was a nice girl than because of my dance technique. I just never was going to be a great dancer." Nor did she want to be, as she says, "a forty-year-old diner waitress, with a name tag. It's cute when you're twenty, but it's getting a little less precious when you're twenty-five." For her ego's sake, Prynn knew that she had to find a job which would give her a feeling of self-esteem. "What do I know about? What am I interested in?" she asked herself.

For two generations, the men in her family had been builders. Her father was in high-rise construction, though he never had his own firm. Her grandfather, whose pet she had always been, was an architect and builder. From the time she was a child, Prynn loved to hang around construction sites. She "helped" her grandfather on all of his projects, and learned to read building plans "really before I could read words. I thought everybody could."

And she had done some building projects on her own. When she was still small, she had reconstructed her bedroom, and built tree houses and huts. In college, where she was self-supporting, to make ends meet Prynn often had to move into a wreck of an apartment. Because beautiful surroundings were important to her, she would take out interior walls, rehang doors to fit, make repairs, spackle, plaster, patch, and paint. "I was a real boon to landlords," she says, laughing. But her family did these things the way other families mow the lawn. That is, the *men* in her family did. Originally, Prynn trimmed her ambitions to fit her sex. She enrolled at Parsons School of Design in New York, and for the next six years she practiced the trade of interior designer.

She practiced first at home, where things were tough for a while. Prynn had gone into her marriage wanting conventional things—a beautiful home, a garden—and expecting her husband to give them to her. When her marriage failed, she gave up her "Cinderella and the prince syndrome," as she calls it, and determined to get what she wanted for herself. For peanuts, she took a longterm lease on a loft in TriBeCa. The place, in the heart of a desolate, undeveloped neighborhood, had been abandoned for ten years. It had no plumbing, no electricity, no heat. Prynn invited her brother to move in with her. They got the plumbing in, and her brother moved in on the bottom floor, while Prynn took the top. They planned to do together what was needed to make the place livable.

Her brother cut a giant hole in the wall to provide access to the roof, but when the weather turned cold he headed for warmer climes. Prynn stuck it out. She paid a plumber a large—for her—sum up front, but he never put in the heating. Then she hired a second plumber, who neglected to tell her that gas lines couldn't be run through frozen ground. He, too, took her money, piddled around, then ran off on the job. "It was awful!" Prynn recalls. "Freezing cold, in an abandoned neighborhood. It was really frightening."

On one occasion, the pipes burst and water began pouring through the ceiling. As Prynn tried to sweep the water down the stairs, "to dissipate this lake on my floor, the drops hit the wall and froze into little ice cubes." Another night the police banged loudly on the downstairs door to question her about a murder down the street. When Prynn came to the door alone, the police were alarmed for her safety. "Get out of here," they told her. "You're going to get killed. You're going to get raped and robbed and murdered." Prynn went back upstairs, climbed into bed with all her clothes on, and shivered till morning, listening for the murderer.

Why didn't she give up and move back to the family home on Long Island, I ask?

She grins that eternally optimistic grin. "I certainly wouldn't give up *then*," Prynn tells me. "Things were so bad, I knew they had to get better."

Soon her first big break came. A friend had just become the president of a union and wanted to redo the executive offices. "Please use me," Prynn begged him. "Putting himself on the line," as Prynn says, her friend agreed to let the fledgling designer have the job. "I know that you would hurt yourself before you would hurt me," he told her.

The job, which took a year, was an incredible boon. Because

she was doing it for a trade union, she worked with the best craftsmen in the city, and gained a great deal of expertise herself. When she had finished redoing the offices successfully, two of the union's lawyers hired her for jobs. That led to jobs for clients of the lawyers, then for friends of the clients. With that kind of word-of-mouth promotion, Prynn was off with a bang as an interior designer.

Her entry into construction work was not calculated. As she worked, Prynn became aware of the costly errors that other interior designers made. Putting in a sub-floor, for example, one experienced designer actually tiled in the whole bottom of a dishwasher. When the dishwasher broke down, full of dishes, the client had to call the carpenters back in to tear up the kitchen in order to get the dishwasher out. Expensive, but avoidable, if the designer had known anything about construction.

As a principle, Prynn had decided in the beginning that she would never charge a client for mistakes she made. She realized that she would make plenty of mistakes unless she learned enough about construction to do a job from beginning to end. So, on every job, she made a point of studying the basic construction as she planned the design. After six years of learning, Prynn, with a male partner who had a few tools, opened North River Construction Company.

The first two years were extraordinarily difficult. The company had zero assets. With the minuscule profits from one job, Prynn and Al, her partner, bought tools for the next job. Prynn never turned down work, however difficult it looked. "Sure, we can do that," she would tell the prospective client optimistically. "I'm a real good faker"—she laughs—"but once you've faked yourself into the situation, then you have to do it. So I would call twenty people, and run all over the city on subways, then stay up all night reading books, to find out how."

When at length she fell asleep, even her dreams most nights were construction dreams. Disastrous things happened in her head all night long. She would close up a wall, and water would start pouring out. Prynn would look for the valve, and there'd be no valves, and she'd be lost in an endless basement, like a labyrinth. And she'd take a subway to the plumber's, but he wouldn't be there, and she wouldn't have any money to get back to the

246

job. And all this time, she knew the water was still pouring out of the wall, flooding every apartment in the building and "they were all going to sue me."

As the head of a construction company, Prynn had two obstacles to overcome. One, "probably the biggest obstacle," was her own naïveté about the business world and what she calls "people's sense of honor." Just as she had been taken by two plumbers at home, she found herself being taken at work also. "I had never believed that anyone would just look you in the eye and screw you. It was a terrible shock to find out that they would. I spent at least six months being very personally hurt that the world wasn't like I thought it was." Then she forced herself to address the situation realistically rather than as a symptom of metaphysical unfairness or degeneracy.

The other obstacle was purely practical. Prynn had no experience with business methods. Since she didn't know the conventional systems for running an office and hiring labor, making estimates, submitting bids, and billing, she had to make up all the systems as she needed them. Fifteen different trades may be involved in a big construction job. The company is contracted to build exactly what's on the plans, but there are myriad changes as the job goes along. Somehow, the construction boss has to keep track of everybody's work, everybody's price, the additions and credits to that price, in order to come in on budget. Learning how to do these things was a huge challenge, but one Prynn met successfully. After nine years, she still uses the same methods, and she's never bothered to ask how a "real construction man" like her father would do it.

As the only woman in her firm—Prynn even has a male secretary—she has brought to the boss's role what may be a feminine interest or skill in suiting the person to the job. At the time she makes her estimate, she is "already figuring which one of my little darlings is going to do which thing. People are just different. If you figure out who's best at what task, your employees will be happier, and you'll be happier, because you'll make more money."

Are the eight to ten men in her employ really her "little darlings," I ask? Prynn's answer is unequivocal. "It's like working with my brothers or something. I mean, they fire me all the time, and hoot my decisions down. But they're sweet and good, and I think they feel kindly toward me. It's a real good company; we do a good job."

Prynn no longer has "construction dreams," but she does dream of other construction. So far, all of her work has been interior renovation. She would like to take on the larger challenge of renovating whole buildings, inside and out. What she doesn't want is a larger company. She's wise enough about herself to know that she wants the stimulation of hands-on work. "I really love building stuff," she says. "I don't want to become a corporation owner rather than a contractor."

Blessed though she is with a strong ethical sense, Prynn says that she is not at all religious. She likes the here and now, things you can touch, and she's too independent to turn her life over to God. "That's not my idea of a good plan of action at all." Her ego is strong enough to make her optimistic about a future she builds herself. "I turned forty last week," she tells me, "and I have big plans for my fortieth year."

Life, Prynn theorizes, is a little like a building. You make plans for it, then you follow them. You're free, of course, to change the plans as often as you need to. But you'll never get anywhere, in her opinion, unless you start with plans. "Most of the people I know," Prynn says, "wait for life to happen to them. But it doesn't just happen. You make life happen. Yes, I think this is going to be a good year for me."

Prynn's talk of the efficacy of plans makes me think of that great planner, Fitzgerald's Gatsby, who is perhaps the most completely self-created hero in American literature. By the time he is ten or twelve years old, little Jimmy Gatz has already set himself on the road to becoming the rich, legendary Jay Gatsby. In the back cover of his copy of *Hopalong Cassidy,* Jimmy outlines a severe regimen for his childhood which pays attention to all the Ben Franklin virtues. Jimmy plans to set aside an hour every day of his young life to "Practice elocution, poise and how to attain it" and no less than two hours to "Study needed inventions." He'll give up "smokeing and chewing," he promises to "Be better to parents," and he'll "Read one improving book or magazine per week."

Fitzgerald knew his Americans well. The Great Gatsby has created himself, bit by bit, out of the raw folk material given to a poor child growing up at the turn of the century on the Minnesota plains. From the early evidence, Gatsby began his mysterious and enigmatic career with a vision of himself as a hero not so much akin to Hopalong Cassidy as straight out of Horatio Alger. The Horatio Alger books, in the wildly popular *Ragged Dick, Tattered Tom,* and *Luck and Pluck* series, recount the stories of poor boys who rise to greatness by the simple application of energy, honesty, and fidelity to duty, as well as, of course, Luck and Pluck.

How is greatness defined in these books? As Gatsby himself defines it—by money. Gatsby, at length, finds that Luck and Pluck are slower means to wealth than crime. To rush things along he takes as his business associate the man who fixed the 1919 World Series. Nevertheless, in spite of Gatsby's eventual failure, Gatsby's dream persists, and looms behind much of the popular culture of America today. Every boy can be rich, the dream says.

And every girl. The person closest to the innocent spirit of Gatsby whom I interviewed began life as a poor girl. Corki Feltman, a composed blonde with a resolute chin and a look of determination, came of age like Gatsby, planning her life under the influence of stories in books, "stories," she tells me, "of people who grew up without any money and didn't have any language skills or job skills, and became filthy rich. And I felt that if they could do that, I could, too. I'm not filthy rich, but I'm a lot better off than 90 percent of the people I knew three years ago."

Corki, only six months away from her fortieth birthday, is clad on this April Sunday morning in a neat pink and gray Western shirt, and pink pants. She sports a big diamond on her right hand. As we sit down to the interview, she hands me her business card which tells me she is "an independent member broker of Re/Max Associates" in Jonesboro, Georgia, as well as an "86–87 Million Dollar Club Member."

"Is money what you want most out of life?" I ask.

"I'm very into power," Corki says. "I want a lot of power, and I want money. But I don't want money for the sake of having the money; I want money for the sake of making it. I like to earn it." And she is good at earning it. The year before she closed on real estate sales totaling nearly $2 million—not bad for a girl who grew up, as she says, by the seat of her pants, who really brought herself up on the city streets of America.

The first thing Corki remembers is a beating. She was four or five years old on an excruciatingly hot afternoon in a small town in Maryland. She had been put to bed for a nap, but "it was so hot you couldn't breathe, much less sleep." Across the scorching room, her little brother, just as restless as she was, stood up in his crib, reached through the bars to the dresser, grabbed the dresser scarf, and jerked. With the scarf came a lamp, which crashed to the floor and broke.

At the noise, Corki's mother came flying into the room and snatched up, not the little boy, but Corki, lying quietly and miserably in her hot bed. "Why did you let him do that?" Corki's mother shouted. She picked Corki up by an arm and a leg and slammed her daughter into the wall. As Corki cowered in fear and shock, her mother stood over the small girl and began to beat her with angry fists.

"And my father came into the room and pulled her off me. And then they went into another room and started fighting. It was at that point," the grownup Corki says coldly, "that I decided that I did not like my mother, and that I didn't want any more to do with her, ever."

The beatings continued on a regular basis throughout Corki's childhood. "It was as though my mother was very frustrated by life, and she took it out on me." Her little brother was spared because he was "the perfect child," Corki "the bad one." Corki escaped through books, which she began to devour from the moment she learned to read "about three weeks into the first grade." Consciously or not, Corki was looking for a way out of the cramped, shabby house, the seedy working-class neighborhood, her father's drinking, and her mother's beatings. She wanted another life.

By the time Corki was ten years old, she was doing all the housework. Then when Corki was twelve, her mother died, Corki doesn't know why. Her parents had been fighting a lot. And all of a sudden Corki's mother was in the hospital.

"No one told me anything," Corki says. In spite of the treatment her mother had given her, for about three weeks Corki hung around the hospital. She would grab the doctor as he was coming out of the building and beg him to tell her what was going on. Sometimes he would stop and talk. Nobody else talked to her. "They just sort of pushed me off in a corner and forgot about me." Meanwhile, at home she was taking care of her brother and the house. Then one day her mother was dead. "It's a dreadful thing to say," Corki says, "but actually I was quite relieved. I knew that I could then take control of my own affairs."

First, however, she had to take control of the family. On the day of her mother's funeral, her father told her that she was going to have to be responsible for the house, the laundry, the cooking, and the shopping, as well as for her brother, who was an eight-year-old handful. Corki said she would. Freed of these burdens by Corki's willingness to shoulder the whole load, Corki's father started drinking "very very heavily." For days at a time he would disappear, then show up drunk, sober up, and be off again. Corki had no idea where he went or what he was doing. When he came home, he would give her a small money order. Corki soon realized that she would have to open an account at the grocery store, charge till the money order came in, then pay up. That way, she and her brother could eat until her father came home again.

Things went from bad to worse over the next three years. Corki became less and less able to handle her brother, who chased her with a baseball bat, shoved her down the stairs, and beat her up. He wouldn't go to school, and Corki couldn't make him. The money situation became so unstable that at fifteen, Corki took her first job, working after school in a pizza shop. Before long, she was making $50 or $60 a week. Corki figured that if she could make $50 a week serving pizza for few if any tips, she could make a lot more serving drinks. So she lied about her age and began working in a nearby nightclub. Her salary remained $60, but she was bringing home an additional $200 a week in tips. Almost incidentally, she dropped out of high school about the same time, at the end of the ninth grade. School bored her, and interfered with her work.

After a while, Corki took a job in another nightclub, the Pirate's Den. She started as a waitress, but before long became an unofficial manager. "They never gave me the title," Corki says, "but I just took over." In her managerial capacity, Corki, who was by now sixteen, decided the town needed live entertainment. She rounded up some local bands, and two or three nights a week she put on a floor show—that is, she became the floor show—at the Pirate's Den. Corki worked out her own exotic dance routines with which to entertain the regulars.

"I went out and bought bathing suits, and I'd attach fringe and sequins to them," she says. "I was well endowed physically, and I loved to dance. So I would just do a whole production—choose the music, hire the musicians, and set up a scenario, slow and dreamy or faster and hotter, according to my feelings of the night." Then Corki would dance. After a while, she hired another girl, Sandy, to dance with her or to spell her, but it was clearly Corki's show. By this time, Corki was sixteen going on thirty.

At home, the problems with her brother accelerated. Very angry, very hostile to the world at large and to his bossy sister in particular, the twelve-year-old boy was playing truant, shooting the windows out of people's homes, and heading toward serious scrapes with the law. Corki felt powerless to prevent the tragedy she sensed was coming. She went to the counselor at her brother's school, but the counselor dismissed what she said as sibling rivalry. On several of the rare occasions when their father showed up sober, Corki tried to talk to him about his troubled son, but her father didn't really hear a word she was saying. It seemed impossible to get help for her brother.

"The only way I'm going to get this kid out of trouble," Corki told herself, "is to leave. As long as I'm here, they'll expect me to take care of him. But if I leave, they'll have to do something." So that summer, Corki left home, going along for the ride with a Pirate's Den regular named Bob who announced one night that he was going to New York City. Her brother was uppermost in her mind, but, Corki says, "I also just wanted to see the world."

Both plans worked. Her brother was alone in the house for five days, then the authorities placed him as an abandoned child in a very structured foster home where he spent the next six years. But Corki was not to learn her brother's fate for several months.

First, she began to see the world, some of the seamier aspects of the world that, for all her maturity, she had not known existed. In New York, while Corki was waiting tables and dancing in joints, her friend Bob tried his hand at forgery. He would buy money orders at a bank in Brooklyn, change the amount, and cash them in other parts of the city. After a couple of months, the police caught up to the sloppy scam. They arrested Bob, and held Corki, who was under age, in a juvenile detention home so she could testify as a material witness at Bob's trial, which was scheduled for late the following month.

Corki spent all of her free time for the next thirty days sitting on the floor in the hall reading books from the center's library. She also attended center classes, and found that it was fun even to do math problems when there was no Pirate's Den to entice her away. The only white girl among the more than two hundred young women in the detention center, Corki was not harassed because she quickly let the others know she was tough. One day in class, a Puerto Rican girl grabbed Corki's pencil. Corki went berserk. She leaped across the table and attacked the girl and her black companion, and beat them both up. After that, nobody bothered Corki, and she was free to read and study.

At Bob's trial, Corki was a witness for the prosecution. She felt nothing toward Bob except anger that he had involved her in such a mess. Bob went to jail, and Corki went on the road, after a stop in Maryland to check on her brother. She earned her own way as she crisscrossed the country several times over the next four years. She worked as a roving photographer, as a barmaid, and, of course, as an exotic dancer, at which she became better and better. "I could start dancing," she remembers happily, "and in fifteen minutes everyone in the place would have slowed down to watch me. I was good."

Some of her friends were strippers, and they used to tell Corki that she could make a lot more money as a stripper than just as a regular dancer. They urged her to let them teach her a couple of strip routines, but "I really didn't want to do that," she says. "Dancing in a bathing suit's one thing; dancing without a bathing suit is another." By the same token, she had a relationship with only one man at a time. Nor would she accept financial help from men. "They could buy me dinner," she says. "That's about it. I always wanted to pay my own way."

By the time Corki was twenty, she had lived briefly in a total of sixteen states. At last, on her way to Florida, she stopped off to see Atlanta. One morning early she walked down Peachtree

Street, and said to herself, "Okay, this is my city. I'm staying." And stay she has, for the past twenty years.

Working in a photo studio in Atlanta as a processor, Corki was the official coffee-fetcher. As she sashayed down Peachtree one afternoon, someone tapped on the window of Number 103. Corki looked up. Behind the glass, she saw an extremely tall, debonair, good-looking man dressed in a green suit. The man motioned that he was coming out, so Corki waited for him. "I'd never seen a man in a green suit before," she explains, "and with such a perfect tie and polished shoes."

The man introduced himself. He was Winston Feltman. Would Corki go to dinner with him?

"Only if I can ask you a couple of questions first," Corki said.

"Fire away," said Winston.

So Corki asked him did he like hot tea, and he said he did. She thought that established a certain sophistication of outlook. Did he like cats, she asked? Yes, he did, his mother had two. "So we discussed cats for a few minutes." Then, because Corki hated pale white hairless men, she asked Winston, did he have a hairy chest? Why, yes, he did, he told her, laughing. "Okay," Corki said, "I'll go to dinner with you." And the two have been together ever since.

Five years after Corki and Winston married, the birth of their only child, a daughter, brought on the major change in Corki's life. Until the little girl was five, Corki stayed home to take care of her. Winston brought home the paycheck each week, and Corki, for the first time since she was fifteen, wasn't earning any money. For someone whose sense of self-worth was bound up in financial independence, the situation was intolerable. "I was deeply frustrated, very angry, very miserable," she says, remembering. "I felt demeaned because I had no money of my own."

Corki describes herself as a perfect housekeeper and a devoted mother, but when her daughter began going to kindergarten five days a week, Corki could see that neither job would take all her time. She wanted work outside the home that would fit with her daughter's school hours. She could hardly go back to exotic dancing and tending bar, so she put an ad in the paper for work cleaning houses.

Pluck and luck, that's what it took. Corki has plenty of pluck.

The luck came in the form of Arlene, a doctor's wife, who hired Corki for housecleaning three days a week, and became her best friend, her mentor, and her model for what Corki describes as "a cultured and civilized life." Arlene was the first educated, cultivated woman Corki had ever known. "She exuded class," Corki says. "When I went to work for her, my hair was chopped off just so it would be out of my way. I thought makeup was a pain in the neck. My language was coarse and vulgar."

Right away, Corki started studying Arlene to find out what made Arlene different from her. She decided that Arlene didn't have anything that she couldn't learn herself, so Corki went to work to improve herself by Arlene's example. "I studied her voice, her language, her manner of dressing, the way she lived, talked to people, carried herself, the way that she existed on earth. And I started copying her."

For example, she says, Corki noticed that Arlene said "fabric" instead of "material," "the market" rather than "the store," "physician" rather than "doctor." Arlene treated even service people with respect and dignity. She entertained easily and comfortably, and was an excellent cook. She was informed about classical music and literature, and she was more than willing, in the six and a half years that Corki worked for her, to teach Corki what she could.

"I still don't have good taste," Corki says, looking down somewhat skeptically at the pink pants she is wearing. "My taste is still questionable at times." Color was always her nemesis, she admits. "Give me a choice between three pairs of pants, one navy, one black, and one red with black stripes, and I'll go for the stripes." But with Arlene's guidance, Corki began dressing more carefully. Arlene taught her to think of clothes as an investment—to stop buying what she liked on impulse and to buy what she needed to project a certain image. "Of course," Corki says, laughing, "my 'investments' were $7.98 or $12.99, very inexpensive. But I managed to convey the image that I wanted."

Arlene taught her other things as well. The two women would sometimes carefully plan their days together. Arlene would be in the kitchen preparing for Passover or cooking for a dinner party while Corki cleaned the house. They would agree on the music they'd listen to together over lunch and "we'd have a delightful day." When Corki went home, she took with her stacks of magazines—the *New England Journal of Medicine, New Woman, Time,* whatever Arlene and her husband had finished with—as well as books Arlene pressed on her. "I've always loved music and reading," Corki says, "but she refined my taste."

This refined taste led to problems with Winston, however. Corki wanted more money. She wanted in her own life some of the things—the books, the clothes, the records, the travel—that she saw in Arlene's. Winston was already working two jobs, but even with Corki's money they were just barely making it financially. And Corki wanted a lot more. "Why don't you get a better job?" she bitched to Winston. "Why don't you make more money?"

After months of enduring her tirades about money, Winston looked hard at Corki one day and said, "Why don't you shut the fuck up? Leave me alone. If you want us to have more money, you make it. Go to real estate school."

"Winston doesn't say an awful lot ever," Corki says, "but when he does, it always has a lot of thought behind it." She knew that if Winston thought she could get a real estate license, she could do it, because he wouldn't have said so otherwise. The question was, how to pay for her schooling? The real estate course she needed would cost $700, a sum way beyond their reach.

Then she thought of the coupons. Corki started collecting coupons "like a crazy person." Corki had her mother-in-law, her sister-in-law, Arlene, her friend Jan, everybody she could think of, clipping coupons. They all saved trash—dog food labels, paper towel and toilet paper wrappers, the zip strips off the orange juice cans, everything. "You can send in ten dog food labels and get back a fifty-cent refund, that kind of thing," Corki says.

Once every two or three weeks, Corki made the rounds to collect "the trash." She took it home, sorted it, put it in boxes, until her dining room looked like a junk warehouse. She formed a coupon club with fifteen other women who got together to swap coupons. Then she opened a savings account. The teller laughed every time Corki came in to deposit her little two-dollar checks or her fifty-cent checks. "You're crazy," she told Corki. "What are you saving these little piddling things for? They'll never amount to anything."

"You just wait," Corki said. "I wouldn't tell her what I was doing, but in about six or seven months I had saved the $700 I needed, from nothing in the world but trash." She enrolled in the best real estate school in the city, "where the big shots went, on Boswell Road."

Corki was nervous about her ability to pass the course and to get her license. After all, she had only a ninth grade education, and she really didn't know how to study. She had to learn how to study before she could learn real estate, which is a very technical field, with a special vocabulary. But she loved it. "It was like I was just born," she says, "the most fascinating, wonderful, difficult thing I'd ever done in my life." Many budding realtors fail to get their license on the first try, but Corki knew that she had to pass. She couldn't afford, financially or emotionally, to fail and have to try again. If she didn't make it the first time, that was it. Corki passed, barely. She needed a seventy-five on the state exam to get her license, and she squeaked through with a seventy-six.

As a salesperson, Corki turned out to be a natural. But she also had the willingness to work harder, read more books, listen to more tapes, and pick more brains than anyone else. She began working for a firm even before her license came in the mail, carefully choosing from among her numerous job offers a company that would give her the best training. She moved early to Re/Max, which has a reputation in Georgia as the best agency in the business. Her second full year in real estate, she made $60,000; the third year, the year before we talked, her commissions totaled nearly $100,000. She wants more, more, more. "I guess I'm an extremist," she says. "Winston says I have two speeds—a hundred miles an hour, and dead."

Her pluck is self-evident. Corki tells me a couple of things about her luck, in which she has an implicit, almost a religious, faith. "I know things without thinking about them," she says.

I ask for an example.

"Well, people," Corki says. "I can tell in five seconds on the phone if someone's going to buy a house or not. Sometimes ten seconds, maybe, but I'll know whether this person is actually serious, whether we will have a good relationship, and whether it will work or not.

"I don't sell houses; I place people in houses. I listen to what they say, I ask them questions to find out what they need, but they may tell me they want one house and I may put them somewhere different. I listen when they say they have a retarded child who needs to be near a special school, or that they have arthritis and can't climb stairs. Then I may show them the house they called about, but I put them where they need to be. And it works, because I have a lucky intuition about people."

She's superstitious about her luck, believes it might desert her if she doesn't give something back to the world. So, remembering the rigors of her own past, Corki will take on hardship cases that other agents might not touch—divorced women, bankrupt couples, people who are very tight financially but desperately need to make a move. "I feel that I'm given these people as a test," she says, "and that if I don't get them into a suitable house, then I'm gonna be in trouble. I won't get the good sales from people who are easier to work with." So Corki makes her own luck.

And she has also created her own identity, has made herself from what might have looked to others like not very promising material. Corki herself has not lost sight of those earlier selves— the abused child, the high school dropout, the exotic dancer, the young mother who hired out to clean another woman's house. She has taken charge of all of those previous incarnations, and put them together in the strong, independent package that is the Corki Feltman sitting before me on this April Sunday. She tells me with some satisfaction that she has come full circle with one of her pending sales. Arlene and her husband have put their house on the market, and have commissioned Corki to sell the house which she cleaned for six years. Being Corki, she takes the measure of that change in monetary terms. "That one sale will probably make me as much money as I made in a year of cleaning it," she says, with a big smile.

"If I can change my life so much," Corki concludes, getting up and smoothing down her pink pants, "anybody can. There's a whole world out there. Take advantage of life. Don't sit there and let it pass you by. Get off your Herculon, and get out there and get some."

14

The Next Generation

What is it like to grow up with parents like the people described in these pages? What influence does the innovator's strong, independent ego have on his or her children? From the adult offspring of several of the innovators in this study, I learned that life in a family with an innovator at the head can be as difficult as it is enriching. Like the innovator, who needs the gumption to establish his own identity in the face of conventional expectations, the child of the innovator must establish his identity against the sometimes powerful pull of his parent's maverick influence. Yet the adult children I talked with all very much admire, and, perhaps more tellingly, think they resemble their innovator parents in significant ways.

From his father, Michael Stanford claims to have learned a total disregard for authority—including that of his father. If Michael sometimes follows his innovator father's example, it's because Michael wants to, not because he thinks he should. "My father can't stand authority figures of any kind," Michael says, "so I got the attitude always to question, and never to take anything on anybody's word just because that person is in a position of authority.

"And what I also got from my father was that there's no need to have a steady job in order to survive."

In other words, Michael absorbed from his father's example at least two skills for change. He learned to listen to his own inner voice rather than to rely on external authority; and he learned to accept the constancy of change rather than to strive for security.

At thirty-five, Michael has been a sheepherder, farmer, and agricultural engineer in England, has bummed his way through India, and now heads his own computer company in Texas. But the variety in his life is nothing compared to that in the life of his father, Dr. Geoffrey Stanford. "Every ten years I change jobs," Geoffrey Stanford says. Dr. Stanford has practiced medicine in London, worked in television and film, designed lenses, taught architecture, pioneered research in waste disposal, and now, at seventy-one, is director emeritus of the Dallas Nature Center, more than four hundred acres of Texas hills allowed to revert to its natural state. "As soon as I know how something works, I lose interest."

Michael Stanford clearly admires his father, and, in fact, as a grown man followed his father to America, then to Texas, then to Dallas. For his own life, Michael has adapted, as well, what he describes as Dr. Stanford's entrepreneurial attitude. "He's a self-starter," Michael says. "If he wants to get something done, he goes out and does it. He doesn't wait for someone else to tell him to. I think that's his greatest strength."

But Michael's father also has a great weakness which Michael has tried to avoid falling into. As Dr. Stanford himself volunteers, he doesn't get along with people very well. A product of the British upper class, Geoffrey Stanford grew up in what he describes as a loveless family. During his early years he was turned over to a nanny. Then he was sent away, at seven or eight, to boarding school. "I might as well have been an orphan," he says. And Geoffrey Stanford thinks like an orphan: asked for family data, he cannot say whether his only sibling, a sister two years younger than he, is living or dead.

For most of his life, Dr. Stanford believes, he has been on a quest for a father figure. When he came to America, he patterned himself for a time on Patrick Horsbrugh, a Notre Dame professor with "astonishing social graces, at ease with a servant, a down-and-outer, or the president of the university." Geoffrey wanted to be as sociable as Horsbrugh. He noticed that people in American society smiled a lot, so he reminded himself to learn to smile. "I tried very hard," he says, somewhat regretfully, "but I've never managed that sort of sociability."

Growing up under his father's influence, Michael, too, found himself in danger of being stuck with what he calls "all sorts of obnoxious quirks of personality and character and mannerisms." Michael's parents, who were divorced when their son was twelve, never gave Michael and his two sisters much help in understanding human nature. Michael's mother, a teacher, is a stable and conservative person, his father just the opposite, and communication between the two most commonly took the form of argument. "You're totally wrong, I disagree, that's really stupid," was the way Michael learned at home to defend his position on an issue.

In their family, Michael says, they never actually discussed other people, or what they were like, or what they did and how to react to it, never really had the sort of ordinary "You'll never believe what that guy did the other day; he's such a jerk" conversations that go on in most families. "Some people get to be socially skilled very early," Michael says, "just because their family discusses all sorts of people. In that way, you discover what a slob is, and what somebody obnoxious is, and you learn how to make a point without being abrasive and alienating other people." In Michael's family, however, whatever sensitivity the children had to the nuances of human behavior and motivation, they had to learn on their own.

As an adult, Michael has tried with some success to moderate his antisocial behavior. Through observation, he has trained himself to be attentive to the finer points of human closeness that he missed growing up. Women, he believes, are more skilled in this way than men, and he has learned a lot from

THE SKILLS FOR CHANGE

female friends and especially from Lorraine Adams, the news-woman he married in February 1988. Though Michael says he's still "not any paragon in getting on with other people," he has learned to accept criticism and to make the kinds of changes in his behavior that his less tolerant and less accommodating father has often found impossible.

Nevertheless, in other respects father and son are similar. Both believe in, as Michael puts it, "maximizing their options," and these two British immigrants feel that America is the place with the most options. Michael speaks of the virtues of America's government and of its open-hearted, generous people. And to contrast the British and American attitudes toward change, Geoffrey Stanford recalls the response of an elderly retired English gentleman to one of Dr. Stanford's proposals to the Greater London Council for the recycling of waste. "But, Dr. Stanford," the gentleman said, "don't you think if this were possible, it would have been done already?"

"I realized there was nothing more to be said," Geoffrey declares. "That was absolutely the way the poor sod thought. In America, people say, 'That's astonishing. I wish you all luck. Go to it, boy!' "

"Never say no to adventure." Ann Ross, the minister's wife in a small Michigan town, was reading aloud from *Chitty Chitty Bang Bang* to her four children. As the four pairs of eyes widened, she repeated the phrase for emphasis, "Never say no to adventure."

"I remember Mom said something like, 'Life is a source of never-ending surprises. Ask for things, let them happen, open yourself up. Life is out there for the taking, and nobody's going to hurt you,' " says Deborah Ross, the second oldest of Ann's four. And Ann's children have said yes to adventure: Deborah took a trip around the world alone; James, the youngest, joined a Buddhist monastery in Thailand.

But, perhaps most amazingly, Ann paid attention to her own injunction. When she first told her children, "Never say no to adventure," she was Victoria Ann Boothby Ross, the very proper wife of an Episcopal priest. She has become Victoria Boothby, a successful New York actress with a Broadway role in *Stepping Out.*

Victoria's minister husband was an alcoholic. During the fif-

262

teen years of their marriage, Victoria found herself increasingly drawn into the role of an "enabler." She kept up a good public front, found a substitute when her husband could not perform his duties as a clergyman, and, as she says, "maintained the dignity of the church, the dignity of his position, the dignity of our family." Very serious about her own religious faith, Victoria believed that playing this role was her duty.

Gradually, she began to see that enabling her husband to continue to drink by covering for him was a disservice to him and especially to their children. This truth was first brought home to her at a party for the oldest child's ninth birthday. "We had both worked to make it a wonderful, wonderful party," Victoria recalls, "but he was so drunk by the time the party actually happened that he was practically falling down." The son of the local judge told the birthday girl, "I've never seen anybody that drunk in my life."

After the party, the little girl repeated this remark to her father. She wanted an explanation. Victoria's husband responded, "Oh, Sarah, people are always lying. You just have to get used to that." Something snapped in Victoria's mind when she heard this self-serving lie. "How could I bring children up when someone was denying the evidence of their own senses?" she says. "I mean, that way lies madness. I thought that was absolutely appalling, not to mention the embarrassment of the actual situation." But her youngest child was only four at the time, and Victoria Ann stuck it out for years before she could finally bring herself to divorce her husband. "The divorce was because I had to live," she says. "Divorce was against all my beliefs, but I had to survive, and I knew I would not survive the way things were."

Their church was in the small town where both Victoria and her husband had grown up, and Victoria was a social pariah when she finally filed for divorce. The church asked Victoria's husband to step down as rector. When he left the church, he left town as well. The rest of the family stayed. Daughter Deborah, who was twelve at the time, remembers the terrible isolation that followed, even in church. "This was the family parish, but we would literally have our own little row; nobody would sit near us, and maybe three people, at the most, would speak to us after the service." The townspeople had known about the minister's drinking, but they preferred hypocrisy to public revelation of the truth.

Before her marriage, Victoria had studied acting at Barnard College and had had a Fulbright Scholarship to continue her studies at the Old Vic in London. During her years as a minister's wife, she had done amateur theatricals for the church and the community. One summer when she was working on a play for the parish, a visiting director from Yale told Victoria, "You know, you remind me of a plant that's been put in the wrong soil."

Years later, in the awful aftermath of the divorce, Victoria remembered that remark. On a visit to New York, she impulsively auditioned for the role of the mother in *A Scent of Roses*. She didn't get the part, but she was a serious contender. "I don't think until that moment I thought I had a chance of making a life in the theater," Victoria says. With that encouragement, forty-year-old Victoria brought her four children to New York.

Deborah remembers the years of difficulty while her mother tried to get a start in the most competitive profession in the country. Sarah, Deborah's older sister, was away at boarding school, paid for by her grandparents, so Deborah, the second oldest, became, she says, "Mother, Junior" to her two younger brothers. When her mother finally began to work in "those little off-off-Broadway theaters on Avenue A and those great places," after Deborah put the two little boys to bed she would lie awake worrying that something would happen to Victoria. "I would get into her bed, because I knew then that if I accidentally fell asleep she would have to wake me up when she got home, so I'd know she was safe."

When Deborah was fifteen, Victoria at last had the chance to go on the road for several months with a show. The children refused a babysitter. Instead, in her mother's absence, Deborah took over the house, getting her brothers off to school, shopping for food, preparing meals like macaroni and cheese, fish sticks, hamburgers, or hot dogs. Though she had a hard time making her brothers mind, Deborah didn't feel put upon, she says. She did often feel sorry that things were so hard for her mother, to whom she has always felt very close—"we could be friends even if we were not related"—and she missed her mother terribly.

But it did Deborah good, as the years passed, to see Victoria survive and eventually triumph. Like her mother, Deborah is in the arts, but backstage, in public relations and production. Deborah is enormously proud of Victoria. "She really had to work very hard," Deborah says. "She didn't just come in and all of a sudden star in some show, and live happily ever after. She's paid her dues twice over, I think."

Deborah was thirty when Victoria finally got her first Broadway show. The night *Stepping Out* opened, all four of Victoria's children were in the audience. James had even come from Thailand for the occasion. "We were all so overcome with emotion," Deborah says, "it was just too much. You know, it was really her dream come true. It was our biggest celebration ever."

Another bond between mother and daughter is a shared religious faith. Although they go to different churches in New York, both have remained faithful Episcopalians. In fact, Victoria credits her religious beliefs with pulling her through the hard times. "I am a believer," she says. She believes that Jesus lived, that he performed miracles, that he survived death, and "that in some way if we believe we participate in that. We take strength from what he did, and we live on."

Victoria connects her religious faith with her life as an innovator. "Jesus said, 'I have come that you might have life and have it more abundantly,' " she says. "I think about that a lot. By 'abundance,' I think he meant more realization of the wonder of who you are. To me, the change I made was an affirmation of life. If that took courage, then call it courage. But to me it was just—I believe that life is beautiful and wonderful and I don't believe we were meant to sit and be miserable forever."

Through changing her life, Victoria has created a strong, independent ego which is a model for her children. "If you're a performer," she says, "the closer you are to your real self is where you really belong. Whatever I'm doing, even my talking to you right this minute, the closer I am to my gut feelings and my ability to give them to you, that's what I'm after. Because then I'm being the truth of myself. That's where I've always wanted to go with my acting—to that kind of truthfulness."

From the hypocrisy of the alcoholic minister's wife to the truth of herself she finds in her acting—is it any wonder that Victoria Boothby wants to keep working as hard as she can? "Victoria," her agent told her the other day when she pressed him to find another role for her, "why don't you just sit back for a few minutes and be grateful for what you have? Be proud of yourself for what you've done. Take a breather."

But Victoria doesn't want a breather. She's ready for another adventure.

Apparently, there is no one right way for parents to create an innovative child. Many of the innovators I interviewed claim, like Rabbi Emily Korzenik, that the stable, traditional family in which they grew up gave them the self-confidence, the strength of ego, necessary to lead an innovative life. Others, like Sylvia Averbach or Waldo Gurewich, credit a repressive family which by its very conservatism made them rebellious pioneers. Still others, like Martha Ritter, first protested, then recapitulated, the innovative patterns in their family.

Alma Whitman, the black woman who decided to have a child by artificial insemination, worried at first that society would see her not as an innovator, but as the follower of an all too familiar path for underprivileged black women. "Being a single woman," Alma says, "I thought most people would say, 'Oh, my God, there's another one that got knocked up; there's another one that something happened *to.*'" And because she was over forty when her son Cedric was born, Alma kept expecting to hear, "Look how long you waited. How did you get knocked up at this late date?"

Oddly enough, it was the example of the very conservative grandmother who raised her that gave Alma the independence to take the route she did. Alma's grandmother was an Alabama farmwife who would have had trouble comprehending the option of artificial insemination, but Alma remembers not her grandmother's conservatism but her strength and independence. "In our family, she was the leader. And she wanted good things for all of us children. She was a very smart woman, and I think she would approve of what I did."

Alma fully expects her son, when he's old enough to hear the truth about his conception, to have the strength and independence to understand and approve as his great-grandmother would have. People have cautioned her not to tell Cedric that she was inseminated artificially, but Alma, who has the courage of her convictions, thinks that's foolish. She wanted a husband and a home, but when they didn't come along, she says, "I tried to have Cedric the best way possible. I couldn't get just what I wanted, but what Grandma taught me was that if one thing doesn't work, you try something else. So I tried the next best thing.

"When any parents do their best, then there is nothing for the child to be upset over. If Cedric doesn't want to accept what I did, then I think that there is something wrong with Cedric. You do the best you can in life, that's all. Grandma always said, 'Don't never be afraid to try something new.' "

She can't give Cedric a strong, independent ego, Alma realizes, any more than her grandmother gave such an ego to her. But Alma can act in such a way that Cedric is provided with a readily accessible model of a strong, independent human being, taking charge of her life, doing the best she can.

As we approach the conclusion of this study of innovative people, let's return to Bill Emerson, the journalist, college professor, and freelance writer with whom this book began. Bill told me that he made a major change even oftener than Geoffrey Stanford's every ten years. Lest he fall into the trap of boredom, Bill said, he changed his life drastically every *nine* years, "especially when I'm happy." Impressed by his daring and curious to know how living with the expectation and atmosphere of constant change affected family members, I arranged an interview with Bill's daughter, Lucy Emerson Sullivan. Like her father, Lucy is a journalist, with experience as a reporter on a large newspaper and, for the past seven years, as an editor for women's magazines. What effect, I ask, has her father had on Lucy's personality and on the choices she has made in her life?

"Profound," says Lucy, a pretty, delicate blonde in her mid-thirties. "I feel a mystical camaraderie with him—that we're kindred spirits." Ever since she was a little girl, Lucy says, she has adored her father. First, as little girls do, she wanted to marry him. She didn't see her mother, for whom she is named, as a problem; Lucy Senior "fit right in and brought out the best in him too." Then, when little Lucy realized that marriage to "Papa" was not quite the thing, she wanted to be *like* him, to be a writer—"I found him to be exciting and funny and original, a kind of classic, and I was just eager to share his life."

Lucy, who is the second oldest of five children, says she and her siblings are divided in their feelings about their father. Three of the children back off from Bill's strong personality, either by distancing him as, in Lucy's words, "a wonderful funny old bear" or by resisting him as "chauvinistic" or "oppressive." But nothing pleases Lucy more than being her father's daughter. She and a brother who also became a journalist "have a lot of concrete things to share with Papa. He tells stories and we tell stories, and he likes our stories and we like his."

And, indeed, the stories are the first thing I notice when I interview Bill Emerson in the comfortable home in Columbia, South Carolina, that he and Lucy Senior are preparing to leave. After more than ten years as a professor of journalism at the University of South Carolina, Bill is completing the circle of his life by moving back to Atlanta, his hometown. He is also, at the age of sixty-three, becoming once again a freelance writer answerable only to his own conscience and discipline. Bill is looking forward to the change as eagerly as a child awaits the end of school. But it is only human nature, as Shakespeare wrote, "To love that well which thou must leave ere long," and on this scorching July day in Columbia, Bill remembers vividly coming to the university.

In the early spring of 1975, Bill and several of his old friends, who were all working as freelance writers "and suffering all the outrages and the goddamned execrable problems of that trade," met for lunch in a diner on the outskirts of Larchmont, New York, where the Emersons were living. For the previous six years, since *The Saturday Evening Post,* where Bill was an editor, folded in January 1969, Bill had been on his own and was involved in miscellaneous entrepreneurial activities. With partners, he created a corporation called The Learning Child, specializing in systems of learning for young children, based on the theories of Piaget and other developmental psychologists. He had begun a publishing company, had written for radio and magazines, had ghosted or co-written several books, and had done consulting for foundations and other groups. But for quite a while, two or three of his children had been in college at the same time, and even as "a very hardworking freelancer," Bill was "really scrambling."

He and his friends, who all had similar problems, eased into the diner seats with their usual exchange of raucous greetings. Then one of them announced, "I've got a letter in my pocket from the University of South Carolina. They're looking for a distinguished professor of journalism."

"My God!" a second man exclaimed. "I've got a letter in my pocket from the University of South Carolina too. Distinguished professor of journalism, it says right here. But I'm not interested. I want to be a foreign correspondent."

"Don't think I've been left out," a third said. "Do you think it would make any difference to them that I never graduated from high school?" The others assured him that it wouldn't, that "academicians wouldn't worry a goddamned bit about a little thing like that."

Bill had gotten his letter too. Unlike the others, however, who hooted at the idea, he was intrigued by the prospect of teaching in a university. Here was an adventure he hadn't had. "I'm going to think about it," he told his friends. When he got home, he asked Lucy, "How would you like it if I went to Columbia to teach?" She was enthralled. "And get an apartment in New York?" she asked, thinking he meant Columbia University. "No, a house in South Carolina," Bill said. "Good heavens," Lucy said. "Are you serious?"

Bill thought he might be. He flew down to talk to the people at the university. The trip decided him. "I was very hazy about the whole thing," he says, "but I was brilliantly illuminated by the South Carolina sun. There were birds and crickets and tree toads and everything hollering and screaming on the runway at the airport. I could smell the flowering shrubs, and bees were buzzing by, and it was a marvelous, tropical wonderland." His talk with the university officials went swimmingly, "and then and there," he says, "I began really seriously considering changing my life.

"I have the feeling that you wear out a number of lives, and I'd sort of worn the other one out. I've always, from the time I was a child, been afraid of being bored, much more afraid of being bored than of being poor or unknown."

Once Lucy got over her shock, she was amenable. "Lucy has

been a great force," Bill says, "very gutsy, very realistic. You've got to have an undaunted partner in this sort of thing. A lot of people are held back by their terrified wives." But when Lucy saw Bill eagerly planning a new life adventure, she busied herself with selling the house in Larchmont and arranging for the move to a pleasant but far more modest domicile near the campus in Columbia, South Carolina.

Leaving was hard. The Larchmont house was home. Lucy and Bill had lived in the great old three-story Victorian edifice on Prospect Street, with its seven or eight bedrooms and comically prepossessing tower at the top, for nearly fifteen years. From that house they had sent their children into the world. Yet coming to Larchmont had been an even greater change for the family. For the ten years before they went North in 1961, Bill, Lucy, and their steadily growing family had made their home in their native Atlanta. The family on both sides could be traced back to the city's founding in 1846. They had hundreds of friends and relatives in the environs of the city.

Bill, as an enlightened thinker who was also at home with Southern mores, was, as Southern bureau chief for *Newsweek,* in charge of civil rights coverage during the fifties. "It was a great time to be alive and to be engaged in my business," he says. He thrived on getting up in the middle of the night and going to Mississippi or Alabama, loved being hardy and aggressive enough to get out and cover the story, was proud to be able to see events in perspective. But after nine years or so, he was physically weary. "I realized I'd worked all night till six in the morning at least a thousand nights."

That difficult decade taught him something, however, about the possibility of change. "I came to believe that people can change," he says, "because I saw it happen in the South during the segregation and desegregation struggles. I knew the Southern mentality, and I saw Southerners come to understand the situation and turn about." So when *Newsweek* offered to make him a senior editor if he would be willing to come to New York, Bill decided that he too could make a change.

Even today, he's not sure that he and Lucy made the right decision for their children. "We can be satisfied that we did the right thing when we change," he says. "But we are always haunted by the thought that we may not have done the right thing for our children. I worry about that." The children had an idyllic life in Atlanta, with aunts and uncles and both sets of grandparents. There were twenty-one first cousins, no telling how many second cousins, and maybe hundreds of Southern "kissing cousins" in the extended family. The five little Emersons had constantly mixed with people who had known them always. They were never left with a babysitter, never taken to a strange, friendless environment. And now off they went, the little boys in their knee pants and the girls in their starched dresses, to what Bill calls "the rambunctious, bad-mannered North."

Lucy Junior remembers that the children were in a state of shock for at least a year. Night after night, she recalls, they would slip downstairs in their nightgowns and plead with their father, "Now can we go home? When will you take us home again, Papa?" And all the Atlanta relatives were calling and saying, "When do you think that you will come back home? We miss you all so much."

The whole family felt out of place in suburban New York. Mother Lucy came down with a serious case of whooping cough, so serious that for weeks she had to have an oxygen tent with a vaporizer over her bed. The children felt lost without their pragmatic, energetic mother on hand. "Mama was always such a great sport," her daughter says. "She realized early the kind of man she had, and she picked up the other end of the load. She saw him through so many potential crises, paid all the bills and didn't tell him how close to the edge we were—she made it possible for him to have the kind of life he wanted. And I don't think this was an unreasonable sacrifice for her, because it's one she wanted to make."

With their mother sick, problems plagued the children that Mama might have been able to put in perspective. "Our clothes were all wrong, and we were very unsophisticated," Lucy Junior says. She and her sisters wore dresses that tied with bows in the back and played with dolls, while the Yankee girls wore skirts and sweaters, and giggled and passed notes to boys. Even the teachers, amused by the outlandish new arrivals with their strange habits, picked on the little Emersons. The school officials wanted to put them all back a grade even without testing

271

them, on the grounds that any Southern child must be at least a year behind Northern children. The Emersons of course refused, and the children's work subsequently proved their parents to be right about their offspring's capabilities.

But parents, however vigilant, could not prevent other stupid, thoughtless cruelties the children suffered during that year of transition. Lucy remembers being brought up in front of the class to answer questions when they had visitors so that everyone could hear her Southern accent and smile at her "Yes, ma'ams," and "No, sirs." Even at nine years old, "I knew exactly what they were doing," she says, "but I couldn't help saying it." Manners are important in Southern families, and those funny "ma'ams" and "sirs" had always been required of her. Little Lucy was sharply aware of the bad manners of the adults who tormented her.

The other children asked the Emersons if they had slaves of their own, unable to think of the South except as a plantation myth. To offset this myth with another, a history teacher referred to Lucy's home state as "a highway bordered by shanties." Lucy and her siblings felt doomed to be misunderstood on all sides.

"We would come home every day, and tell Papa these terrible stories, and you could see it just broke his heart," Lucy remembers. "And he was unhappy, too, a misfit in suburbia. Papa's was the only laugh you would ever hear on the platform waiting for the train. I'm sure he was questioning the whole time, 'Am I out of my mind? What am I doing with these slick Yankee bastards? My children are being ruined; they're all social outcasts, and they cry themselves to sleep every night. My wife is miserable and probably going to die. What are we doing here?'"

But Papa himself sometimes embarrassed the children. "Ho, tiger," he would say loudly and cheerfully on the station platform to another man, who would look at him as if he were mad, according to his daughter. He frequently addressed women as "Peaches." "You can't believe how he stood out," Lucy says. Bill wore a Beatles wig when he took the children to a Beatles concert at Shea Stadium. He bought a pair of earmuffs with little birds on them which he wore to walk the children to the bus stop —Lucy would stand across the street and pretend she didn't know him. Sometimes he rode her brother's little rickety, outgrown bike to the train station. "He thought all those things were hysterical," Lucy says. "He was rebelling against this tight commuter world."

Bill was perhaps also rebelling against his own father's example. He describes his father, an executive for Westinghouse, as "a great company man," who wanted his son to do the conventional thing, to be an intelligent, resourceful, competent employee for a company—"to do what he understood," Bill says. He was probably "horrified" at every turn in his son's life, from Bill's decision to leave Georgia and go to Harvard on the GI Bill, to the move to New York. "He was a Democrat, a moderate, and an independent thinker, but he was very much bound by Southern tradition, very familial."

If the elder Emerson's desire to hold his son close backfired, oddly—or perhaps not so oddly—the seven Emersons became a closer family because of the changes they made together. "We were bonded to each other," Lucy says, "because we had to survive; we knew we had each other." She believes they became a much tighter family than "some families I know who have all stayed in comfortable, cushy little places, camouflaged into surroundings that they're very much a part of and never really needing to rely on each other the way we did."

What are the qualities that Lucy Emerson Sullivan hopes to gain for her own life from her "mystical camaraderie" with her innovator father? First, she values the complex view of the world she has attained, the sort of view that enabled Bill Emerson to write objectively about his beloved South in the throes of the civil rights movement. After high school in New York, Lucy and her sisters all went South to college. Lucy found that, just as because of her Southern roots she had more perspective about the North than her New York friends had, because of living up North she also had a take on the South that her Atlanta friends lacked. "They just had never gone anywhere, some of them, and they were in awe of the things I would bring up in all innocence to talk about."

One aspect of this broad perspective is an interest in other people that Lucy has inherited from her father. Bill gets chatty, his daughter says, with the man selling tomatoes on the highway, becomes friends with the guy at the Gulf station. This democratic interest in others Lucy regards as "the secret formula" for feeling the way her father does about the world. "Papa makes everybody part of the fabric of his life," she says. "When he comes onto the scene, he brings people to life, even people who look stone dead. I like to watch that, and I love to believe I can do that too."

Lucy also values her father's craft as a writer, in particular his innovation and daring with language. "He just explodes his limits," she says. "The effect of his language is so powerful because he uses words in ways you've never heard them used before." She identified with her father so strongly in this respect that when she was younger she began peppering her conversation with some of his pet obscenities.

On her first newspaper job, when she was still in college, Lucy was asked by a paternalistic male editor to tone down her salty language. "Honey, you've got to stop talking like this," the fatherly man told her. "You're a lady, but you're not acting like one. It makes me sad to see somebody as pretty as you talk so ugly."

At the time, Lucy resented this reprimand, and she protested hotly. "The guys around here all talk exactly the way they want to," she said. "I'm no worse than they are. Why don't you fuss at them?" Now she realizes that she "must have looked pretty stupid," but she was trying diligently to be Bill Emerson's daughter.

Being Bill Emerson's daughter has created other trials for Lucy. With his incorrigible optimism, Bill hates to be the bearer of bad news. Once, when Lucy was in college, Bill let her make all the preparations for a junior year abroad before he got up the gumption to tell her that he simply didn't have his share of the ready money she needed. Lucy was actually packing when she got the bad news. After planning the adventure for a year, working weekends and nights, saving her money, she was bitterly disappointed. "I hate you," she told her father. "It's unforgivable to lead me on and lead me on, and then let me down at the last minute. This is the meanest thing you have ever done." She walked out of the room, and for several months, she says, "he didn't exist for me." Another kind of father would not have disappointed his daughter in that way.

Nor would another kind of father have made Lucy as jealous

as she has been of some of Bill Emerson's students. With his obsessive enthusiasm for whatever project he's involved in, Bill absolutely doted on his students. They were going to do great things, he told his daughter.

At the time, Lucy and her husband Chris were living in Baltimore. She was trying her hand at freelancing, like her father, and the young couple "had absolutely no money. I would go to the grocery store with seven dollars, and get tuna fish, tuna fish, and tuna fish." They had gone out on a limb to buy an old house which they were renovating. For a while, they had no refrigerator, and Lucy cooked on a hot plate. In the middle of dust and plaster, she was trying to write stories that would sell, and she desperately needed some guidance.

Lucy went to visit her folks in South Carolina. Sitting with her father on the porch, she tried to tell him about one of her ideas for a story. She wanted to get his professional help, like a young fighter asking an old fighter for tips. But Lucy was surprised that her father didn't seem very interested in her problem. He wanted to talk about his own concerns. "Your story idea's a total waste of time," Bill told her bluntly. "Who in the world would want to read that? Now one of my students is working on something that I just know she's going to be able to sell to *Playboy* or *Ms.* or somewhere big."

Lucy burst into tears, and "at the very same moment, a yellow jacket stung me on the knee." She stormed into the house, holding the swelling on her knee and the swelling in her heart. The next day, she went back to Baltimore, and again it was several months, after Bill had written her a lengthy apology offering his help, before she was reconciled with her father.

If another kind of father might have been less wrapped up in himself and his own ego, neither would another kind of father have given his daughter the valuable lessons Lucy has had from Bill about the possibility of change. "Moving and changing jobs and starting over is a pattern I've seen all my life," she says. "You land on your feet, and the more times you land on your feet, the more confident you are that you will land on your feet next time.

"I think watching my father evolve has been liberating. It shows me I'm not in a rut, that I can learn different things and live different places—there's always another chapter."

"Staying with one set of problems forever is like living forever in a bad marriage," Bill Emerson says. "You can do it if you don't inhale." He congratulates himself on his own choice of a mate. Lucy Senior he describes as "a tremendous companion—tough, gallant, bright, right about things, and amazingly unneurotic." Lucy is a planner who thinks of the future. She'll say, "I have an idea; let's do this." Bill denies that he ever thinks abstractly about the future. "What I'm doing right now, at this moment, is the most important thing to me. I wouldn't go across the street to see Genghis Khan when I'm absorbed in the job at hand."

On the other hand, it is Bill who feels the need to try something new. He thinks of humankind as naturally nomadic. "Metaphorically, you use up the grass and the water, and you move on, just like a damn tribesman on the Serengeti plains. You get a signal in your viscera to get out of there." In this respect, he thinks of himself as typically American. "We just don't have the knack that Europeans have had to create rich, permanent, sacred places. We're always spiritually packed and ready to go—to cross the mountains, stake out new land, clear forests, raise new crops. And we're curious. We're also looking for a new territory of the mind to explore."

Characteristically American in his restlessness, in his curiosity, his interest in "the human hieroglyphic" around him, Bill also recognizes that his sense of himself doesn't depend on his job. He moves through the world as a free-booter. "I don't identify myself with what I do, so I can move on or change without losing my identity." He does identify himself with his use of language, and speaks of having created himself with thoughts and words. "When I was little, I thought I'd never be anybody, never go anywhere, so I decided that at least I'd teach myself to converse, to talk, to think. I struggled to isolate a personality."

That personality turned out to be strong and independent enough to defy time. At an age when other people retire, Bill Emerson is returning to the life of a freelancer, still striving, still dreaming. "I have more freedom than I ever had before. I don't want to sit around and drink and make conversation. It irritates the hell out of me to be conceived to be old."

From the dining room, Lucy Senior calls us to lunch. "I'd really like to be a tremendous, late-life success!" Bill booms happily. "I'd like to be a goddamned Browning or somebody, and do something really brilliant, sweep up a couple of piddling little Pulitzers, and then wipe off a Nobel Prize toward the end."

Then he grins a little wryly at his own hubris. "I'm being terribly self-indulgent," he says. "But I really want to *do* something. I think it's going to be a hell of an adventure."

"Never say no to adventure," the life of the innovator says to the next generation. Innovators cannot be created by their parents, of course. A parent who makes frequent changes can frighten a child into lifelong immobility, just as a parent who never makes a change can propel his offspring into a rabid desire for constant mobility. The stimuli and response of child rearing never follow a predictable pattern. But a parent can summon the awareness and courage to act out in his own life the truth of his deepest self. Thus, whether that truth is to move or to stay put, the parent provides for his child a model for honest, brave behavior.

Whether to follow the model provided is a matter of personal choice. Innovators create themselves. They perform this act of self-creation by developing the skills which are discussed in the second half of this book—accepting the constancy of change, listening to the inner voice, recognizing and exploring opposites, developing an independent ego. By learning these, the innovator rewards himself with, as Victoria says, "more realization of the wonder of who you are." And when we come to know as fully as possible the wonder of who we are, we will have life and have it more abundantly.

15

Starting Over

Elephants were in the bride's dowry when Bubu Arya's mother married Bubu's father. The bride was fourteen, the groom thirty-four, and the match uniting two princely Indian families had been arranged by their parents. After the ceremony in the bride's village, the bridegroom transported his new wife to Calcutta. There he employed an English governess to educate the child-woman whom he had married and the children who were to come, first the essential son, then Bubu and her sister.

The new husband, like his father before him, like all the males of his father's aristocratic family, had been educated in England. He adored his young wife. Although he had been a businessman before his marriage, after the wedding he never worked a day in

278

his life, Bubu says. Instead, he devoted himself to his pleasures and his family. He didn't need to work, he reasoned, so why should he?

Bubu's mother didn't work either. Her only task was to keep herself beautifully groomed, which she did with the help of personal servants. Other servants looked after the house and the garden, prepared meals, and tended Bubu and her brother and sister. As the children grew up, the family retinue traveled often, to England, to Europe, and to cities all over India. But in spite of the supposedly broadening effects of travel, "we were very conservative," Bubu remembers, "very snobbish, even more snobbish than our British rulers, I think."

Bubu's upbringing was strict. As she and her sister reached adolescence, they were carefully chaperoned on all social occasions. On a family holiday in Bombay, when Bubu was fourteen, she met Grandhi Arya, India's first pilot. Grandhi, who was to become Director General of Civil Aviation in India and then Indian ambassador to the United Nations, was fifteen years older than Bubu. Somehow, in spite of the onmipresent chaperones and the age difference, the two fell in love.

For the next three years, however, in accordance with family conservatism, Bubu was allowed to see her suitor only in her home under the watchful eye of her parents. Although her parents liked Grandhi, her father insisted that the dashing pilot was too old for his daughter. "Look at your marriage," the spirited young girl protested. "You've done beautifully! I want a man who'll pamper me the way you pamper my mother."

That's what she got. At seventeen, Bubu became the wife of a serious and important government official. She presided as lady of the house. Every evening, she and Grandhi went out or entertained at home. Entertaining was easy with a staff which consisted of a cook, a cook's assistant, a butler, a butler's helper, a sweeper, two maids, two gardeners, two chauffeurs, and three watchmen. The servants did everything. "I never poured a glass of water from the refrigerator for myself," Bubu says. "If I was brushing my hair and the brush flew across the room, a servant picked it up." Bubu also discovered at one point that Grandhi literally did not know the location of the kitchen oven.

In this incredibly luxurious life, Bubu's main jobs were to look beautiful and to be gracious. After the children were born—a daughter, Mona, when Bubu was eighteen, and two years later a son, Jai—Bubu involved herself with them. "My whole life was exactly like my mother's."

Then the children went to school and gradually became more and more absorbed in life outside the home. At first, they came home for lunch and raced into the house asking the butler, "Where is my mother? Is Madame at home?" After a time, they no longer came home for lunch. Then there were cricket matches and friends after school. Bubu began to realize how empty her life had become, as she whiled away the long days waiting for the children to come home and for the evening round of parties with Grandhi to begin. At length she spoke to her husband about doing what no woman in her family or social circle had ever done: getting herself a job.

Grandhi was amused. "Of course, Bubu," he said, "by all means work. What will you do?"

"I don't know," Bubu said.

"You haven't got any skills," Grandhi said. "Nobody's going to hire you. Come, Bubu. Be reasonable. We are together, we go out a lot, we travel, you've met foreign dignitaries all over the world—what more can you ask for? Why can't you be content just being the perfect wife that you are?"

Bubu tried to make her husband understand. "I wanted to do something that came out of my life," she says, "something to do with my own identity and not as my husband's wife. I wanted a career, some recognition, a feeling of accomplishment." Finally Grandhi gave his reluctant permission, and Bubu found her first job as a stock girl in the fashion department of the Indian Trade Commission.

Her first day on the job, Bubu came to work in her pearls over a diaphanous yellow sari made of French chiffon. She wore matching yellow Dior sandals, and even a yellow band on her Piaget watch. In this dress-for-success outfit, she was sent to stock fabrics in the "godown," a dark, hot, airless, musty basement. Day after day, through the Indian summer, Bubu toiled in the godown, coming home like a wilted flower in her rumpled, sweaty sari to join her husband for some party or other.

"This is absurd," Grandhi said. "Look at you—you are exhausted, I'm a neglected man, and my poor children are becoming orphans. And for what? For less money than my chauffeur makes! Give this nonsense up, Bubu."

But Bubu stuck it out. "I don't know why," she says. "I wanted to show everyone I could do a job. But, of course, I had wanted something with glamour in it. Here I was, with my husband and the prime minister, meeting Richard and Pat Nixon when they came to India, and the rest of the time ruining all my saris in that godown."

Her stubborn refusal to give up paid off. A superior noticed her eye for clothes and her dependability as an employee, and Bubu was given a dramatic, overnight promotion to a position created for her as fashion consultant for the Commission. Her job of coordinating Indian fabrics with Western fashions gave her a place in the fashion industry. She worked with such designers as Pierre Cardin, Ferré, Carol Horn, and Hanae Mori. For the next seven or eight years, she traveled to fashion shows all around the world for ideas, brought back designs to be copied, created other designs of her own, oversaw the work of two hundred tailors, hired models and put on fashion shows, and was also responsible for public relations. The woman with "no skills" discovered she had many, and no one was more happily surprised at the discovery than Grandhi Arya.

Eventually, Bubu began to manage a Madison Avenue shop owned by the Indian government. By that time, her family, except for her son, Jai, had relocated in America. Grandhi was at the United Nations. Though he traveled frequently, New York was his base. Jai, who had married an Indian girl, was living in India, but Bubu's daughter, Mona, was working in New York and living in her own apartment, very much a modern young woman. Then, in 1977, Indira Gandhi was beaten at the polls by Morarji Desai, and a new government came into power in India. Over the next several years the program for which Bubu worked underwent some drastic changes. The Madison Avenue store was closed, and Bubu was out of work.

Grandhi had been enormously proud of his wife's success, but now he begged Bubu not to submit herself to the rigors of finding a new job in New York. "You've proved yourself," he told her. "Retire, and travel with me." But Bubu wasn't interested. She had been everywhere already. If she traveled with Grandhi on his business trips, she knew there would be parties and dinners in the evening, but what would she do with herself during the day while Grandhi went to meetings? She wore only saris, so shopping didn't interest her, and how much time can you spend browsing in museums and walking city streets? "No," Bubu told Grandhi, "I will find work."

Her work for the Indian government didn't translate into real job experience, by New York standards. So this elegant woman in her forties, one of the beautifully dressed and jewelled beauties of the world, who had dined with presidents and kings, with movie stars and astronauts, went to work managing a discount retail store in Manhattan. Nevertheless, working in a situation her mother would have found inconceivable, Bubu didn't lose sight of who she was. The owner of the discount store asked her to clean the toilet every morning before the arrival of customers. Bubu refused; a manager does not clean the toilet, she told him.

This dignity and sense of fitness she extended to her employees also. Horrified at the working conditions for her sales staff of older women, Bubu revolutionized the organization. During their entire working day, the "girls" were not permitted to sit down, smoke, make personal phone calls, or even to talk to each other. "What do you run here—a concentration camp?" Bubu asked the owner indignantly. She lifted all the rules, and counted on her employees to justify her trust. They did.

When, at length, Bubu applied for the manager's position at a better store, she maintained the pride of her independent ego. The potential employer asked her to take a routine polygraph test. She refused. To Bubu, such a request was tantamount to calling her a liar. "How dare you?" she asked. "Get yourself another person." She walked out and went home. As she came in the door, the owner was on the phone offering her the job. She accepted, and the polygraph test was never mentioned again.

In 1985, Bubu gave up her latest job, and she and Grandhi returned to India for an extended family visit. On the flight back to the States, two hours out of Kennedy, Bubu's husband of nearly thirty years suffered a cardiac arrest. Grandhi "just shut his eyes" and died. Even in her shock, Bubu could see the poetry of his death. Her husband had loved planes all his life. He had been a pilot for Air India when she met him, then head of the airline. What better way for Grandhi to die than painlessly, with

282

her at his side, somewhere over the Atlantic, on the Air India flight from London to New York?

Nevertheless, Bubu was devastated. She had lost her husband, her lover, the closest companion she had had since she was fourteen. The trauma of the funeral preparations was increased by all the red tape caused by the circumstances of Grandhi's death. And, as she came through the terrible fresh grief, Bubu realized that she wasn't sure what to do with herself.

Once, Indian women committed suttee, a ceremonial suicide, upon a husband's death. Bubu mourned for Grandhi, but she couldn't believe that his death had finished her. Her son urged her to return at once to India, where her house and all the servants, even the pets, awaited her. Life in New York without her husband's affluent position, Jai argued, would be unthinkable for a well-bred Indian woman. Although Bubu could bring very little money out of India, if she returned to her home in that country she could live in luxury the rest of her life.

In luxury and in idleness, Bubu thought—almost a kind of suttee. Bubu's own mother had been widowed at forty, and Bubu knew very well the routine imposed by convention on upper-class Indian widows, the hours of bridge and shopping, the long lunches with other women, the immersion in the lives of grown children, the boredom and aimlessness. Bubu didn't want such a future.

So Bubu decided to stay in America, where she could work and live in freedom and independence, where she could travel, go to the theater, attend parties, be her own woman. She owned her apartment, and she knew that she could earn enough for her other modest expenses. Tired of the responsibility of a managerial position, Bubu got a job as a corporate receptionist for a New York firm. No typing, no switchboard, nine-to-five, and she loves it. She wears running shoes and uses public transportation, an unfinished woman on her own in the city.

For the first time in her life, Bubu has no domestic help. She has been teaching herself how to do ordinary household chores. Proudly she recites her new accomplishments: "I can cook, though not that great. I can vacuum—my neighbor showed me what to do when the machine sucks up the rug fringe. I can change a light bulb; I had never done that before. I've started washing my own clothes and ironing them. I can shop for groceries." Toilets are still her *bête noire;* she has a little trouble scrubbing the bathtub satisfactorily, but feels confident that in time she will master that task too.

"I like life in America," Bubu says. "My small apartment feels like home."

I tell myself, and you, Bubu's story to remind us all that Americans do not have a monopoly on the ability to change. Like the people of all countries, Americans are chauvinistic. We pride ourselves on the restless, energetic, striving American character, hungering for effort, desiring to test itself, welcoming change. But then there's Bubu, born to luxury in a country on the other side of the world, the child of a family where all the work was carried on by menials. Yet Bubu has exhibited throughout her life what we would call very American characteristics.

Is it significant that Bubu, as an independent woman, has chosen to start over in America? I think it is. The United States is a great country in which to start over. From the beginning, American citizens have not been expected to stay put and endure without reward. Unique among such documents, our Constitution grants us the right to pursue happiness, to chase it into as many new places and as many new lives as it takes for us to find it. If Americans are historically optimistic about their personal futures and their ability to control their own destinies, that constitutional right is a major reason.

There are other historical causes for American optimism. For most of the two hundred years of our history, a frontier existed into which we could move while hotly pursuing happiness. The plenitude of free and open land is gone now, but we continue to redefine the term "frontier" in ways that stimulate our imaginations and accommodate our dreams. After years in New York, Betsy Williams chased happiness to California. Katherine Fanning left Chicago to seek it in Alaska. Bill Cutler ran to Atlanta in pursuit of it. Michael Stanford found it in Dallas. Bubu finds the frontier of her imagination in the challenges of Manhattan. The frontier, which was once a physical actuality of American life, has become a habit of the American mind.

Another historical cause for our national optimism is the absence of a feudal tradition, a tradition which separates princes from peasants before birth. In this country, within certain practical limitations, you can create yourself. You can be a prince or a peasant as you will, someone utterly unlike your parents or grandparents. The Social Register is full of peasants who became princes. And a prince or princess is free to become a peasant, as well, to seek a demotion into democracy if that condition is more appealing. Bubu refused to clean the shop toilet because she was a manager; that's job definition, a term Americans understand. But when Bubu tells me that as an independent American woman she has learned to scrub her own bathroom, I admire her gumption and think her no less princely for performing what she grew up thinking of as a peasant task.

For all this geographical and social mobility, however, it's not very often that an American girl literally becomes royalty. I interviewed one who did. Meet Hope Cooke, the New York debutante who became a queen and is now a social historian living in Brooklyn.

I wrote requesting an interview when I saw a brief note in the press that Hope Cooke, former Queen of Sikkim, had become a consultant at the Museum of the City of New York and would be leading walking tours of the city in the spring of 1987. Hope Cooke! With a start, I remembered the fanfare in 1963 when Hope, two weeks after graduating with honors from Sarah Lawrence, flew off to Asia to marry Maharaj Kumar Palden Thondup Namgyal, the Crown Prince of Sikkim. Chogyal, the Sikkimese term Hope uses for her former husband, who is now dead, was a forty-year-old widower with three children from an arranged marriage. He was also a royal scion who would before long be King of Sikkim and who would also become, as the religious head of that tiny Himalayan land, a senior incarnation of the Buddha. What a story! The American press had a field day with the romantic tale, and I had been fascinated.

In 1980, Hope had published *Time Change*, an autobiography. I had followed up on the Hope Cooke saga and found *Time Change* a wonderful, wise book about a girl becoming a woman under the strangest of circumstances. In her memoir, Hope described her early history, her eleven years in Sikkim, and her escape to America with her two children when the tiny principality was violently annexed by the Indian government. When I closed the book, I wanted to know more. What had happened to her since? Had she divorced the King? Had she done anything with what her Sarah Lawrence teachers called her "brilliant" mind? How were her cross-cultural children managing? Did Hope have a lover, a husband? How did such a woman fare, I wondered, when she started over in America?

Now, with Hope alive and well and living in New York, I had a chance to ask the woman herself.

On the warm May afternoon of our interview, fourteen years after her return from Sikkim, Hope bustles into my apartment and divests herself of the paraphernalia that busy New York women manage to accumulate during the course of a day. As I seat Hope at the dining room table, the tape recorder between us, I study this, to me, almost mythical figure—the girl who gained and lost a throne. A little older than the picture on the cover of *Time Change,* Hope otherwise has the same slender, pointed face surrounded by a mass of curly hair. There are the same humorous yet piercing eyes, the same high cheekbones, the same sensitive, sensual mouth belied by a stubborn chin. A trusting, intelligent, strong, vulnerable face, a face as contradictory as, perhaps, Hope herself.

"When I came back to America, I was thirty-two years old," Hope tells me, "and I thought my life was over. I had really stopped expecting anything for myself."

From the beginning, her expectations were never great. What Hope mostly wanted, as a girl growing up, was "something that lasted in my life." Her parents split up when she was two. Her beautiful mother, who was a flier, died not long afterward—a suicide, Hope believes, because her mother took off with the gas tank of her Piper Cub nearly empty. Hope was grown when she learned this fact from a magazine article. No one ever told her as a child anything about her mother's death, not even where her mother was buried, and all the photographs of her mother were summarily removed after her death. Hope remembers seeing her father only twice in her life, and both times she fled from him.

She and her sister, Harriet, made their home, if home is the right word for its cold, repressive atmosphere, on Park Avenue with their wealthy maternal grandparents. The little girls lived in a separate apartment across the hall from the apartment of their grandparents, and saw very little of the old couple. Hope and Harriet were mostly cared for by a series of nannies. Because Hope's grandmother was "difficult," no nanny lasted very long. A few of these nannies were kind, especially Johnny, whom Hope loved. Others were at best dutiful and some were downright sadistic. But what tormented Hope most was not the periodic cruelty but the constant change.

As she would come down Park Avenue on the school bus, her chest would "freeze up" in terror that there would be an unfamiliar person waiting to meet her. "I think I'm the only grown person who can still read *Mary Poppins* and be frightened," Hope says. "There's that prevailing North Wind which Mary Poppins is always saying she will go off on, and which she does go off on at the end." Hope would listen to the story in terror—after all, her mother had gone off and never returned. "Even now," she says, "it gives me the chills to think about it."

So Hope grew up with an orphan's mentality. She dreamed either of becoming some family's little mother or of being adopted herself. Sometimes she fantasized about herself as a child/mother like Wendy in *Peter Pan,* a figure who had the magical strength in that double role to hold things together. "I always saw myself as the elder sister or the little mother, in a covered wagon, maybe, feeding children, looking after them, in a time of some uncertain danger, like Indians."

Another fantasy was of being found by a missing relative, or of being adopted. The Edwardian children's stories her grandparents supplied were full of orphans. A favorite (for which Hope later learned she shared a fondness with another wealthy orphan, Gloria Vanderbilt) was *Sara Crewe, or the Little Princess,* in which orphaned Sara is befriended by the Indian servant of an old gentleman who eventually turns out to be Sara's missing grandfather.

To satisfy these fantasies in some fashion, with a child's halfconscious cleverness, Hope developed a "chameleon-like ability" to fit in, to make herself charming and ingratiating so that "people would always adopt me. I could board a bus and get myself adopted by a busload of people." But she found it an exhausting and risky business, psychologically so difficult that, Hope now realizes, she had no sense of herself at all. Hope

287

describes her young self as a mix of Penelope and Ulysses, dependent like Penelope, "waiting to be subsumed," independent like Ulysses, traveling through adventures toward a dream of home.

The Indian servant in *Sara Crewe* turned out to be a prescient detail. When her grandparents died, Hope and Harriet became the wards of their Aunt Mary and Uncle Selden. Selden Chapin was the United States ambassador to Iran. Living at the embassy in Teheran with her affectionate guardians, Hope wrote, "Every minute is precious, lapidary, like the very art of Persia." Small wonder that before long the needy young girl "gave to life in Iran all the imaginative power" of her pent-up longings for a place. The East became her first home.

Hope carried that love for the East with her to Sarah Lawrence, where she concentrated on Asian studies, read Oriental philosophy, and eventually became a Buddhist. "I was engrossed in India," she says, "living more Indian than American, which was a great trial to my friends." Her friends wanted her to have some balance, some perspective, but balance and perspective were not on Hope's agenda. She wanted a cult, to be subsumed.

In the bracing intellectual atmosphere of Sarah Lawrence, Hope began to develop real intellectual strengths. Her professors, impressed with her genuine gift for history, encouraged her to go on to graduate school, possibly at the School of Oriental and African Studies in London. But Hope had some reservations which were born of her lack of personal identity.

"I was scared of my cerebral strengths," she says. "That was the only really strong asset that I knew I had, and I felt top-heavy with ideas and reading. I had no sense of any physical context— no family, no roots, no sense of daily-ness. I was afraid of being, like the figure in the Saul Steinberg cartoon, a person made entirely of books."

So instead of going on to study history, when she met and married the Crown Prince, she began making history herself. "I needed a place, a mission," Hope says. Her husband so closely identified himself with his tiny country that, in his case, Louis XIV's famous *"L'État c'est moi"* could have been reversed. As the wife of her husband, Hope made Sikkim her mission. She became caught up in Sikkimese history and culture, and in the ongoing struggle for Sikkimese autonomy. Until her immersion in Sikkim, Hope had been a thinker, not a doer. As Queen of Sikkim, she became a doer.

She took on many jobs. In addition to caring for her new family, she was, of course, her husband's official hostess. Because of the romance of her marriage, she also became an unofficial public relations figure for Sikkim. She did research into Sikkimese history and published at least one scholarly article on the subject. She coordinated the manufacture of Sikkimese handicrafts so they were available for export. She worked with children in the schools.

One of her projects was reworking the social studies textbooks from a Sikkimese perspective, replacing a picture of a British railroad, for example, with an illustration of Sikkimese transport. Such changes would not only strengthen the Sikkimese sense of national identity, Hope believed. They had the added advantage, touted by Piaget and Bank Street, of beginning a child's education with what the child already knows, working from the child's point of view outward rather than imposing the outward world on the child. Ironically, when the end of her time in Sikkim came, it was this thoroughly Western notion which was most attacked in the Western press; Hope was accused vaguely of maliciously "rewriting Sikkimese history."

In her years in Sikkim, Hope worked hard, and felt that her work was intensely important. Today, she says, she feels the same kind of significance in her work for the Museum of the City of New York, a significance that comes from helping people to understand their connection to the place where they live. She likes the sense of legitimate work heightened, she says, by "the joy of collectivity. There is an extra urgency in working for something larger than just earning a living." Marrying Chogyal, Hope had also married Sikkim.

And, of course, in marrying someone with children she had married a family. The marriage, which seemed to an outsider an exotic thing to do, was for Hope, "completely the opposite. It was a basic drive for home." Coming into the responsibility of Chogyal's three children at barely twenty, in the next five years Hope added two more children, a son, Palden, and a daughter, Hope Leezum, to the family. Until she married a Himalayan and became the mother of a brood of Asian children, Hope's identification with Asia had been abstract—wishful thinking, or, as she puts it, "an imperative growing out of my circumstances." Now she had to take charge, to evolve into the woman these children needed. Hope had become the "little mother" of her fantasies. There was even "an uncertain danger, like Indians."

As the years progressed, dangers of various kinds became more and more certain, until, in the late summer of 1973, Hope Cooke, with her children, Palden and Hope Leezum, returned to the United States. With them came Yangchen, Hope's step-daughter, who was to attend college in this country, and three other Sikkimese youngsters. Chogyal and his two sons remained behind in Sikkim. Hope promised to return, but in her heart she knew she had no intention of doing so, though she did intend to send her children back to see their father every summer.

What went wrong with the fairy-tale romance? The marriage itself had been in danger from the beginning, Hope says, and, in fact, the Crown Prince danced and laughed with his paramour and snubbed his bride even at the wedding festivities. The vast cultural differences and the personal disagreements mounted with time, and drove Hope and her husband further apart. The age difference perhaps played a role, too. Chogyal had married a wistful, lonely, untried girl; ten years later, he found he was married to a self-confident, experienced woman. As Hope grew stronger, her husband seemed to grow weaker.

Hope also grew homesick for her native land. After a visit to New York in 1972, for the first time Hope felt "culture shock" upon her return to the East. Even the presents that she brought back—party decorations, toys, books, records—served only to remind her of her distance from America.

But another part of the trouble in the marriage was surely political. *Time Change* has a great deal to say about the internal politics of Sikkim, and about the political relationship between Sikkim and India. Hope refers to an Indian intelligence plot to cause widespread disturbances in Sikkim so that it would look as if the Sikkimese themselves were rebelling against their government and calling for reform of the monarchy.

The Indian government, Hope believes, seized on the idea of Chogyal's American wife as a handy ploy, with which the Western press fell in line, to discredit the internal government of Sikkim. A particularly vitriolic attack on Hope, referring to her

as "a Himalayan Marie Antoinette" and accusing her of extrava-
gance and megalomania, appeared in *Newsweek* in July 1973.
Though Hope says that the reporter responsible for the article
later apologized to Chogyal, accusations of this kind did their
damage. For two months before she and the children left Sikkim,
the whole family was held hostage in a siege of the palace. Hope
felt that under the circumstances she could best help her beloved adopted country by leaving it. A year and a half after her
departure, Chogyal was deposed and the little principality's an-
nexation by India was completed. Though in 1978, the new
Indian prime minister was to apologize publicly for the takeover
of Sikkim under the previous regime, Sikkim today remains part
of India.

So we're back to Hope Cooke, an ordinary American citizen
with an extraordinary past, coming home at last. During her
eleven years in Sikkim, Hope had worn the long skirts of Sikkimese dress. Friends met her at the airport carrying two short
dresses for her, as if she were coming out of a convent. Her
children, who had never seen their mother's legs, were embarrassed, but Hope was delighted with the dresses. One was red,
the other green. "I wore them both for years," she says, laughing, "changing them like traffic lights."

Returning to America, Hope felt not so much like an ex-nun
as a prisoner of war leaving a detention camp. After five weeks of
house arrest, she had such an enormous sense of freedom that it
was frightening. Things that had been so difficult in Sikkim were
surprisingly easy here in America. Travel, for example. In the
East, you could be stuck for days on a road which was rained out.
In New York, if you missed a train, you just took the next one.
Shopping was simple, but had its own perils. There were so
many *things* on the supermarket shelves that Hope found making
a choice almost impossible. She began ordering her groceries by
phone, and for years the big brown bags delivered weekly from
D'Agostino's or Sloan's were the symbols of security and plenty
to her children.

"All my Sikkimese friends said the same thing," Hope recalls.
"Life was so easy here that it was kind of like using all your
weight, as if you're breaking into a safe, to go through a swinging door. We brought the same sort of intensity to life here that

was necessary in Sikkim, and then felt ridiculous. You just land on your face because there's no resistance."

Thrilled with the ease of communication, Hope found herself spending a lot of time on the phone with friends. The luxurious ease of keeping in touch with the people she cared about, friends going all the way back to high school, was one of her greatest pleasures. In Sikkim, she claims, the Indian government had placed hidden microphones in their home and had read their mail. The international newspapers they got were three weeks old. "I was absolutely bowled over by the disparity of liberty here," she says, "with what I'd been used to. I felt like I had both hands plugged into a socket. I wanted to be like a current, to be completely open."

As the years pass since those halcyon days, Hope has become more critical of the incursions on civil liberties in America, and she is quite aware of the poverty and homelessness on the nether side of New York. But in the first jubilant flush of her return, she exulted that "everybody had options. They'd go home after five o'clock, and the time was theirs. With a pint of ice cream and American television, I felt I was living at the height of hedonism."

Hope had serious concerns as well, of course. The most serious responsibility was to her children, those creatures of a dual culture. She was concerned about their psychological well-being, their ability to integrate the polarities of East and West. So, in the summer of 1974, she allowed her children to go back for a visit, which turned out to be a decision that was incredibly dangerous for the children. "I denied to myself," Hope says, "that the royal family in Sikkim had sometimes put a sense of mission ahead of individuals and that there was a certain casualness about human life or safety." After that, the safety of the children came first. Hope wanted them to know their heritage, but she also wanted them to live to enjoy it.

Her fears in this regard were well founded. In 1978, her stepson Tenzing, Chogyal's oldest child, was killed in a bizarre highway accident on a lonely mountain road near the palace. Tenzing, who was twenty-six, as his father's heir had been tremendously involved in the Sikkimese political conflict. There was no inquiry into the accident. But after five years of trouble in

Sikkim, things settled down. Since 1980, the children have been able to go for a visit almost every summer.

Hope's second responsibility was, and is, to herself. She didn't file for divorce for seven years after the split with Chogyal, and not until October 1987, long after Chogyal was dead, did she remarry. On her own, she found "a nesty house in Brooklyn, with a wisteria arbor, very 'Little House on the Prairie,'" where she could be content. Her life had moved so fast that she had the feeling of having more impressions than she'd had time to process, she says, "like having taken rolls of film that you haven't had time to develop. I had no need for new stimuli."

During that time alone, which was difficult but very necessary to her evolution into the person she is now, Hope worked out some strategies for continuity in the face of change. One is her circle of friends, a circle which is itself like a family. "We have this tribal underpinning that takes some of the angst of life away," she says.

Out of her own experience as an orphan, Hope has a fear common to many single parents that "you might die and these kids could be orphaned. It's a really strong feeling." Hope and her friends combat this fear with connections which they carefully keep alive. On the day Tenzing was killed, for example, knowing what Hope and the children would be feeling, her friend Clover came up on the shuttle from Washington. Clover made all the beds, washed the dishes, and cleaned up Hope's house, "just made it a pretty, orderly place to be." Then Clover took the shuttle back to Washington. "That was her gift," Hope says.

Hope's gift to the "tribal underpinning" has been her sense of celebrations. Thanksgiving, Christmas, her June birthday—certain fixed points are always celebrated. "Single mothers with kids would gravitate to our celebrations," she says, "because we were so stubborn about them even in the face of disaster." She and her friends would prepare for a month, and plan a ceremony, with one person responsible for the music and another for the Japanese lanterns and others for the food. These celebrations became an important way to honor constancy in the midst of fragmentation.

Another strategy for continuity in the face of change is her work. The interest in history that Hope had at Sarah Lawrence and in Sikkim has continued, and has become her profession. Her specialty is New York social history, which she has taught at Yale and now, to bring her intellectual quest full circle, is teaching at Sarah Lawrence. She believes that she has a mission in life "to say what it is that I've understood: how important it is not to live blindly but to live to see your environs.

"Everything else in this age is fragmented. We move, we don't write letters, so we erase our personal history. We destroy our cities, so we erase our public history. We don't draw on the past as we should."

Sometimes, what Hope wants to say falls on deaf ears. Recently a history of Brooklyn that she was writing drew the contempt of publishers, she says (one editor wrote her that the very idea of Brooklyn is contemptible). "It's not just learning about Brooklyn history," Hope protests. "It's establishing a paradigm to help learn where we are. People take where they are for granted; they don't notice what they inhabit."

Hope notices what she inhabits. She is an interesting contradiction, a Buddhist who loves the things of this world. Buddhism holds that everything is illusion; Hope agrees, but enjoys the illusions of her own special place. But she is no longer afraid of the flux of life. She even made a limited peace with Mary Poppins when she read that the author described the much-loved fictional governess as the Buddhist principle of disappearing and reappearing energy. Hope looked for fixity in Asia, for a family and a culture to adopt her. As she has grown stronger and wiser, she has come to recognize the enormous privileges of choice and change to be found in America.

Bubu Arya, whose mother brought elephants in her dowry, now lives as an independent woman in the modern world. Hope Cooke, the American orphan, attempted to return to an older culture, but was thrown back by twentieth-century political realities. Each of these women, by starting over in America, has constructed a life for herself that connects one of the world's oldest civilizations with one of the world's youngest.

Conclusion

Take Two

Years ago, on the eve of our divorce, the man to whom I was married wrote me a letter that began, "Why fight it? After all, everything in nature changes; nothing is permanent." And I wrote him back, "How can you say that? Nothing in nature changes; everything is permanent."

We were both right, of course. The great whirling cycle of nature moves from life to death to life, endless changes within an unremitting pattern. We focus our attention on change or constancy according to our individual lights.

When I began writing this book, I characterized myself as a lover of sameness. I still am. In writing about change, I have felt myself at times to be in the enemy camp. Innovators hate being bored, run from routine, fly headlong toward the limitless, fantastic possibilities on the horizon. The stories they tell testify that change is always on the ready, waiting to be grasped firmly in an aggressive palm.

If life has shortchanged them, they simply change their lives. "Take Two," the innovator yells. Shoot the scene again. Life, like a movie, is made up of a series of "takes." A second take is a second chance to get it right, to aim for perfection. The constancy of change thrills and challenges innovators.

Change impresses those of my ilk with the poignant insubstantiality of everything human, Virgil's *lacrimae rerum,* "tears in the nature of things." We lovers of sameness, like Yossarian in *Catch-22,* want our days to be boring so that our lives will seem longer. Even after listening to the inspiring stories of these extraordinary people who made dramatic changes, I choose whenever I can to hold fast. For that reason, I think this book should come with a warning: "Danger. Contents are explosive. Handle with care." Why blow up a life in which one is happy, useful, loved, and loving?

The kinds of changes sought by the people chronicled here are not for everyone. A second take in life is almost always difficult, and it can be devastating. It can disturb your sleep, impede your success in the world, damage your credibility as a sane and responsible person, and diminish or destroy your most cherished human bonds. These possible consequences cannot be taken lightly.

"I had immense, enormous, terrifying doubts about my ability —woke up at four in the morning for about three months, rigid, staring at the ceiling, saying, 'What have I done?'" says A. Bartlett Giamatti. And Giamatti is talking about *becoming president of Yale.* For the twenty years before, Giamatti had been a student, and then a teacher, at the university. Yet, when at forty he became the youngest president in Yale's history, the change was "a tremendous jump," according to Giamatti.

This stocky, powerful man with flashing eyes and a gray goatee, I decide fifteen minutes into our conversation, is, like me, a lover of sameness. I've come to ask about a more recent change in his life, a change which on the surface looks dramatic indeed. Giamatti, the holder of fifteen university degrees (thirteen are honorary), the author or editor of a dozen scholarly books and over sixty articles and reviews, has been an academic all his life. Now, however, after eight years in Yale's presidency, he has just taken on a new job. In December 1986, Bart Giamatti succeeded Chub Feeney as head of the National League of baseball. Two years after our interview, he became baseball commissioner.

But the first big change is the hardest, Bart says, and he thinks I should hear how he felt about taking on the presidency of Yale. As a professor in the English department, he had enjoyed "a life of privacy, in which the imperative as well as the pleasure is a sense of completion—of a class, a semester, a book." When he began his stint as chief administrator of a university beset with budget deficits, faculty feuds, and labor disputes, he moved into "a life by definition of incompletion: of multiple problems, short-term issues, half-hour appointments—of memos instead of books." Moving from the playing fields of university politics to the hallowed traditions of America's national pastime, he insists, was a breeze by comparison.

In spite of the skepticism it aroused in the Yale crowd as well as the baseball crowd, Bart prefers to think of his move to the National League as a natural evolution rather than a particularly daring or innovative jump. He had recent experience heading another major American institution, and he had always loved baseball. Like many American fathers, his father, who taught Italian at Mount Holyoke, introduced his son to baseball. The game gripped the boy's imagination immediately and never lost its power over him as he grew up. Even during the crowded years as president of Yale, while Bart continued to write articles on Dante, Spenser, and Milton, he also published lyrical and philosophical reveries on baseball.

But Bart never set out to be anything other than a university teacher like his father. If being president of Yale, and then of the National League, had been predicted to him in 1975, he tells me, he would have said, "Nonsense. Piffle. I'm very much a creature of habit and tradition, stuck in the mud, and I like it." But he is also what he calls a "principled opportunist." When opportunity arose first to head the university, and then to combine that administrative experience with his love for baseball, Bart took both opportunities.

I have come to rest in this saga with Bart Giamatti, not be-

cause his story is so dramatic—it isn't, at least as he explains it—
but because it represents once again, as all these stories do, a
kind of balance between holding fast and letting go. Bart reveals
that it is possible to see oneself both as a traditionalist and as an
innovator. I quote Emerson, the apostle of change, to him, but
Bart prefers Emerson's friend Thoreau. Thoreau, Bart says,
"was constantly looking for that morning sun that didn't
change," for permanence in the flux. Thoreau knew very well
how much change was in the wind, but "he was looking for
anchors to windward" which he found in Walden Pond.

Everybody will locate such anchors somewhere, Bart insists.
One of his anchors is literature, so he chose to teach it. Another
is the university, so he chose to head it. Another is baseball.
Sure, he gambled when he moved from education into the world
of big-time sports, but it was a gamble underwritten by the
passions and the practices of his past. And, on the most profound level, what he likes about baseball is that that game, too,
combines holding fast with letting go, playing the field yet returning to home base. "Baseball is quintessentially American,"
he writes in one article, "in the way it tells us that much as you
travel and far as you go, out to the green frontier, the purpose is
to get home, back to where the others are. The pioneer is ever
striving to come back to the common place."

As I think back over the people in this book, I know that Bart
Giamatti is right about the universal need for an anchor, a home
base to which innovators return. Sometimes the anchor is religion, as it is for Jack Coleman, the Quaker, or Rabbi Emily
Korzenik. For Kenny Schaffer, with his satellite dish, it's a vision
of world unity; for Hope Cooke, it's the history of a place,
whether that place is the palace in Sikkim or a town house in
Brooklyn. Nancy Schwartz is anchored by her husband, Rachel
Weissman by her adopted children. Art does it for others: Victoria Boothby by her acting, Olive Ann Burns by her writing,
Gilbert Kaplan by conducting a single Mahler symphony.

Yet, at the same time that they need a home base, these people
are pioneers traveling to the frontier of their own experience. As
true innovators, they have special qualities. First is their intensity. Whatever they do, they do with an energy that becomes
obsession. The phrase "to the max" was invented for them.
Even when they are doing something ordinary, like cooking or

clipping coupons, they are excessive. Thus, during her years as a housewife, Lois Grant insisted on making perfect Napoleons from scratch, and Corki Feltman clipped enough coupons to provide herself with the training and the license for a career in real estate. With this intensity, Ed McCabe, a skinny, fatherless, high school dropout, became so respected in the world of advertising that Michael Dukakis sought McCabe out as a consultant in his 1988 campaign for the White House.

A second quality is their willingness to take risks, to gamble on things that may not work, to gamble on themselves. When Job Michael Evans left the quiet of the monastery, he threw everything he had into his new enterprise; he had no fall-back position. But he had an anchor—he knew the canine mind. Without home or job, with only her Christian Science faith to anchor her, Kay Fanning put her three children in the station wagon and pulled out for Alaska. Her enormous success as a newspaper editor began with that gamble.

Innovators have a third quality, imagination, a particular kind of imagination which comes from looking into themselves. They study their hearts and listen to the midnight voice of their psyches to know what they truly want to do. From this self-knowledge comes the power to dream, to use their imaginations to transform their lives.

But innovators are not Walter Mittys, idly playing out impossible fantasies. Innovators know imagination must be converted to action. The fourth quality that distinguishes true innovators is their gumption, the pragmatic application of their fantasies to their lives. They don't just dream; they do. This book celebrates the imaginative, pragmatic, determined, idealistic people who *do.*

Such people, the embodiment of qualities which are often today regarded as characteristically American, have created a model for action which has become global in scope. Countries as well as individuals can practice the skills of the innovator. Geoffrey Stanford left England disgusted with the reactionary attitudes he found there, but in the last decade that country has changed considerably. Thirty percent of English voters gamble by owning shares in the stock market, a higher proportion than ever before.

China, too, has changed since Martha Ritter tried, during the

Cultural Revolution, to convert farmers into English teachers. In the early 1980s, Deng Xiaoping began to institute modern capitalism. Foreign investors and Western advertisers affect the Chinese economy. Western music, clothing, and dancing are permitted. Ordinary people own small shops and family businesses, and the state offers economic incentives for factory and agricultural workers.

With Mikhail Gorbachev's policies of *perestroika* and *glasnost,* even the U.S.S.R. is beginning a new act. The exotic Soviets that Kenny Schaffer watched with such bemusement on his homemade satellite dish have begun a restructuring of the economy that has already drawn the Soviet Union closer to the West. Like it or not, America has become a paradigm for the new century which is just around the corner.

Not everyone likes it. Not everyone likes the idea of constant, inevitable change. There is something "tough," to use Giamatti's word in another essay, in those who can live without even the illusion of permanence, "who have the wisdom to know that nothing lasts." "I am a simpler creature," he concludes, "tied to more primitive patterns and cycles. I need to think something lasts forever, and it might as well be that state of being that is a game; it might as well be that, in a green field, in the sun."

Not all of us are tough, not all of us are innovators, not all of us are any one thing. My mother has told me that in the primitive fundamentalist churches in Mississippi, when she was a girl growing up, at evangelical meetings there were two groups, the holders and the shouters. The shouters shouted out their ecstasy when the volatile spirit of God transformed their hearts and sent their feet flying into the air, and the holders—well, the holders held the shouters fast. Some of us are shouters, some of us holders. Some of us are innovators, and some of us lovers of sameness.

As I listen to Bart Giamatti and think of cycles and circles, it occurs to me that as the players circle the diamond on that green field in the sun, they describe a crude mandala, the ancient symbol for the wholeness of existence.

References

Atkins, Anselm. "From City of God to City of Man." *The Humanist,* September/October 1982.

Bellow, Saul. *The Adventures of Augie March.* New York: Viking, 1953.

———. *Mr. Sammler's Planet.* New York: Viking, 1970.

Bruner, Jerome. *Actual Minds, Possible Worlds.* Cambridge: Harvard University Press, 1986.

Burns, Olive Ann. *Cold Sassy Tree.* New York: Ticknor & Fields, 1986.

Cather, Willa. *My Ántonia.* Boston: Houghton Miflin, 1918.

Coleman, John R. *Blue-Collar Journal: A College President's Sabbatical.* New York: J. B. Lippincott & Co., 1974.

Cooke, Hope. *Time Change.* New York: Simon & Schuster, 1980.

Cutler, Bill. *Into Thin Air.* [Unpublished.]

Davies, Robertson. *One Half of Robertson Davies.* New York: Viking, 1978.

Evans, Job Michael ("Brother Job"). "The Monastic Family." Published by Monks of New Skete in *Gleanings,* Fall 1974.

———. "Obedience Training" and "Learning to Love the Land." Published by Monks of New Skete in *Gleanings,* Fall 1976.

Fanning, Katherine Woodruff. Autobiographical profile (untitled) in *New Guardians of the Press: Selected Profiles of America's Women Newspaper Editors.* Edited by Judith G. Clabes. Indianapolis: R. J. Berg & Co., 1983.

Faulkner, William. *Absalom, Absalom!* New York: Random House, 1936.

Fitzgerald, F. Scott. *The Great Gatsby.* New York: Charles Scribner's Sons, 1925.

Giamatti, A. Bartlett. "The Green Fields of the Mind." *Yale Alumni Magazine and Journal,* November 1977.

———. "Men of Baseball, Lend an Ear." *New York Times,* June 16, 1981.

Goodman, John L., Jr. *Public Opinion during the Reagan Administration.* Washington: Urban Institute Press, 1983.

Illingworth, Monteith. "Uncapping Mr. Kaplan." *Pan Am Clipper,* April 1984.

Jacobson, Mark. "The Birth of an Optimist." *Esquire,* July 1987.

Kagan, Jerome, ed. *Creativity and Learning.* Boston: Houghton Miflin, 1967.

———. *The Nature of the Child.* New York: Basic Books, 1984.

Kaplan, James. "Breaking Away." *Manhattan,inc.,* October 1986.

Kingston, William. *Innovation: The Creative Impulse in Human Progress.* London: John Calder, 1977.

Lebrecht, Norman. "The Conduct of Obsession." *The Sunday Times Magazine* [London], December 9, 1984.

301

REFERENCES

Lowell, Robert. *Day by Day.* New York: Farrar, Straus and Giroux, 1977.

Maddox, Brenda. *Married and Gay.* New York: Harcourt Brace Jovanovich, 1982.

Maslow, Abraham. *Toward a Psychology of Being.* New York: Van Nostrand, 1962.

McCabe, Edward A. "Eight Thousand Miles of Bad Road," *Esquire,* July 1987.

Monks of New Skete. *How to Be Your Dog's Best Friend.* Boston: Little, Brown & Co., 1978.

Ritter, Martha. "Echoes from the Age of Relevance." *Harvard Magazine,* July–August 1981.

Salinger, J. D. *The Catcher in the Rye.* New York: Little, Brown & Co., 1951.

Storr, Anthony. *The Dynamics of Creation.* New York: Atheneum, 1972.

Wilding, Suzanne. "The Lady Is a Newspaperman," *Town & Country,* January 1986.